A HISTORY OF MOD

By the same author

A SHORT HISTORY OF MODERN WALES
John Murray. Third Edition 1961

JOHN FROST: A STUDY IN CHARTISM
University of Wales Press 1939

THE REBECCA RIOTS: A STUDY IN AGRARIAN DISCONTENT
University of Wales Press 1955

JOHN PENRY: THREE TREATISES CONCERNING WALES
University of Wales Press 1969

Frontispiece. THE NAVE OF ST. DAVID'S CATHEDRAL
A drawing by John Parker, 1836. The roof dates from the late fifteenth century.

A History of
MODERN WALES

DAVID WILLIAMS, D.Litt.

JOHN MURRAY

First Edition 1950
Reprinted 1951, 1962, 1965, 1969
Second Edition 1977
Reprinted 1982

Printed and bound in Great Britain by
REDWOOD BURN LIMITED
Trowbridge, Wiltshire

[0 7195 3358 9]

CONTENTS

LIST OF ILLUSTRATIONS

MAP

2

PREFACE

WHEN this book first appeared in 1950 I wrote as follows: 'This book is an attempt to trace, in broad outline, the main developments in the political, the religious, the economic, and the social history of modern Wales. To the people of Wales, themselves, these are matters which still 'come home to their businesses and bosoms'; they are matters on which it is possible to hold conflicting opinions. I have tried to keep the balance evenly between those who approve of the union with England which took place in the sixteenth century and their opponents, as well as between those who commend and those who deplore the religious changes which took place at the same time. The anglicans and dissenters of the seventeenth and eighteenth centuries still have their enthusiasts. This is even more true of the landowners and their tenants, the industrialists and their work-men, whose struggles form such important aspects of the history of Wales in the eighteenth and nineteenth centuries. Finally, in our own day, there are those who advocate varying degrees of autonomy, and those who strongly disagree with them. I cannot hope to have written to the satisfaction of everybody. No attempt has been made to include the history of Welsh literature, since a discussion of this would be of little value to those unable to read the literature itself, and, for those who can do so, there is already available Professor Thomas Parry's *Hanes Llenyddiaeth Gymraeg*, to which I hope that this book may be considered a companion volume.'

Of the nine writers to whom I then acknowledged most indebtedness (having 'put my sickle in other men's corn') all but one have since died. I gratefully acknowledge their share in the book's success. Needless to say I accept responsibility for any errors or misunderstandings.

I have been most fortunate in securing the help of my successor in the Sir John Williams Chair of Welsh History, Professor Ieuan Gwynedd Jones, who has brought the final chapter up to date. He has also ensured that due attention has been given to recent research on the subject, and I am greatly indebted to him for his assistance.

David Williams.

Aberystwyth.

CHAPTER I

INTRODUCTORY

THE extent of Wales in the later middle ages is not easy to determine. The dominion of Wales (to use a term familiar to Tudor lawyers) comprised the land west of Gloucestershire, Herefordshire, Shropshire and of the County of Chester, but the boundaries of these territories were themselves indefinite. Still more uncertain were the limits of the Welsh people, as no clear line of division between the English and Welsh settlements had ever emerged. For the English conquests had neither driven the Welsh solidly to the west nor entirely exterminated those who stayed behind. Protected by high ground or thick forest, groups of Welsh-speaking people had continued for some time to exist within the areas conquered by the English, and these groups became increasingly numerous as the invaders pushed on westwards. Thus in the hilly district of what was to become southwest Herefordshire the Welsh language continued to be spoken not only until the Tudor period but well into the nineteenth century. Even Offa's Dyke, the traditional boundary of Wales, did not provide a permanent frontier. Built in the eighth century as a line of demarcation rather than for military defence, it marked the westernmost limits of Mercia, but with the decline of that kingdom the Welsh again infiltrated beyond the Dyke and reoccupied a wide belt of land which has remained part of Wales to this day.

The Anglo-Norman conquest introduced new racial and linguistic factors into Wales. The rapid military advance of the Norman lords, up the river valleys which open on to the English lowlands and along the coastal plains, brought with it a French-speaking element in the Norman magnates, and a fresh English element among their followers. Then, by the grant of exclusive trading rights in the new boroughs which they established, the Normans induced English merchants to settle in Wales. Moreover, in the first decade of the twelfth century, the Norman king, Henry I, planted a colony of Flemings in south Pembrokeshire, who, through combining with earlier settlers, soon abandoned their own tongue and became English in speech. For over eight centuries they have remained a separate unit within the body of the Welsh nation.

The defeat of Gwynedd by King Edward I at the end of the thirteenth century was but the culmination of the Anglo-Norman conquest of Wales, a process which had taken two centuries to complete. Edward's victories facilitated the intrusion of still more English influences. In particular, the boroughs which he set up in North Wales remained alien to the Welsh countryside, and were regarded by the Welsh people with unconcealed dislike, though, in course of time, some of them, Caernarvon in particular, became almost entirely Welsh. From this time onwards the English speech crept up the valleys. Like an incoming tide among the sand-dunes, it left the higher ground untouched at first, and its progress was slow, so that it was only in the sixteenth century that the Welsh language finally retreated from the lower Severn. Throughout the Tudor period, while English was spoken in the market towns of Wales, it can safely be assumed that the countryside remained almost entirely Welsh in speech.

The Anglo-Norman conquest had been piece-meal in character, each Norman lord having been allowed to obtain what land he could for himself. William the Conqueror had carefully prevented the continental type of feudalism, in which the barons were virtually independent, from taking root in England, but in Wales it was this system which he adopted. As soon as the conquest of England was secure he sought to control the three avenues into the mountainous land to the west by establishing great earldoms at Hereford, Shrewsbury and Chester. The earls then proceeded to conquer the territories of the Welsh chieftains, one by one. These new lands they held by right of conquest and not by grant from the king. Therefore they exercised palatine powers, that is, they were sovereigns within their own domains. Almost inevitably, the earl of Hereford, and, later, the earl of Shrewsbury, revolted against the king, and when they were defeated, their lands were converted into shire ground. Chester, however, remained a palatine earldom, though in time it, also, passed into the possession of the crown. And it was not only the great earls who possessed these palatine powers, or *jura regalia*. The lesser barons, also, held their lands primarily by right of conquest. Moreover each one of them assumed the quasi-regal powers which the Welsh chieftains whom they displaced had exercised under the old Welsh law. The king's writ, therefore, did not run in their lordships.

In this way the Welsh March came into existence. It consisted of an intricate pattern of almost independent states, separating the territory of the Welsh princes from England. Succeeding English kings sought to curb the power of the barons, and, with the conquests of Edward I, the reason for their existence, namely the need for defence against the Welsh, had passed away. Yet so dependent was Edward on their support, that even he found it necessary to reward his followers by creating new lordships out of part of the territory which he had conquered. Nor did he unite the remaining lands of the princes of Gwynedd, or the possessions of the crown in south Wales, to the realm of England. Therefore, when his son, Edward of Caernarvon, became prince of Wales, he held his principality as a separate marcher lordship. His subjects were not represented in the English parliament, nor were they subject to the English common law.

Edward I's preoccupations and the weakness of his son consolidated the power of the barons, which was further strengthened by the dependence of succeeding monarchs on their help in the wars with France. But they now served no useful purpose, and the division of the land among them into small areas subject to differing jurisdictions reduced the administration of the country to a state of confusion, which their greed, rapacity and turbulence intensified. Their extinction was a reform which was long overdue.

At no time before 1500 can the population of Wales have greatly exceeded a quarter of a million. Wales was therefore very sparsely populated, and its inhabitants were fairly evenly distributed, as there were no large towns. The boroughs, although some of them were slowly growing in importance, were little more than straggling villages. Gerald of Wales noted in the twelfth century that the majority of Welsh people did not live in towns, nor even in villages, but in scattered homesteads. This was due to the fact that they were mainly pastoral in occupation. 'The people,' he said, 'almost without exception live upon meat, oatmeal, milk, butter and cheese. They eat great quantities of meat, but bread somewhat sparingly. . . . Most of their land is used for grazing, a little for tillage, less still for gardening, and for the growing of fruit trees hardly any at all.' The country, in fact, was unsuited to the growing of corn, since two-thirds of it is over five hundred feet above the sea, and the rainfall is heavy. The native industry of Wales has, therefore, always been the rearing of cattle, and, in later centuries, of sheep. As the people moved in summer to the uplands with their herds and flocks, villages and towns had not the same opportunity to develop as in settled lands where corn was more extensively grown, and where the fields were ploughed by the villagers in common.

Within this rural community two differing social systems continued for centuries to exist side by side. Over a large part of the country the old Welsh system prevailed. This was based on kinship. The people were divided into tribes, some of which were large and powerful, particularly in north Wales, while others were smaller and less important. All members of the tribe were united by real or supposed descent from a common ancestor. Within the tribe there were smaller divisions, or clans, based on a closer blood-relationship. These smaller groups were responsible for the payment in common of a variety of dues to the chieftain. Their members were freemen, though their economic condition might be poor indeed, and their standard of life lower than that of serfs on the manors of the Norman lords. For land was divided equally among the sons of each father, and continued subdivision had reduced the amount held by individuals until it was insufficient to provide a livelihood. Subsistence then became possible only through cultivating the waste land in the territory of the tribe. In addition to the freemen there were also townships of bondmen, who were subject to further dues and services, but their numbers were always very small, and in the fifteenth century they disappeared.

The Norman lords took over in their entirety the individual territories of the Welsh chieftains whom they conquered, and with them the dues and services to which these chieftains had been entitled. In the remoter areas of each lordship the old Welsh customs persisted. But in the lowlands, particularly in the neighbourhood of their castles, the Normans introduced a manorial organisation. On the manor there were free tenants who had to make certain payments, but who could dispose of their land if they desired and go elsewhere. The great majority of the inhabitants of the manor, however, were serfs, who were tied to the land and were unable to leave. They had to render fixed dues to their lord, and perform detailed services on his demesne. In this way they cultivated the land of the manor together. Moreover, as well as being an economic unit, the manor was the medium through which local government was administered.

But the social structure, whether tribal or manorial, was never entirely static, and changes were already taking place before the Edwardian conquest, even in Gwynedd itself. As the power of the prince increased, his law displaced the system by which a man relied on the protection of his blood relations, and was himself held responsible for their misdeeds. Groups based on kinship thus tended to break up for their original purpose was vanishing. The dues which these groups had rendered in common were being converted into money payments, and through a natural disinclination on the part of everyone to be accountable for the share of a defaulting neighbour, these payments came to be regarded as attached to the holding of individual portions of land. Through the growth of commerce in the tiny boroughs which the princes set up, the people also became more used to the handling of money. This made cash payments easier, and thereby helped to break up the old way of life. Besides, although the keynote of Edward's policy was to make as few social changes as possible, his conquest opened the door to English influences, which proved still more disruptive of the old order. In those areas where a manorial organisation prevailed, the same processes were at work. Dues and services were being converted into money payments, and the difference between free tenants and serfs became less evident. Wealth accumulated in commerce, small though it might be, was used to buy up land, particularly on the outskirts of the towns.

This development was greatly hastened by the Black Death and the recurrent pestilences which swept over Wales in the fourteenth century. Free tribesmen died in large numbers, and the lords thereupon seized their lands and leased them to strangers. So great was the mortality among the serfs on the manors that the lords found themselves unable to cultivate their demesnes as hitherto, and were forced to let out land in individual farms. Poverty, also, due to the pestilence or to the continued subdivision of land, led many a free tenant and free tribesman to surrender his share to a more fortunate neighbour. So a society gradually emerged in which the classes were based on a difference in wealth and not on a difference in birth or on blood relationship as hitherto.

This disruption of the old way of life produced a social upheaval and was naturally accompanied by disturbances. Of these, the greatest was the revolt of Owen Glyn Dŵr in the first decade of the fifteenth century. Its causes are obscure for the very reason that it arose out of these social changes, but it was, itself, more devastating in its course than even the Black Death had been. Owing to the revolt land remained uncultivated, homesteads were destroyed and tenants abandoned their settled habitations for more inaccessible areas. The manor as an economic unit almost ceased to exist. The vengeance of the rebels fell particularly on the hated towns, and in them they wrought such destruction 'that green grass grew on the market place in Llanrwst . . . and the deer fed in the churchyard,' as Sir John Wynn records in his *History of the Gwydir Family*. The revolt was also futile in its results. When it was over, much of the land of the rebels was seized by the king, while heavy fines and the poverty caused by all this destruction led others to abandon their patrimony. The old way of life was gone beyond recall.

As a consequence of the revolt, also, laws proscribing Welshmen as Welshmen appeared for the first time on the English statute book. In order to strengthen the border towns as garrisons against the Welsh, Henry IV's parliament forbade Welshmen to acquire land within them or to become citizens of them. Moreover if the merchants of any of these towns were robbed in Wales, and the stolen goods were not recovered within a week, the townspeople could retaliate on any Welshman whom they could seize. Even in Wales itself Welshmen could not acquire land within the boroughs or hold any municipal offices. Nor could they carry arms nor fortify their houses, nor, indeed, hold responsible offices in the service of any English lord, while Englishmen who married Welsh wives became subject to the same disabilities. Welshmen could not obtain the conviction of an Englishman in the courts, except by an English jury. Finally Welshmen were not allowed to assemble together for any purpose without special permission.

Despite the valiant service performed by Welsh soldiers in the armies of Henry V and of his son, these laws remained in force, although it is difficult to say how stringently they were applied. Individuals, it is true, obtained letters of denizenship which gave them the rights and privileges of Englishmen. Many of these belonged to a new class of officials, or stewards, in the service of the crown and of absentee English lords. They were intensely unpopular with their own people, partly because they were the instruments of foreign oppression and partly because, in the turmoil which prevailed, they took advantage of their position to acquire land for themselves. The nucleus of many a large estate was formed by them at this time.

The partisans of Glyn Dŵr had meantime become outlaws, and as the century wore on their ranks were replenished by soldiers returning from the wars in France, proficient in the arts of pillage and robbery. The varying fortunes of the Wars of the Roses added greatly to their numbers, for the armies of each side brought desolation in their train, and with defeat hastily dissolved and took to the woods. A captain on the Lancastrian side, one Dafydd ap Siencyn of the Vale of Conway, was much celebrated by the bards. His castle, they said, was the depth of the forest; his towers, the oaks of the vale. He and his followers were clad in green, so that the country folk, says Sir John Wynn, seeing them walking by night, took them for fairies and ran away. These outlaws kept the land in constant disorder, and accustomed the people to violence. Blood feuds, so graphically described by Sir John Wynn, were therefore fomented, and 'so bloody and ireful were quarrels in those days, and the revenge of the sword at such liberty as almost nothing was punished by law whatsoever happened.' Small wonder that Sir John maintains that no one 'went abroad but in sort and so armed as if he went to the field to encounter with his enemies.'

The revolt of Owen Glyn Dŵr lacked the justification of ultimate success. It should not, however, be condemned merely because the cause was lost, nor even because of its destructiveness. It served to awaken in the Welsh people a dormant sense of nationality, and this national consciousness, confused and indeterminate though it remained, was fostered by the Wars of the Roses. Both sides in this struggle derived much support from Wales, the Yorkists from the vast Mortimer estates on the Welsh border, and their opponents from the Lancastrian lands in the south. In the early stages the Welsh favoured the Yorkist side, for the Yorkist claimant traced his descent from Gwladus Ddu, daughter of Llewelyn the Great. Moreover the powerful leader, Sir William Herbert of Raglan, who dominated the government of Edward IV, had great influence in Wales. His defeat at the battle of Banbury was a national disaster, so many were the Welsh gentry who were killed on the field or were executed afterwards with their leader. But when, two years later, the Lancastrian claim to the throne devolved upon young Henry Tudor, Welsh sentiment veered quickly to his support.

The house of Tudor arose to importance only in the fifteenth century. Meredith Tudor, of Penmynydd in Anglesey, was steward to the bishop of Bangor. He was a cousin to Glyn Dŵr, in whose revolt the Tudors actively participated. This did not prevent his son Owen from entering the service of King Henry V, and securely establishing his family's fortunes by his spectacular marriage with the king's widow. His sons, Edmund and Jasper, were made by their half-brother, King Henry VI, earls of Richmond and of Pembroke respectively, and Edmund was married to Margaret Beaufort, a descendant of John of Gaunt. It was through her that her son, Henry Tudor, derived what claim he had to the English throne, and this claim became of supreme importance when the heir to the throne was killed at the battle of Tewkesbury and the king himself murdered.

Henry Tudor's ultimate success was in large measure due to the patient work of his uncle, Jasper Tudor, earl of Pembroke, who immediately took him to Brittany. For fourteen years they and their impoverished band of followers remained in exile. But during this period the Welsh bards conducted an active propaganda on their behalf. The bards claimed prophetic vision, and they had long foretold the coming of a deliverer from Saxon oppression, possibly Arthur, or Glyn Dŵr, whose mysterious disappearance gave rise to hopes that he would return.

Now their expectations were concentrated on the exiled prince, and to him they referred in esoteric terms whose significance has long been lost to us. No less than thirty-five bards wrote these 'vaticinatory' poems, but the most prolific of them all was Dafydd Llwyd ap Llywelyn of Mathafarn. Their work, passed on from person to person by word of mouth, kept the Welsh people in a ferment of expectation, and served greatly to deepen their national consciousness.

After twelve years of exile Henry's opportunity seemed to come in the revolt of the duke of Buckingham against Richard III. Buckingham was a great feudal lord in south-east Wales who had helped Richard to obtain the throne. Richard had, in fact, entrusted the defence of the west country to him, but Buckingham's ambitions led him to take up arms on his own account. Henry determined to take advantage of this and his fleet set sail, but it was dispersed by strong gales, and the Severn floods prevented Buckingham's own advance from Brecon. The revolt therefore ended in failure and in Buckingham's execution.

Two years elapsed before Henry tried again. His emissaries had now obtained a promise of support from Rhys ap Thomas of Dynevor, the greatest magnate of south-west Wales, who, like many another in those insecure times, had wavered between York and Lancaster. At last, on August 1, 1485, Jasper and Henry left the mouth of the Seine with a motley army of two thousand men. They landed at Dale on the north side of Milford Haven on Sunday, August 7. Although the attitude of Rhys ap Thomas was still uncertain, their landing was not opposed, and the army moved on to Haverfordwest and thence to Cardigan, where some of Rhys's men seem to have joined them. Proceeding along the coast, Henry crossed the Dovey near Machynlleth, and, if tradition can be relied on, had recourse to the prophetic wisdom of Dafydd Llwyd at Mathafarn. By August 13, Henry was at the Long Mountain near Welshpool. This was a convenient and, probably, a prearranged meeting-place, for there he was joined not only by Rhys ap Thomas and a substantial force from mid-Wales, but by the Herberts and their levies from the south-east, and by the tribal followers of the north Wales chieftains, William ap Griffith of Penrhyn and Richard ap Howel of Mostyn, who brought droves of cattle with them to feed the army, and added greatly to its motley character.

Henry's success then depended largely on the attitude of Sir William Stanley, a shifty and uncertain person who had become a great magnate through grants of land by Richard III. He was as important in north-east Wales as Rhys ap Thomas was in the south-west. Should he choose to do so, he might well prevent Henry's advance. Stanley, however, made no move, and on August 14, Henry reached Shrewsbury. Three days later, at Stafford, Henry had an interview with Sir William and his brother, Lord Stanley, who was Henry's own stepfather. They still hesitated, and it was not until August 20 that Sir William Stanley came out openly for Henry, while it was only in the battle of Bosworth itself, two days later, that Lord Stanley threw in his forces on Henry's side, thereby deciding the issue. Crowned on the field of battle, Henry then proceeded to London, and celebrated his victory with a *Te Deum*, 'not meaning,' as Bacon says, 'that the people should forget too soon that he came in by battle.' To the Welsh people, his victory was theirs; they had thereby regained their liberty. Even foreign observers were of this opinion. 'The Welsh,' so a Venetian emissary reported to his own government, 'may now be said to have recovered their former independence, for the most wise and fortunate Henry VII is a Welshman.'

CHAPTER II

FIFTY YEARS: 1485–1535

On his march to Bosworth Henry Tudor had sought to rouse the Welsh chieftains to his support by sending to them messengers bearing a proclamation of his intentions. He expressed his confidence in 'the nobles and commons of this our principality of Wales', and his determination, when 'that odious tyrant, Richard, late duke of Gloucester' had been overthrown, to restore not only 'our said realm of England to its ancient estate, honour and prosperity,' but also 'our said principality of Wales and the people of the same to their former liberties, delivering them of such miserable servitudes as they have piteously long stood in.'

The new king was, in fact, not unmindful of his debt to Wales. His grandfather, Owen Tudor, had been of pure Welsh descent, and although Henry was otherwise of mixed English and French ancestry, he had nevertheless been born in Pembroke castle. He was brought up, also, by a Welsh nurse, the wife of one Philip ap Howel of Carmarthen, who may, indeed, have taught him to speak Welsh, and of whom he had so pleasant a memory that he granted her a pension when he came to the throne. The first fourteen years of his life were spent exclusively in Wales, and if the fortunes of the Wars of the Roses did afterwards allow him to visit the court of Henry VI it can only have been for a few months. For the next fourteen years he was an impoverished exile in Brittany and France. So, when he ascended the throne, a young king, twenty-eight years of age, Henry knew much of Wales and but little of England. He was at pains to stress his Welsh connections. At Bosworth he unfurled the standard of Cadwaladr, a red dragon on a field of white and green sarsenet, for this almost legendary king of the seventh century he considered to be the last of his British predecessors to rule over the whole of southern Britain. He appointed a commission of three men to enquire into the ancestry of his grandfather, Owen Tudor, and they took evidence of men learned in Welsh genealogy, notably of Gutyn Owen, the bard. Moreover he named his eldest son Arthur, 'in honour,' says Bacon, 'of the British race of which himself was,' thus making it possible that there should once more be a King Arthur in Britain.

Henry's character had been formed in the difficult years of his childhood and adolescence. Their uncertainty had made him so cautious that he had become 'a wonder for wise men.' Yet Bacon adds that 'what he minded he compassed,' and it was these two qualities of caution and determination which securely established his dynasty on the throne. His thriftiness was a virtue born of his early poverty, and was not admired in a Renaissance monarch. Yet he was no ascetic. He was an ardent sportsman and had a Welshman's love of music. He was a patron of learning and of the arts, and he encouraged the new craft of printing. Nor was he ungenerous, as his rewards to his supporters amply demonstrate.

The architect of his fortunes was Jasper Tudor, his companion and constant adviser. Jasper now became duke of Bedford, and had restored to him the earldom of Pembroke, the lordships of Glamorgan, Newport, Abergavenny, Haverfordwest and Cilgerran, as well as becoming chief-justice in the king's dominions in south Wales. It is doubtful whether Jasper lived in Wales in the ten years which elapsed between Henry's accession and his own death, but his interest in his lordships is shown by the fact that he built the great tower of Llandaff cathedral, and by his bequests to the friaries of Cardiff, Newport and Haverfordwest.

Second only in importance to Jasper came Rhys ap Thomas. He had been knighted on the field of Bosworth, and offices were now showered on him. He became chamberlain in the king's dominions of Carmarthen and Cardigan, and was, in reality, the ruler of this southern principality. He also became constable and lieutenant of Brecon, and seneschal of Builth, and had various lordships conferred upon him. In time he was made a knight of the garter. Yet, although he lived in regal state in his castle of Carew, he was never granted a peerage. This may have been due to Henry's cautious policy of preventing any one of his subjects from acquiring too much influence. Certain it is that the Anglo-Norman domination of south

Wales, which had continued unbroken since the conquest, was suspended in Rhys's lifetime only to be restored at his death.

A great many of Henry's followers were rewarded with letters of denizenship, extending to them the rights and privileges of Englishmen and freeing them from the penal enactments of Henry IV. Even more important was the fact that the lesser offices in Wales were now granted to Welshmen. For the first time in a century Welsh names appeared on the lists of sheriffs of the three North Wales shires, and the tribal chieftain, William ap Griffith of Penrhyn, became chamberlain of the principality of North Wales. Henry also realised the propriety of appointing Welshmen to the Welsh sees and interrupted the almost unbroken sequence of alien bishops. In his reign four Welshmen were collated to St. David's and St. Asaph, among them John Morgan of Tredegar, one of the most active of his partisans in his years of exile, whom Henry made his first clerk of the parliament and afterwards bishop of St. David's.

But it was not only in Wales that Henry's Welsh supporters reaped their reward. They followed him to court and obtained many minor posts. So numerous were they, and so indecorous their scramble for offices, that they became objects of dislike and satire to the English courtiers. The poet, Skelton, ruefully recorded the device of St. Peter, who, being tired of the clamour of Welshmen in heaven, arranged that someone should shout the two Welsh words, *caws pôb*, (toasted cheese) outside the gates, which were quickly shut when the Welshmen had all rushed out. The chieftain, Richard ap Howel of Mostyn, it is true, disdained to abandon his old way of life and seize the glittering opportunities which now offered themselves. 'I dwell,' he said, 'among my own people.' But he was an exception. For when the king formed his celebrated body of attendants, the yeomen of the guard, to secure his personal safety both in his palace and on his journeys, many of them were Welshmen chosen from among those who had faithfully served him in exile, and more than once did the king give his guard a substantial sum out of his privy purse 'towards their feast' on St. David's day. Among them was one David Seisyllt, of Alltyrynys in Ewias, who is recorded to have 'fled out of England with Henry of Richmond.' He became a sergeant of the guard and a landowner in Northamptonshire. His son was a page at court, and he, in turn, was the father of William Cecil, Lord Burghley, Elizabeth's greatest statesman, and ancestor of the earls of Exeter and Salisbury.

Nevertheless, the Welsh bards were soon recording their mortification that the king had not done more for Wales, for, in fact, he gave the country very little attention. His time was occupied in ensuring the stability of his throne, as he could not afford to assume that Bosworth would prove to have been the last battle of the Wars of the Roses. The danger came from the over-mighty subjects whom he was determined to suppress, and one of these was closely associated with Wales. This was Sir William Stanley, who had played so enigmatical a part before Bosworth. Although he can never have trusted Stanley, Henry allowed him to keep the vast estates in north-east Wales which he had received from Richard III. Stanley was thus one of the greatest landowners in the kingdom, and since he was allowed to keep the spoils from Bosworth field (which he stored in Holt castle) he was also one of its richest men. Henry had thought fit to make him chief-justice of the principality of North Wales. But his power was too great, and when Henry considered himself sufficiently secure on the throne, ten years after his accession, Sir William Stanley was executed on a very slender charge of treason, and his enormous possessions passed to the crown.

Henry's ability as an administrator lay not so much in the creation of new organs of government as in the adaptation of old expedients to meet new situations. He showed this in the way in which he reorganised and developed the judicial aspect of the king's council, meeting in the Star Chamber. This was his main instrument in suppressing the over-mighty subjects, and although the Star Chamber was little concerned with Wales in his reign, or even in that of his son, hundreds of Welsh suitors flocked to it in the reign of Elizabeth, when its activities were as beneficial as they were popular. The same powers of adaptation were shown in the revival of the Council in the Principality and Marches of Wales. Like the Star Chamber this was not a new creation, and just as the Star Chamber represented the judicial side of the king's council, so did the Council of Wales represent an extension of it functioning in a particular locality.

Like the Star Chamber, again, its activities were popular. Elizabethan writers were all agreed that Henry's motive was to remedy the oppression of the poor by placing a court in their midst and thereby removing the almost insuperable difficulties involved for poor suitors in a journey to London. It was the misuse of both courts by the Stuarts which brought them into disrepute.

It is true that each succeeding prince of Wales had had a body of advisers to help him and act in his absence. But in 1471 the Yorkist king, Edward IV, had made an entirely new departure. Having finally defeated the Lancastrians, as he thought, at the battle of Tewkesbury, he was in a position to put his house in order. He felt powerful enough to curb the barons of the March. The civil war had considerably reduced their number, and the king, himself, through the inheritance of the Mortimer estates and the confiscation of those of the house of Lancaster, was in possession of many border lordships, in addition to the principality itself. Moreover his heir, born the previous year, was an infant, and obviously could not govern. So Edward nominated a council of fifteen persons (increased two years later to twenty-five), with wide powers both to administer the prince's revenues and to try offenders, and the queen with her son went down to Wales. But the death of Edward in 1483, and the murder of the prince, suspended the council's activities.

Henry VII resembled Edward IV far more than he did his Lancastrian predecessors. Like him he was typical of the new monarchy which was arising in Europe, and was impatient of any feudal survivals which limited his sovereignty. He, also, even more than Edward IV, had a great part of Wales under his immediate control. He ruled over the three shires of Anglesey, Caernarvon and Merioneth which constituted the principality of North Wales, and over the crown territory of Cardigan and Carmarthen which formed the southern principality. The shire of Flint had been formed out of the county of Chester, and was directly governed by the crown. He had inherited the vast estates of the duchy of Lancaster, and the Mortimer lands had passed to him on the death of Richard III. The great estates of Jasper Tudor had, on his death, reverted to the crown including the lordships of Glamorgan and of Pembroke, and by the attainder of Sir William Stanley, Henry had secured the Stanley lands in north-east Wales, including the lordships of Chirk and of Bromfield and Yale. As in the case of Edward IV, Henry's heir also was a minor. Prince Arthur had been invested with the principality and with the county of Chester in 1489, and had entered upon all the feudal grants and privileges which this involved. Like his predecessors he had a body of advisers who administered his properties. But, in 1501, Henry decided to reconstitute the prince's council along the lines adopted by Edward IV. The prince was now fifteen years of age, and his father wished him to gain experience in government. So, on his marriage with Catherine of Aragon in November 1501, Arthur proceeded to Bewdley on the borders of Wales, and took with him a council of ten, under the presidency of William Smyth, bishop of Lincoln. But within five months the prince was dead.

The council nevertheless continued to function. Its centre came to be the magnificent castle of Ludlow, in the heart of the Mortimer lands and conveniently accessible from all parts of Wales. Little is known of its activities in the succeeding years, but its procedure gradually became stabilised, and in the absence of a prince the president acquired greater authority. He came to be known as the lord president, and the council itself ceased to be regarded as a personal body of advisers to the prince, and became known as the Council in the Marches of Wales.

It was not until Henry had been on the throne for twenty years that he began to redeem his promise to deliver his Welsh subjects from the 'miserable servitudes' imposed upon them by the penal legislation of Henry IV. He had, it is true, granted letters of denizenship to individuals. He now issued charters of enfranchisement, though still restricting them to certain lordships in his possession. The first, dated August 1505, was granted to the lordship of Bromfield and Yale, acquired ten years previously on the attainder of Sir William Stanley. It annulled the injunctions of Henry IV, and allowed the inhabitants of the lordship to acquire land and hold offices without restraint, either in the boroughs in Wales or elsewhere. It also exempted them from certain services and tribal dues which had long lost their significance but to which the inhabitants were still liable. Furthermore, gavelkind, or the division of land among male heirs, which had reduced land tenure to such chaos that it had long been abandoned in practice, was declared abolished, and inheritance was to be henceforth according to the common law of England. In July of the following year similar charters were given to the lordship of Chirk, also acquired on the execution of Sir William Stanley, and to that of Denbigh, which had formed part of the Mortimer inheritance.

A more comprehensive charter was granted in March 1507 to the inhabitants of the principality of North Wales. They, also, were exempted from the penalties of the laws of Henry IV, and the boroughs were thrown open to them. In addition all bondmen in the principality were declared to be emancipated, and all the exactions to which they had been subject (and which were here recited in detail), were declared abolished. Bondage had, in fact, become extinct in the principality, and the land of the bondmen had passed into the hands of freemen who had been prepared to make the payments into which the dues and services of the bondmen had been commuted. The inhabitants of the principality were also freed from tolls levied on their trade by the boroughs, and they had complete equality with Englishmen before the law, so that an Englishman could now be tried before a Welsh jury. Four months later, Henry confirmed two charters which had been granted sixty years previously by Richard, duke of York (the father of King Edward IV), to the people of the lordships of Kerry and Cydewain, which also formed part of the Mortimer lands. Finally, in June 1508, Henry, who had purchased the lordship of Ruthin from the insolvent earl of Kent, gave its inhabitants a charter similar to those of the neighbouring lordships of Denbigh and of Bromfield and Yale.

Together these charters covered the greater part of north Wales, and it may well be that Henry would have added to their number had he not died the following year. Not that they were granted without payment. The inhabitants of Chirk paid the huge sum of a thousand marks for their privileges, and the others probably paid similar amounts, for Henry made even his generosity serve the interests of his treasury. Even so, the grants were not made without protest. The burgesses of Caernarvon, Conway and Beaumaris protested vigorously against the loss of some of their special privileges, and in other towns there were scuffles on market days when the country-folk tried to assert their newly acquired rights.

Writing a century after Henry's death, George Owen, the historian of Pembrokeshire, records the tradition that on his death-bed he 'gave in charge, as it is thought, to his son, Prince Henry, that he should have a special care for the benefit of his own nation and countrymen, the Welshmen.' Henry VIII's solicitude was none too apparent in the early years of his reign, for he was immersed in the joyful activities of his court and in wider affairs of state. He did however continue his father's policy both of acquiring marcher lordships and of suppressing his over-mighty subjects. In the year of his accession he bought the lordships of Arwystli and Cyfeiliog, and, in 1521, the duke of Buckingham, the last of the great marcher lords, was executed. It was the duke's father who had helped Richard III to get the throne, but had later revolted against him and paid the penalty for so doing. Henry VII restored to the son the great lands of the family in Wales, including the vast lordship of Brecon. The new duke had an unenviable reputation for oppressing his tenants. He was also highly ambitious, and may even have had aspirations to the throne. The charges made against him were trivial but they sufficed to secure his downfall, so that his great estates passed to the crown. The family thereafter never recovered its influence. Thus, apart from the lands of the earl of Derby in north-east Wales, and the lordships of Chepstow, Raglan and Gower belonging to the earl of Worcester, the March was now almost entirely in the hands of the king.

The rule of the house of Dynevor in west Wales also came to an end. Sir Rhys ap Thomas died in 1525 in his seventy-sixth year. At the same time Princess Mary was sent to Ludlow with a council of fifteen, whose president was John Voysey, bishop of Exeter, but whose most active member was Walter Devereux, Lord Ferrers. Rhys's lands passed to his grandson, Rhys ap Griffith, but his important office of chamberlain of the principality of south Wales was granted to Lord Ferrers, partly, no doubt, because of Rhys ap Griffith's youth, but mainly to curb the power of his family in west Wales. Developments in the king's divorce affair led to Princess Mary's recall, and Lord

Ferrers acquired greater authority. This seems to have exasperated the young Rhys ap Griffith, so, when Ferrers was holding the king's sessions in the town of Carmarthen in June 1529, and a scuffle had arisen between the servants of the two men, Rhys, with some forty armed followers, burst into the hall in which the sessions were being held, but was promptly disarmed and arrested. His wife, Lady Katherine Howard, the sister of the duke of Norfolk, brought a body of retainers to effect his release, but they, also, were dispersed and Rhys was then brought to trial in London. Through high influence he obtained a pardon, but he continued to live in London and was soon afterwards rearrested. Once more he was released, and once more, in November 1531, he was arrested again and charged with treason. He was alleged to have conspired with others to obtain help from Ireland and Scotland to establish himself as ruler of Wales. Improbable though these charges were, they were sufficient to ensure his death, and in the next month he was executed.

This disaster to a great house stunned the Welsh magnates. They realised that the pleasant days when their Welsh blood was sufficient to bring them royal favour were at an end. The government also regarded the situation with extreme gravity. Ireland was seething with revolt, and the unrest must not be allowed to spread to south Wales. Rhys may, indeed, have fished in these troubled waters; at any rate the later activities of his kinsman, James ap Griffith, were carefully watched. The latter had played a shady part in the affair, either as conspirator or as informer, or possibly as both, and then had fled to Scotland. He remained constantly in touch with south Wales during his wanderings, and his movements in Flanders, in Germany, in Italy and in Austria were reported on by English spies with a care which showed the solicitude of the government. For the religious changes had now brought with them the possibility, once more, of foreign intervention, and the king could not forget that his father, Henry VII, had chosen to land his invading force in Pembrokeshire. Besides there were rumours, unfounded though they proved to be, that the Welsh might resist the Reformation.

If there was but little religious disaffection in Wales, there was sufficient lawlessness and disorder. A government report of about this time attributes the state of Wales to three causes. The first was the irresponsibility of juries. If a crime were committed by a magnate no jury would convict, either because of intimidation or through corruption. Murder, itself, went unpunished except by the Council of Wales. The second abuse was arthel or advowry. This was the practice of the magnates of keeping in their household a number of disreputable persons, often related to them by blood, who took advantage of the variety of jurisdictions in the March to slip from one petty lordship to another to escape justice. It was these men who were mainly responsible for the stealing of cattle which at this time was endemic in Wales. The president of the Council reported, in fact, that in 1534 there were kept at one and the same time, in the lordship of Magor, five men who had committed wilful murder, eighteen others who had committed murder and twenty-five thieves and outlaws who had committed a variety of crimes. So valuable were these malefactors to their masters that Sir John Wynn records that they kept them 'very choicely . . . as very precious jewels.' The third abuse noted in the report was the levying of forced gifts or commorthas, notably on those occasions when a magnate had been convicted of murder or theft and had succeeded in compounding for his felony, for he would then obtain the money for his fine by exactions from the poor. Indeed, the government came to regard commorthas with suspicion even when their ostensible purpose was to aid a neighbour in distress, for they were the excuse for large gatherings of people which might have seditious purposes in view.

As the crisis of the Reformation deepened, the government could no longer allow this dangerous situation to continue, and Thomas Cromwell's memoranda repeatedly indicate that he felt the need, when the pressure of business would allow, to look into the state of Wales. So, in 1534, in the year of the final severance with Rome, he decided to take strong measures, and these were twofold in character.

In the first place he appointed a strong man, Rowland Lee, to be president of the Council of Wales. Lee, although on his own admission he had never entered a pulpit, had, a few months previously, been made bishop of Coventry and Lichfield, on the borders of Wales, no doubt as a preliminary to his new appointment, and to strengthen his position he was empowered, although a priest, to inflict capital punishment, despite the injunctions of canon law. He proved, in fact, to be, next to Cardinal Wolsey, the most striking example of a secularised prelate even in the Tudor period, and it has been said of him that he was more at home at the head of his troopers chasing cattle-thieves than when performing his spiritual duties.

For eight and a half years, from May 1534 until his death in January 1543, Lee strove to restore order in the marches of Wales, aided by Thomas Englefield, Sir Richard Herbert and others. He proved 'an extreme severe punisher of offenders,' and the terror which he inspired is reflected in the exaggerated opinion of a contemporary that he hanged five thousand men in these years. With an eye for the spectacular he, on one occasion, caused the dead body of an outlaw to be 'brought in a sack trussed upon a horse' to a market town and hanged on a gallows in the presence of three hundred people. 'The manner thereof,' he sardonically informed Cromwell, 'had not been seen heretofore.' He was not to be restrained by the rank of an offender, and he boasted that he had hanged 'four of the best blood in Shropshire.' But his activities were confined to the Welsh border, especially to the Radnor Forest, 'among the thickest of the thieves.' He is not known ever to have visited the three shires of North Wales, nor the southern principality of Cardigan and Carmarthen, and it was but seldom that he came as far south as Brecon. Without question Lee proved himself to be a vigorous and capable administrator, but he showed no gifts of statesmanship. He relied entirely on repressive measures and had no appreciation of the reasons for the condition of Wales. He dealt with the symptoms of disorder and not with its causes.

In the year of Lee's appointment, Thomas Cromwell also obtained the passing by parliament of a number of measures to meet the emergency in Wales. Juries suspected of having given false verdicts could now be summoned before the Council of Wales and severely punished. In order to prevent cattle raiding there must be no movement after dark across the lower reaches of the Severn. No one was to be allowed to carry arms in any circumstances. Nor must there be assemblies of people under cover of a commortha, even for a marriage or a child's first communion or for games, and exactions of money must cease. The custom of arthel was to be abolished, and offenders escaping from one lordship to another must be handed back. The power of the remaining marcher lords was seriously infringed by a measure by which their officials could be tried before the Council of Wales for wrongful imprisonment or the exaction of money. Most important of all was the entirely novel device by which crimes committed in the marches could be tried in the nearest English shire.

All these measures bore the obvious marks of emergency legislation, and were in no way a solution of the Welsh problem. For fifty years the attitude of the Tudor government towards Wales had been purely opportunist, and as late as 1534 there was no evidence of any enlightened or even consistent policy. Throughout this period Wales was governed as a dependent territory, having no voice in its own affairs. In 1535 parliament did not meet; when it reassembled in 1536 it became clear that new methods were to be tried.

CHAPTER III

THE UNION OF ENGLAND AND WALES

THE new approach to the problem of Wales bore fruit in a series of acts passed by parliament between 1536 and 1543, which completely unified Wales with England. This union was to have momentous consequences for both countries. It has determined the course of the history of Wales until our own day, and for England it initiated the development which brought the whole of the British Isles under the central government in London. For the union with Wales was but a prelude to that with Scotland, and with Ireland. There is no doubt that it was, in a large measure, the result of conscious policy. Henry VII had already shown by his marriage alliance with Scotland and by his treatment of Ireland that he sought to extend his control over them. Moreover both he and Henry VIII were typical of the new monarchy which was arising in Europe, and were impatient of any feudal survivals which limited their sovereignty. They consciously desired uniformity in government. Elsewhere in Europe, in France and in Spain, in particular, the same development could be observed, and the modern unified sovereign state was emerging. It was not an accident that in 1532, only four years before the so-called Act of Union of England and Wales, the Breton branch of the Celtic peoples, separated from the Welsh for a thousand years, was assimilated to France by the treaty of Vannes.

By and large the new policy was intended to be conciliatory. If Wales was to be assimilated to England, then Welshmen must be entitled to all the rights and privileges of Englishmen. They must be allowed to govern themselves through their representatives in parliament. They must also have the benefits of the common law of England together with the English system for the administration of justice, including justices of the peace chosen from among themselves. Nothing better illustrates the fact that a change in policy had taken place than the opposition which the new measures encountered from the king's officials

33

in Wales, particularly from Rowland Lee himself. It is evident that he had not been consulted about them. When, in March 1536, he first heard that the king proposed to appoint justices of the peace in Wales he wrote immediately to Cromwell protesting that this would undo all his work. It would be setting one thief to try another, he said. He felt that conditions in Wales were such that they could not be redressed by the common law, for the gentry from whom justices would be chosen were those who, themselves, harboured thieves and malefactors. Besides, they had neither the authority nor the property qualification for the office. 'There are very few Welsh above Brecknock,' he maintained, 'who have ten pounds a year in land,' and he added disparagingly that 'their discretion is less than their land.' To the very end Lee opposed the new measures.

That they were introduced despite this opposition is, in itself, proof of the urgency of the situation. The position in the marcher lordships had become intolerable. Order could not be firmly established until the conflicting jurisdictions of the courts of these petty lordships had been abolished. With the growth of trade there were increasing complaints that the disorder in the March and the exactions of the officials were proving a hindrance, particularly to the cattle trade with England. Moreover, the fact that several boroughs and ports lay within the lordships meant a considerable loss to the crown of revenue from tolls. But far outweighing these considerations was the need to ensure the success of the Reformation. The danger of foreign invasion was increasing, and the government was showing much concern about the defence of the coast, particularly in the west. A uniform administration was necessary in order that the religious changes could be introduced. Moreover the king felt the need, in this crisis, to secure the goodwill of the people. A pacified Wales would both increase his strength and help to make the western approaches safe against attack. Some conciliation was necessary, and in the summer of 1535, while parliament was still prorogued, the king himself was reported to be 'on the confines of Wales, hunting and traversing the country to gain the people.'

Demand for union came, also, from Wales itself. In Edward Lord Herbert of Cherbury's *Life of Henry VIII* there is preserved a petition from Wales to the king 'craving to be received and adopted into the same laws and privileges which your other subjects enjoy.' After a passing reference to resistance under Owen Glyn Dŵr, and to the adherence of the Welsh to the house of York, the petitioners protested their unfailing loyalty thereafter to the Tudors. They asked for union as a reward for this loyalty. That the Welsh spoke a different language, they claimed, should be no bar. 'Your highness,' they said, 'will have but the more tongues to serve you.'

There is no way of ascertaining who were the authors of this document or of the change in outlook which now took place. The preservation of the petition among the Herbert papers may point to Edward Lord Herbert's great-grandfather, Sir Richard Herbert, one of the most enlightened men of his day. That his family had supported the house of York may explain the reference in the petition, and, if so, would be some slight confirmation of this surmise. Tradition has always, on very slender evidence, attributed much influence to young John ap Rhys, a member of an old Breconshire family, who, at the dissolution of the monasteries, became possessed of Brecon Priory, and came to be known as Sir John Price of Brecon. Price's wife was related by marriage to Thomas Cromwell through both her father and her mother, and Price may well have had access to him through her. Price was, moreover, a protégé of Sir William Herbert, who later became earl of Pembroke. However there were many other Welshmen at court and in London who were equally influential. In truth, although this legislation is the most important of all relating to Wales on the statute-book, we know the names neither of those responsible for the policy embodied in it nor of those who drafted the acts themselves.

It is typical of the tentative nature of much Tudor legislation that the first act to embody the new policy, passed by the Reformation Parliament when it reassembled for the last time in February 1536, was very limited in its application. It arranged for the appointment of justices of the peace in the County of Chester, in Flintshire, in the three shires of North Wales, in Cardigan and Carmarthen and in the lordships of Glamorgan and Pembroke. Within a few weeks this was superseded by the comprehensive measure which goes by the name of the Act of Union. Yet this act itself was tentative in nature.

It bore marks of haste in its numerous contradictions. It established commissions to ascertain the facts on which the act itself should have been based. Besides, the king was granted the right to suspend or revoke it in whole or in part within three years, should need arise, a clear indication that no well-thought-out policy had been determined upon. Finally, it threw the administration of the country into confusion. It was not until six years later that union was completed in the act of 1543. The two acts are, in fact, complementary. That of 1536 indicated the broad lines of policy, while that of 1543 worked out this policy in the minutest detail. Neither is more entitled than the other to be called the Act of Union.

The most obvious indication of the disappearance of feudalism which this new legislation involved was the conversion of the petty lordships of the March into shire-ground. Various lordships were attached to the border shires of Shropshire, Herefordshire and Gloucestershire. In the main these lordships had always been associated with the shires concerned, except in the case of Ewias Lacy which was now arbitrarily united to Herefordshire, but which remained Welsh in speech for another three hundred years. As the purpose of the acts was to assimilate Wales to England, the question of a frontier between the two countries did not arise, but, in fact, the frontier of Wales was thereby determined. It coincided with the limits neither of the Welsh language nor of the Welsh dioceses, but it has remained unchanged until our own day.

Various lordships, including that of Gower, were attached to the county of Glamorgan, and others to the county of Pembroke. Some were united to Cardigan and some to Carmarthen, among them Laugharne and Llanstephan, which had been joined to Pembrokeshire in 1536 but reverted in 1543 to Carmarthenshire, with which they had long been associated. The mountainous lordship of Mawddwy was united to Merioneth, despite the fact that the two areas were separated geographically by the great heights of Aran Fawddwy, while historically, also, Mawddwy had formed part of Powys, the core of the new shire of Montgomery. It can only be surmised that this arrangement was adopted because of the particularly wild and disturbed state of Mawddwy, for in Merioneth there was already a settled administration capable of suppressing disorder, while the new shire of Montgomery would take some years to become stable. Out of the remaining lordships the entirely new shires of Monmouth, Brecon, Radnor, Montgomery and Denbigh were created.

Thus a much needed reform was accomplished, and the administrative and judicial powers of the feudal lords came to an end. This marked the close of the long struggle between the crown and the marcher lords, a struggle which went back to the time of Edward I and beyond. That the crown was now successful was due to the fact that most of the lordships were in its own possession, while no marcher lord remained who was powerful enough to resist its wishes. To soften the blow, certain pecuniary rights were still reserved to the lords, and an act of the reign of Queen Mary confirmed these to their descendants.

The abolition of the rights and privileges of the feudal lords introduced equality before the law as between them and their former subjects. Of far greater importance in the eyes of contemporaries was the fact that Welshmen were granted equality with Englishmen. This, indeed, was the supreme achievement of these acts. The penal legislation of Henry IV still remained on the statute book, but it was entirely superseded. Letters of denizenship were no longer necessary, for Welshmen now obtained full rights of citizenship. Henceforth they could participate in the economic life of the towns both of Wales and of England, and these towns acted as a magnet on all classes. To the Welshman of the day the removal of inequality before the law far outweighed any disadvantages which were involved in the new legislation, or were caused by the abolition of the ancient Welsh codes of law. There is little evidence that the people of Wales wished, even in the areas where tribalism had persisted, to retain the provisions of the laws of Hywel Dda. It is true that arrangements were made in 1536 for a commission to examine these laws and decide which should be preserved. The king was even granted authority to implement the recommendations of the commission without further recourse to parliament, and his power to suspend the operation of the act within three years may well have been in order to enable him to do this. But we have no knowledge that the commission ever met, or, if it did, of any outcome to its deliberations. Certainly its activities had no effect on legislation.

It is against the background of equality before the law that the language provision of the act of 1536 must be considered. This ran as follows: 'all justices . . . shall proclaim and keep . . . all . . . courts in the English tongue; . . . all oaths shall be given . . . in the English tongue; . . . no person or persons that use the Welsh speech or language shall have . . . any office . . . within this realm of England, Wales or other the king's Dominion . . . unless he or they use and exercise the English speech or language.' Its purpose was, with the introduction of uniformity in the legal codes of England and Wales, to have uniformity also in their administration. The Tudors were greatly concerned with administrative convenience, and it seemed convenient to them that the courts should be conducted in one and the same language. How far this provision was rigidly applied it is difficult to ascertain. From the beginning it was assumed that 'latimers', that is to say, interpreters, should be employed, and Elizabethan officials even advocated that at least one justice of assize should understand Welsh because of the difficulties involved in hearing evidence from Welsh witnesses.

To assume that those who framed this legislation had any deliberate intent to suppress the Welsh language would be to attribute to them the ways of thought of a later age. National consciousness in Europe was still far too indefinite and ill-defined for this to have been possible. Nevertheless the consequences of the stipulations with regard to language were deplorable. The number of Welshmen who became officials was small but a premium was placed on their use of the English language, and this added to the many other factors which produced a breach between their class and the peasantry. More serious was the fact that in the courts cases were conducted in English although they related to a people who were at this time, almost entirely Welsh in speech. Although it was, again, only a minority among the Welsh people who were involved in litigation, the language of the courts served to emphasise the fact that the legal system was, in reality, an alien one. The legal code did not therefore win from the people of Wales the respect which an indigenous system would have gained, for they could not understand it, and were apt to regard it as a means by which they could be tricked out of their rights.

They were, therefore, less unwilling than they might otherwise have been to infringe its provisions.

Uniformity in law meant the introduction of the English system of land tenure and the abolition of gavelkind. The practice of the partition of inheritances had already largely fallen into disuse, and the act of 1536 did little more than recognise this. Nevertheless, although it declared the Welsh system of inheritance to be abolished, it accepted as a compromise that it should be continued where it had been practised 'time out of mind.' The act of 1543 admitted of no such compromise; gavelkind was abolished outright. In spite of this it still continued as an extra-judicial survival in many parts of Wales.

Equality before the law also involved participation in the framing of the law by Wales's representatives in parliament. Hitherto representatives had been called from Wales only exceptionally to two parliaments of Edward II. Yet it was always held that parliament could legislate for Wales, as well as for other palatine lordships, since parliament was but an extension of the king's council, and the palatine lords owed fealty to the crown. The act of 1536 was itself passed by a parliament which had in it no Welsh representative.

Each Welsh shire was now to have one knight of the shire, with the exception of Monmouthshire which obtained two, and each shire town was to be represented by one burgess, with the exception of the shire town of Merioneth which had no representation. Wales did not therefore have the same representation as England, which had two knights for each shire and two burgesses for each borough. This, however, far from being an injustice, was probably regarded as a concession on account of the poverty of Wales. The act was passed at a time when representation was only just ceasing to be regarded as a heavy burden. The expense involved was considerable, both for the representatives and their constituencies, and members frequently asked to be excused from attending. Merioneth, in particular, was the remotest part of Wales, more so than Caernarvonshire and Anglesey which were on the route to Ireland, and Harlech, the shire town, had fallen into decay when its castle ceased to be of importance. It was, no doubt, glad to avoid this additional burden of representation. Both the knights and the burgesses were to be paid, although this was ceasing to be the practice in England, and in the boroughs the burgess's wages were to be levied not only on the shire towns (another act of 1536 enabled the king to determine which these should be) but on 'all other ancient boroughs,' although these had no voice in the election of the member. This was an evident injustice, and an act of 1543 removed the anomaly and gave these towns the franchise. A system of 'contributory boroughs' entirely peculiar to Wales thus came into existence. Willingness to contribute no doubt determined which boroughs were to participate in elections, and this proved a matter of great importance later on, when the right of election was greatly coveted and the payment of members had ceased. The franchise was to be regulated 'in like manner as in England.' In the shires this meant that the forty-shilling freeholders had the vote. The position in the boroughs was not so clear, but in time it became apparent that in the majority of Welsh boroughs the franchise was vested in the freemen, that is, in those who were burgesses through birth, marriage or apprenticeship. By the act of 1543 Haverfordwest was given separate representation, which it retained until 1885. It was also made into a separate shire. Tradition has always attributed the latter arrangement to the influence with the king of the mother of Sir John Perrot of Haroldston nearby. The fact that it is three times stated in the act itself that it should continue only at the king's pleasure seems to indicate that it was intended to be temporary and, to some extent, corroborates the tradition that it was granted as a personal favour.

Although the codes of law of England and Wales were assimilated, Wales was allowed to retain its own system of law courts, which was extended to cover the whole country with the exception of Monmouthshire. Here again the guiding principle was one of administrative convenience. The statute of Rhuddlan of 1284 had established a chancery and exchequer at Caernarvon, and the justice of North Wales had held the great sessions regularly in the three shires. A similar arrangement had come into existence in the principality of South Wales, with its chancery and exchequer at Carmarthen. The system had worked well, and owing to the remoteness of Wales from the courts at Westminster it was decided that it should continue. The act of 1536 therefore established new chanceries and exchequers at Brecon and at Denbigh, and by the act of 1543 these four administrative units were converted into circuits, thus bringing into existence the king's Courts of Great Sessions. The justice of North Wales was to continue to hold his courts twice a year for six days in the three shire towns of Anglesey, Caernarvonshire and Merioneth, and, for the time being, the justice of Chester was to do so in the shires of Flint, Denbigh and Montgomery. Two new justices were appointed for the circuits of Cardiganshire, Carmarthenshire and Pembrokeshire, and of Glamorgan, Breconshire and Radnorshire.

These courts were to be held 'in as large a manner' as those of Westminster, of which they were entirely independent. The justice of North Wales had been empowered to administer the law on grounds of equity, as was done in the Court of Chancery in Westminster, in cases where ordinary justice might miscarry. This 'equity jurisdiction' was retained by the Courts of Great Sessions. The new system remained popular in Wales throughout its history, for by it justice was both cheap and speedy. But in time the Westminster courts, which were constantly striving to extend their powers at the expense of each other, began also to encroach upon the authority of the Welsh courts, and ultimately, in 1830, these were abolished.

By the act of 1536, Monmouthshire had been made subject to the courts of Westminster. It was therefore not included in the arrangements for the Great Sessions made in 1543. The shire has, in consequence, been placed in an anomalous position since that time. Ecclesiastically it has always remained part of Wales, but while it has been included in the provisions of most acts of parliament relating to Wales, it has been excluded from certain others. As it was the intention of the Acts of Union to absorb not only Monmouthshire but the whole of Wales into England, it cannot have been intended to separate Monmouthshire from Wales in any particular way. The different arrangements were made merely because Monmouthshire was, in the words of George Owen, 'the nearest part of Wales to London,' so that its suitors could appear at Westminster without undue hardship; possibly, too, this was done because Monmouthshire did not fit into the neat pattern of three shires to each circuit.

Meanwhile the Council of Wales continued to function,

and the act of 1543 gave it a statutory basis, so that it was not, as hitherto, merely a body established by the exercise of the king's prerogative. The act, however, did not define its authority, other than to say that it was to attend to 'such causes and matters' as might be referred to it by the king. After Lee, its only great president was Sir Henry Sydney who acted in that capacity from the accession of Queen Elizabeth until his death in 1586. In time the Council's activities became divided into two categories. It acted as a court of law, especially when appeal was made to it by poor persons unable to obtain justice because of the wealth or influence of their adversaries. Many such cases arose out of oppression by the new officials in Wales, especially in disputes relating to land, for, in the confusion brought about by the social changes and the changes in the laws relating to land tenure, these officials took advantage of their position to despoil their neighbours. Even so, as many of them were either members of the Council or associated with it, poor suitors found it better, despite the expense, to bring their cases before the Court of Star Chamber, and in the reign of Elizabeth, alone, the Star Chamber dealt with over a thousand cases relating to Wales.

The Council of Wales, however, came to be primarily an administrative body. It was the Council which carried out the instructions of the king's privy council and administered acts of parliament. It supervised the activities of officials, such as sheriffs and justices of the peace, and punished their defaults and misdemeanours. It levied troops and arranged for the defence of the country. When the new office of lord lieutenant was established, to represent the crown in military matters, the president of the Council acted in this capacity for the whole of Wales as well as for the border shires. The Council also sought to suppress piracy off the coasts of Wales, though with little success; to supervise alehouses, which were considered to be sources of disorder; to arrest vagabonds; to punish recusants, and to discharge a great variety of other duties. Its authority extended not only over the thirteen shires of Wales, but over Gloucestershire, Herefordshire, Shropshire and Worcestershire. These four shires strove to break away from its jurisdiction, and in 1604 the Westminster courts, jealous as ever of any rival authority, decided in their favour.

Their decision was upheld by parliament, but King James I asserted the rights of the Council, which was still regarded as a prerogative court. The dispute therefore continued until it was merged in the struggle between king and parliament which culminated in the Civil War. During the war the Council fell into abeyance. It was revived in 1660, but it had only very restricted authority until the revolution of 1688 brought it finally to an end.

The breaking up of feudalism and the decay of the manorial courts made necessary the introduction of a system of local government. The king's courts replaced the manorial courts, and the king's officers replaced those of the marcher lords. The representative of the king in the new shires, as had been the case in the old shires of North Wales, was the sheriff. He was chosen annually by the Council of Wales, and was subject to the control of that body. His duties were many and various. He arrested suspects, enforced the decisions of the courts and was responsible for keeping prisoners in the shire gaol. He was the supreme financial officer of the shire, and saw to both the assessment and the collection of local taxes. He also acted as justice in his own courts held monthly to decide cases in which sums under forty shillings were involved, while twice a year he held the sheriff's tourn, or court of enquiry to ascertain if any misdemeanours had been committed. Finally he was responsible for musters and the defence of the shire. His military duties were however taken over in Mary's reign by a new officer, the lord lieutenant. The president of the Council nominally held this office for all the Welsh shires, but he delegated his authority to deputy-lieutenants, while special commissions were still frequently directed to the sheriff in military matters. The sixteenth-century sheriffs had an unenviable reputation for corruption, and in the course of the century their authority became more and more curtailed, as their duties were taken over by the justices of the peace. In time the office of sheriff became purely ornamental.

The most efficient instruments employed by the Tudors to maintain their authority were the justices of the peace, and nothing illustrates better the change in Tudor policy from intimidation to conciliation than the introduction of this office into Wales. Hitherto Wales had generally been governed by Englishmen, either as royal officials or as the officials of alien marcher lords. Local administration was now placed in the hands of men drawn from local families, and, although it is true that in Elizabeth's reign many of them neither administered justice nor kept the peace, nevertheless the energies of these families were now directed to the prevention of disorder rather than to its perpetration as hitherto. The granting of wide powers of administration to laymen, a system which was entirely unique and which became one of the best features of public life in England and Wales, developed in these men a sense of responsibility and provided them with experience in government. It may well be that this was the most important of all the practical provisions of the Acts of Union. Certainly it was the justices of the peace who exercised greatest authority in Wales, an authority which they were to retain until 1888.

Eight justices of the peace were to be appointed in each Welsh shire. They were chosen on the advice of the Council of Wales, and, again as a concession to the poverty of Wales, the property qualification of twenty pounds a year was waived. One among them was chosen as keeper of the rolls (*custos rotulorum*), and he acted as chairman. Their duties, again, were both administrative and judicial. They carried out the injunctions of the Council of Wales, and supervised the application of the statutes concerning recusants, trade regulations, wages and prices, alehouses, vagabonds, enclosures, paupers and innumerable other matters. Commissions to hold enquiry into various occurrences or to take special action in certain cases were constantly directed to them by the privy council acting through the Council of Wales. More and more they took over the functions of the sheriff, and, in time, when a separate lord lieutenant came to be appointed for each shire, he held, in practice, the office of *custos rotulorum*.

The justices met four times a year, in quarter sessions, to perform their administrative duties. These quarter sessions also had power to try cases of importance and could, in the sixteenth century, even inflict the death penalty. Moreover the act of 1536 had established a commission to divide the shires into hundreds, and within each hundred the justice of the peace had great authority. Here he held his petty sessions, and, with the aid of two constables, appointed by himself from among 'substantial gentlemen or yeomen,' administered the law and saw that the king's peace was kept. Minor offences could be dealt with summarily by the justice of the peace in petty sessions.

Each hundred was made up of a number of parishes, but the parish officers are not mentioned in the Acts of Union, for it was not till the Reformation that the parish became a civil unit. Hitherto it had been entirely ecclesiastical, but the Tudors, not wishing to give power to the manorial courts of the feudal lords, gave more and more duties to the parish officers in purely local affairs. The churchwardens, in addition to their ecclesiastical duties, supervised the morals of the people and saw to their attendance at church. When the needs of expanding traffic made it necessary to improve the roads, an act of 1555, in the reign of Philip and Mary, threw this duty on the parishes. The parish vestry had to appoint annually two surveyors, whose function was to apportion to each parishioner his share in keeping the roads in repair. This was so unpopular and invidious a duty that it was difficult to get men to act in this capacity. The Elizabethan poor laws greatly extended the work of the parish. Overseers of the poor were appointed by the vestry, and they were often the churchwardens. Finally the township, which generally coincided with the parish, appointed a petty constable. He also was chosen annually, and under compulsion, so great was the loss of time and odium which the office involved. It was he who summoned juries, raised the hue and cry, saw that there was no tippling on the Sabbath day, arrested vagabonds and put them in the stocks, and kept watch and ward from sunset to sunrise so that the king's peaceful subjects should come to no harm.

CHAPTER IV

THE CHANGES IN RELIGION

THE Act of Union of 1536 was passed in the last brief session of the Reformation Parliament, and henceforth the changes in government and in religion were inevitably associated together in the minds of the Welsh people. To a great extent union had been brought about to facilitate the introduction into Wales of these religious changes. But the connection between them went far deeper than that, for both were aspects of the unified sovereign state which was now emerging. King Henry VIII had brought to an end the long struggle with the barons by eliminating those feudal rights and privileges which had restricted his sovereignty. The struggle with the papacy was similar in nature, for the claims of the universal church had also infringed the sovereign power of the king. Whenever there had been a powerful ruler on the throne of England there had always been a struggle over the investiture of bishops, over the authority of the ecclesiastical courts and over the taxation of the clergy. The Act of Supremacy of 1534 was the culmination of this struggle. It indicated the complete triumph of the state, and was the high water mark of Tudor despotism.

In the Reformation as a political movement in this wide sense there is no evidence that the people of Wales took any interest. Nor were they very much concerned with the immediate question of King Henry VIII's divorce from Catherine of Aragon. It is true that Princess Mary had resided for some time in the March, but very little is known of her life in this period or of the attitude of her subjects towards her. One of the Emperor's correspondents does speak of their devotion to her, and to the king's great antagonist, Reginald Pole, who was descended from the princes of Powys, but there is no evidence of this from any other source. The Welsh accepted the breach with Rome and the establishment of a state church, as they accepted union with England, with hardly any opposition. On the other hand, there is even less indication that they

46

actively desired the new religious changes than that they resisted them.

Neither was there any dissatisfaction with the doctrines of the Roman catholic church. On the continent of Europe, and, to a lesser extent, in England, the breach with Rome had been due to the abandonment of mediaeval dogma, and the return, so the reformers claimed, to a purer form of the Christian religion. These reformers had had several precursors, so that Luther's revolt was remarkable mainly because it was successful. Among his forerunners in England was John Wyclif. He had taught at Oxford in the later fourteenth century, and had asserted the rights of the individual conscience before God, without the need of any human intermediary, whether priest or pope. There were many Welsh students at Oxford in his day, and some must have accepted his ideas, but little is known of any Welsh Lollards. Among their leaders in England, however, was Sir John Oldcastle, who is closely associated with the lower March. He was condemned as a heretic, but managed to escape to Wales in 1415, and attempted to incite a rebellion against the church and the king. He is known to have been in touch with the sons of Owen Glyn Dŵr, and to have plotted with them in the hopeless cause of Welsh independence. But he was captured in 1417 in the neighbourhood of Welshpool, by Sir Griffith Vaughan, a burgess of that town, and was put to death as a heretic and a traitor. Of those followers who suffered with him, nearly all came from west Herefordshire and the Welsh border.

Lollardy had flourished during the ferment of opinion caused by the breaking up of the old social system which, in England, had brought about the Peasants' Revolt of 1381, and, in Wales, the revolt of Owen Glyn Dŵr. This social ferment found expression in English in the poetry of William Langland, and in Welsh in that of Siôn Cent. Tradition has always associated his name with Kentchurch in west Herefordshire, and with the family of the Scudamores, of whom one had married a daughter of Owen Glyn Dŵr. It cannot be proved that Siôn Cent was in touch with the Lollards, but, unique among the Welsh bards of his day, his constant themes were the uncertainty of life and a contempt of the world, and he gave expression to a puritanism which came near to their teaching.

Later in the century, Lollardy found one of its most formidable opponents in Reginald Pecock. He was a priest of the diocese of St. David's, and is reputed to have been born in Laugharne. From 1444 to 1450 he was bishop of St. Asaph. He tried to reconcile the Lollards by argument, appealing to reason, as against their constant recourse to scripture. He was led to defend many abuses, such as absenteeism, the adoration of images, and the neglect of preaching, on the grounds of their reasonableness. But reason can be an effective instrument not only against scripture but against authority, and, in 1457, while he was bishop of Chichester, when changes in the political situation had removed his patrons, he was charged with heresy. He recanted and saved his life, but was kept in rigorous seclusion until his death. Since it is unlikely that he spent much time in the diocese of St. Asaph, his influence in Wales was small.

Thus, on the eve of the Reformation, there was little demand in Wales for doctrinal changes. The people were scarcely aware of their religion as a body of doctrine. They accepted the religious practices of the universal church as a system which was permanent and immutable as the universe itself. In no sense was the Reformation for them a liberation of the human spirit. It was a change in the religious system introduced from the outside by the action of the government. Nevertheless they accepted the changes both in doctrine and in religious organisation with a willingness which is as strange as anything in our history. To understand why they did so, it is necessary to examine the condition of religion in Wales.

Wales was divided into the four bishoprics of St. David's, Llandaff, St. Asaph and Bangor, forming part of the province of Canterbury. Of these four the largest was St. David's, which stretched from the headland on which the cathedral was situated all the way to Herefordshire. The others were scarcely less difficult to administer, because of mountainous country and wide stretches of open moorland. They were sparsely populated, with few large towns to act as centres of religious activity. Moreover they were poor in comparison with the English bishoprics. On any reckoning, St. Asaph and Bangor were the poorest in the kingdom, while Llandaff was scarcely better, and even if the annual revenue of St. David's was about double that of Llandaff, nevertheless it was poorer than all but two or three of the English sees.

In view of the remoteness and poverty of the Welsh bishoprics, it is small wonder that their bishops should regard them merely as stepping-stones to better preferment elsewhere. In consequence their stay in Wales was generally short, and they took but little interest in their duties. In many cases a Welsh bishopric was only an empty title, coveted for reasons of prestige by rich ecclesiastics in England, such as abbots and priors of great monastic houses, who had no thought of abandoning their other dignities. Some bishops were appointed for political services, among them Henry Standish, whom Henry VIII made bishop of St. Asaph as a reward for his defence of the king's authority in ecclesiastical matters. Some received Welsh bishoprics in compensation for the loss of other posts, notably Richard Rawlins, who in 1521, was 'deprived of the wardenship of Merton College, Oxford, by the archbishops for many unworthy misdemeanours . . . and soon after, because he should not be a loser, had the bishopric of St. David's conferred upon him.' The number of Welshmen among those appointed was very small. In the great majority of cases they were Englishmen who had but little sympathy with their monoglot Welsh clergy. One, Athequa, the Spanish chaplain to Catherine of Aragon, who became bishop of Llandaff, did not even speak a word of English, a disability, it is true, which he shared with most of the people of his diocese.

The inevitable consequence of this state of affairs was non-residence and neglect. Precise evidence is difficult to obtain, but it is certain that non-residence was the rule rather than the exception among Welsh bishops in the hundred years before the Reformation. In their absence they farmed their dioceses to others in return for a fixed stipend. Athequa, for example, farmed his see to John Smart, the abbot of Wigmore, who was said to have thrown the diocese into confusion by ordaining a thousand priests in seven years. When Wolsey's agent visited Bangor in 1529 he reported that Bishop Skevington had not visited the diocese in fourteen years. He had farmed the see to Dr. William Glyn, archdeacon successively of Merioneth and Anglesey, and a member of the powerful local family of Glynllifon. Conditions in Wales were not unusual, and the pre-Reformation bishops do not compare unfavourably with their successors, but, apart from a few exceptions, they contributed little to the spiritual welfare of their people.

The great majority of the lower clergy were drawn from the people themselves and were Welsh in speech. There is ample evidence that the ecclesiastical authorites considered it desirable that they should speak Welsh, even in the border parishes within the diocese of Hereford. Their numbers, however, were inadequate, and their sparsely populated parishes too large. Even so, there was some pluralism, and Welsh parishes, as well as cathedral offices, were held by non-resident English clerics. On the whole, the standard of education of the parish priest was not high. Many, no doubt, taught their flocks the simple elements of the faith which they unquestioningly accepted themselves. But there is evidence that many were regarded with little esteem and some with dislike. The vexed question of celibacy rendered matters more complicated. Priests were forbidden to marry by canon law (although they took no vows of celibacy), yet in Wales this rule was constantly violated, and the fines which the offending priests paid to their ordinary had come to be regarded almost as licences. In Archbishop Warham's visitations of the dioceses of Bangor and St. David's in 1504, which are still extant, no less than eighty clerics were indicted for incontinence, and threatened with penalties unless it was discontinued. There is no doubt that it was far more prevalent in Wales than in England in the later middle ages, and that it was regarded as improper both by the church and by the laity.

The parish priest was entitled to his tithes. There were the greater tithes on corn, hay and other crops, the lesser tithes on cattle, sheep, wool, poultry, milk and cheese, and the personal tithes on wages and on the profits of trade and industry. Generally speaking, it is true to say that all tithes were paid up to the Reformation, although personal tithes have since completely disappeared. The priests were also entitled to other fees, such as marriage fees, and burial fees, or mortuaries. The latter were considered particularly exorbitant, and priests were accused of withholding the last sacrament until they were paid. One of the first actions of the Reformation Parliament was to abolish mortuaries in Wales. Benefit of clergy, also, had become an abuse. It extended to all orders of the clergy, not only to priests and deacons, but to sub-deacons, readers, door-keepers and the like. If an accused man could read a verse of scripture he could get his case transferred to the ecclesiastical courts, where he might escape punishment by compurgation, if twelve clerical sympathisers would swear to a belief in his innocence. An act of the Reformation Parliament severely restricted this privilege, and special provision was made for its application in Wales.

In addition to the secular clergy various regular orders had established houses in Wales. First had come the Benedictines, who were represented at Brecon and Ewenny priories. The Augustinian Canons had established themselves at Llanthony, and the White Canons at Talley. But in Wales, all these were overshadowed by the great Cistercian order of White Monks. To name only the greatest of its houses there were Tintern, Whitland with its three daughter houses of Cwm Hir, Strata Florida and Strata Marcella, which, themselves, established branches at Cymer, Llantarnam, Aberconway and Valle Crucis, in addition to Neath, Margam, Basingwerk and Dore. All these orders were of alien origin, but the Cistercians became Welsh in sentiment and were great patrons of Welsh learning. Possibly because they established themselves in secluded areas, far from the towns, they came into closer touch than the other orders with the native element in the population, and took the Welsh side in the struggles with England. Then, in the wake of monks, had come the friars. The Black Friars had houses at Bangor, Cardiff, Brecon and Haverfordwest; the Grey Friars at Cardiff, Carmarthen and Llanfaes in Anglesey; the Carmelites at Denbigh, and the Austin Friars at Newport in Monmouthshire. In all, on the eve of the Reformation, the regular orders had in Wales some fifty houses, large and small, including the three nunneries of Usk, Llanllugan and Llanllyr.

In their day the monks and friars had rendered great service to the religious, the intellectual and also the economic life of Wales. They had provided havens of peace where Welshmen could live the contemplative life, undisturbed by the disorders and uncertainty of the world around them. They had encouraged learning and had provided the channels through which con-

tinental ways of thought had reached the remote Welsh countryside. They had extended hospitality to wayfarers. Even the
king of Portugal is said to have thanked the priory at Carmarthen for hospitality to his merchants. They gave alms to the
poor. They introduced new methods of cultivation. Not the
least of their contributions to the life of Wales was their development of sheep farming, for which they found admirable
breeding grounds in the open moorlands, and they greatly
extended the wool trade.

Nevertheless, the conclusion is inescapable that by the late
fifteenth century the monasteries had reached a period of decline,
and had largely outlived their usefulness. In a poor country,
with a population of scarcely more than a quarter of a million,
their number was excessive, and they had become an intolerable burden on its economy. They had great wealth. They
owned large tracts of land with numerous granges; they held
property in the towns; their mills brought in considerable
revenue, and they had the right to hold fairs and levy tolls.
Moreover they had impropriated the tithes of numerous
parishes, and among their bitterest enemies were the parish
priests. Yet there is reason to suppose that the careful estimate
of Professor Savine that, on the eve of their dissolution, the
English monasteries spent no more than three per cent of their
revenues on alms is equally applicable to Wales.

Besides, the number of monks in the various houses was
unexpectedly small. In the great monastery of Tintern there
were at the dissolution thirteen monks. Carmarthen and St.
Dogmel's each had nine monks, and Margam, Whitland and
Neath had eight. In the forty or more other houses the number
was even smaller. Some monks may, it is true, have left their
houses before the dissolution, determined not to accept the new
changes, and prepared on that account to sacrifice their pensions, but if so, the reports of Henry VIII's visitors are entirely
silent about them. These reports are known to have been prepared to justify the dissolution. It would be well to disregard
any evidence they produce of abuses in the monasteries. But
this does not make invalid evidence from sources prior to the
divorce affair, when the question of a breach with Rome had
not arisen. The records of Archbishop Warham's visitations
of 1504 show that the abbot of Penmon and two of his monks

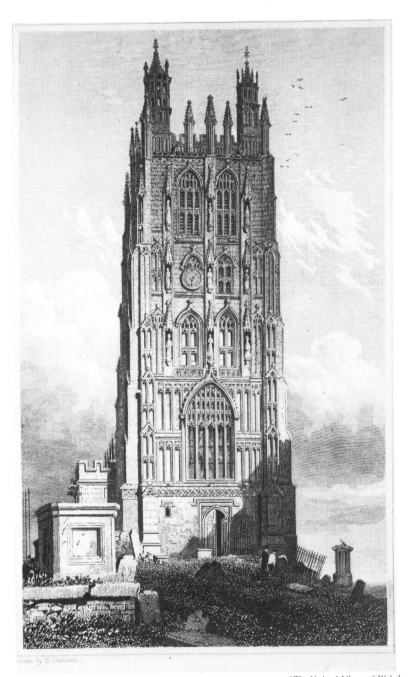

THE TOWER OF WREXHAM PARISH CHURCH
Late fifteenth century

TINTERN ABBEY

were presented for incontinence, despite their vows of chastity. At the time of the dissolution, Nicholas Pennant, the abbot of Basingwerk, was the son of his predecessor. They were both remarkable men, and both despoiled the abbey without scruple. When Abbot Nicholas wished to get the living of Holywell for his own son, he organised a party of men to waylay the bishop's nominee and drove him out by force. In 1532, before Henry VIII's visitors had arrived, one of the five monks of Strata Florida had been placed in Carmarthen gaol for counterfeiting in his cell, and in May 1535, Abbot Salisbury of Valle Crucis was arrested for highway robbery in Oxfordshire, and consigned to the Tower. The recital of these distressing facts would be unnecessary did they not go far to explain the attitude of the people to the new religious changes.

Written evidence of this attitude it would be difficult to find. Poor and inarticulate, the people have left few records of approbation or condemnation. They obeyed unquestioningly the summons of their priest as he called them with his handbell to prayer in their little, whitewashed clay churches in wooded valley and on windswept hillside. Little did they understand of the mysteries of the sacrament performed in Latin at the altar. Sometimes the priest would instruct them in their meaning or in the articles of faith, but seldom would there be a sermon other than from a wandering friar.

In its outward aspects the religion of Wales was similar to that of the other countries of Western Europe. There are many instances of Welshmen who had gone on pilgrimage to Rome, and even to the Holy Land. It was somewhat easier to visit the great shrine of Santiago in Spain, and Welsh pilgrims would travel there by sea from Bristol, or even go direct from Milford Haven to Coruna. Far more numerous were the pilgrimages to shrines at home, undertaken to accomplish a vow, or as penance, or to obtain the intercession of a saint. They had a festive as well as a devotional side, particularly in the gatherings on saints' days for the patronal feasts. Among the innumerable centres of pilgrimage in Wales were St. Winifred's well at Holywell, the shrine of our Lady at Penrhys, the shrine of our Lady at Cardigan, before which a taper burned continuously without diminution, Llandderfel, where there was an image of Derfel Gadarn who had the power to rescue souls from hell, Bangor,

D

where Malchus's ear was preserved, and Strata Florida which had the cup of healing, believed to have been made from the wood of the True Cross. In addition friars roamed the countryside selling images of St. Seiriol, which could cure diseases, and of St. Curig, which drove away evil spirits. Others went around selling indulgences. The people of Carmarthen and Haverfordwest were much exercised in 1474 by the activities of one Thomas Hochekyn, who sold indulgences without authority. 'Of late days,' they complained, 'divers persons have come into our coasts usurping upon them by feigned and coloured writings great power to assoil *a pena et a culpa*, and afterwards found fickle and untrue unto their great rebuke and shame.' The earliest printed sheet relating to Wales is an indulgence issued in 1528 or 1529 by the abbot of Strata Marcella, with the authority of the pope and of Cardinal Wolsey, to raise funds for the monastery. Those who contributed had the right to choose their own confessors with powers to absolve from all offences, except those reserved to the Holy See. They could commute any vow (except the four chief vows) to other works of charity. They might eat eggs, butter, cheese and other milk products, and even meat, in Lent, and they participated in all masses for the dead sung at the monastery.

Towards the end of the fifteenth century there appears to have been a religious revival. This is shown in an outburst of genuinely religious poetry, much of it in praise of the Virgin and of the miraculous powers of various shrines. Many churches were built at this time, often with double naves, one of which was reserved to the cult of the Virgin. This time also saw the building of Jasper's tower at Llandaff, of the tower of St. John's church at Cardiff, of the churches of Mold and Gresford and of the tower of Wrexham parish church which is numbered among the seven wonders of Wales. But, despite this late flowering, the religious life of Wales in the later middle ages was formal and inert. It was not such as to lead men to sacrifice everything in resistance to the new religious changes.

The clergy of Wales, both the parish priests and the regular orders, seem to have subscribed to the Act of Supremacy of 1534 without exception. As various payments which had hitherto been made to Rome were now appropriated by the government, it was desirable to have a valuation of them, and, in

1535, commissioners systematically went around the country, and compiled what is known as the *Valor Ecclesiasticus*. The government therefore had knowledge of all monastic revenues before the dissolution of the monasteries. But even before the *Valor* had been completed other commissioners had begun a tour of the monasteries to enquire not only into their revenues but into the morals and religious life of their inmates. It is no exaggeration to say that they were expected to produce evidence to justify dissolution. Among them was young John Price. To his credit it may be said that his reports were mild, and that he praised the monasteries, and especially the nunneries, for their educational work. He is not known to have visited any Welsh house, although he wrote a letter on behalf of the monastery at Neath.

The visitation of the Welsh houses took nine months to complete, from August 1535 to April 1536. There were three visitors. One was Dr. John Vaughan, who is thought to have been a Carmarthenshire man. He used his position in his own interests, for he begged Cromwell to give him 'some of the abbeys to farm,' adding, in justification, that 'everything is so dear in Wales.' He reported very favourably on Carmarthen priory, saying, perhaps significantly, that there 'we had best cheer of any house.' With him was Dr. Adam Becansaw, a canon of St. Asaph. But much better known than either was Dr. Ellis Price, a Cambridge graduate, known in Wales on account of his red doctoral gown as 'y doctor coch.' He was the son of one of Cardinal Wolsey's chaplains, and his grandfather had borne Henry VII's standard at Bosworth. It was Ellis Price who sent to London the wooden image of Derfel Gadarn, which was used in burning Friar Forest at Smithfield. Price succeeded in intimidating the abbot of Aberconway and obtaining his resignation, substituting for him his own brother who was abbot there for the last few months before the dissolution. His two colleagues protested vigorously against his enormities and against his scandalous behaviour in taking a concubine along with him on his visitations.

In February 1536, the lesser monasteries were suppressed by the same parliament which passed the Act of Union of that year. 'In the larger and solemn monasteries,' stated parliament, 'religion, thanks be to God, is right well kept and observed.'

An annual revenue of £200 was fixed upon as a standard. All the Welsh houses were thereby dissolved, but Strata Florida, Neath and Whitland were allowed to continue on payment of a heavy fine. Many Welsh abbeys, among them some of the most important, such as Brecon, Cardigan and Ewenny, were 'cells' of English monasteries, and were surrendered with their mother houses from 1537 onwards. They were all alike dissolved in 1539. In the meantime had come the turn of the friaries. Richard Ingworth, bishop of Dover, had paid a hurried visit of three weeks to the friaries of Wales in August and September 1538, and had secured the surrender of them all.

In this way a great chapter in the history of Wales, as of England, was brought to a close. However much the monasteries had fallen into decay, it would be foolish to suggest that they had been dissolved on that account, or that less drastic measures would not have sufficed. Many of the monks must have felt heavy at heart as they passed through the monastery gates for the last time. What became of them is not easy to say. Some, no doubt, returned to their kinsfolk. Others, it is more than probable, took their holy vessels with them and sought to continue the observance of their rule in wild and desolate places. In 1536, the monks were allowed, if they so desired, to go to the larger monasteries, and one Welsh monk is known to have gone to Fountains Abbey. They could also ask the archbishop to licence them as parish priests, and it is probable that the great majority of them did so in Wales, as they are known to have done in England. The abbots received pensions, ranging from £24 a year paid to the abbot of Valle Crucis, to £3. 6s. 8d. a year paid to Rose Lewis, the prioress of Llanllugan. In 1539, both the abbots and monks of the remaining three monasteries were pensioned. Leyson Thomas, the abbot of Neath received a pension of £40 a year together with the living of Cadoxton, worth £21 a year. Richard Talley and William Vayne, the abbots of Strata Florida and Whitland, also received pensions of £40, and the monks received sums varying between £2. 3s. and £4 a year. These pensions were paid with commendable regularity, and when it is remembered that the sums should be multiplied by about thirty to arrive at their present-day value, it cannot be argued that they were inadequate.

The monasteries were dissolved because the king coveted their wealth. Very little of their land was given to favourites; his need for money was too great for that. Most of it was disposed of at market prices, and since competition was keen these prices were high. Very little was sold outright. The usual practice was to let the land on lease, and so it frequently changed hands in the years immediately following the dissolution. In this the government was but continuing the practice of the monasteries themselves. The monks had long ceased to cultivate their own land, and had leased much of it to neighbouring families. The Augustinian Canons, for example, had abandoned Llanthony in Ewias for their new house near Gloucester, and had leased its lands. As the possibility of dissolution became evident, the abbots of other monasteries sought to get what they could for themselves by arranging for leases to their friends, while the abbot of Strata Marcella sold his monastery to Lord Powis, buildings, land and all. So widespread was the practice that parliament was forced to declare 'all such leases made within one year of dissolution utterly void and of none effect.' The buildings were often sold by the government to speculators, who dismantled them and sold the lead, the glass, and the iron. Many a beautiful edifice disappeared, leaving no trace behind, while the ruins of others testify to the irreparable loss to our cultural heritage. Here and there the monastery church continued to be used, and sometimes the monastery building became a country mansion.

Many of the families which were to dominate Wales in succeeding centuries profited by the dissolution, and this was true of both Roman catholics and protestants. The Somerset family, earls of Worcester, and later dukes of Beaufort, the leading Roman catholic family in Wales, drew much of its wealth from the sequestered lands of Tintern. Sir Edward Carne, the last British ambassador to the Holy See, obtained Ewenny priory, which remained in the possession of his family for centuries. Margam passed to the Mansels. John Price obtained his reward in Brecon priory, and Neath went to his wife's cousin, Richard Williams, Cromwell's nephew, at a nominal rent of £3 a year, one of the very few cases of the kind in Wales. Dr. John Vaughan, who had found everything so dear in Wales, obtained the lease of Grace Dieu in Monmouthshire.

The most iniquitous aspect of the dissolution of the monasteries was the great extension it gave to the lay impropriation of tithes. The monasteries had accumulated livings, to the intense dissatisfaction of the parish priests, and had themselves made provision, very often inadequate, for the spiritual needs of the parishioners. At the dissolution these tithes were not returned to their spiritual uses. They were regarded as property, attached to the land, and they passed with it into the hands of lay owners. This continued in the reign of Elizabeth. One of her courtiers obtained a lease of the tithes of Llanddewi Brefi together with those of twelve other associated livings, on the grounds that Llanddewi Brefi had been a collegiate church, and that this had been concealed at the dissolution. By the eighteenth century, it was calculated that in no less than two hundred and fifty out of the three hundred parishes in the diocese of St. David's, the tithes were in the hands of lay owners, mostly members of the local gentry. These tithe owners made very inadequate provision for the cure of souls in their parishes, and in some cases made none at all. Much of the subsequent history of the church in Wales was determined by the fact that its wealth had passed into the hands of the gentry.

In 1536 there were rumours in the alehouses on the border, said to have spread from Wales, that the king proposed to pull down the parish churches and seize their property. This proved to be untrue, but ten years later commissioners did enquire into the revenues of the chantries of England and Wales, for their original purpose had ceased when the offering of masses for the dead became regarded as a superstitious practice. Among these commissioners were the four Welsh bishops and John Price. Their work was interrupted by Henry VIII's death, but new commissions were issued in December, 1547, whereupon the property of the chantries was confiscated, much of it again passing into private hands. This proved to be the last episode in the official spoliation of the church, for though commissioners were appointed by Edward VI to take over the plate and valuables of all cathedrals and parish churches, their work was stopped by the return of Roman catholicism under Queen Mary. By this time many of the treasures of the churches had already been despoiled, among them the magnificent shrine of St. Teilo, the glory of Llandaff Cathedral.

Henry VIII's chief instrument in carrying through the religious changes in Wales was William Barlow. Through the influence of Anne Boleyn he had been made prior of St. Thomas's, Haverfordwest, and there had preached advanced doctrines, which had met with much opposition locally. He was transferred to Bisham in 1536, but in the same year was made bishop of St. Asaph, and, within a few months, removed to St. David's. So attached was he to the Reformation that the chapter at St. David's denounced him as a heretic to the Council of Wales. He was active in suppressing pilgrimages and the adoration of relics, and saw no reason why the centre of the diocese should remain in 'a barbarous and desolate corner' at St. David's, merely on account of the presence there of the relics of the saint, for he doubted if St. David had ever lived. He removed the bishop's residence to the collegiate church of Abergwili, near Carmarthen, and caused the ruin of the bishop's palace at St. David's, possibly the most beautiful building in Wales, by stripping the lead from its roof. He surrendered the bishop's other palace of Lamphey to the king, who then leased it to Barlow's god-son, Richard Devereux, heir to Lord Ferrers. In view of his advanced ideas it is remarkable that he survived the last years of Henry VIII, when the king became more and more conservative in doctrine. Two years after Henry's death he was transferred to Bath and Wells.

That the Reformation was making some advance doctrinally in Wales is shown by the martyrdom in Cardiff in 1542 of Thomas Capper. It is probable that he died because of his denial of transubstantiation, but this is only a surmise, for his supreme sacrifice would have passed into complete oblivion had not the bailiffs of Cardiff recovered from the corporation the sum of four shillings and four pence spent in burning him. Tyndale's translation of the Bible had now been published in English, and in 1545 there appeared the 'King's Primer,' containing the Creed, the Lord's Prayer and the Ten Commandments. It may well be that it was this which caused John Price to translate these into Welsh. His work, which has no title, is known by its first four words as *Yny lhyvyr hwnn* (In this book), and was the first Welsh book to be published. Its title page bears the date 1546, though it may not have appeared until the following year. When it was set up in type, the author, who was now possessed of Brecon priory, found that he had significantly forgotten to include the eighth commandment.

Yny lhyvyr hwnn was immediately followed by a book of proverbs in Welsh, edited by William Salesbury, a literary lawyer of Llansannan, who had been educated at Oxford, and had there adopted protestantism. This book is notable because in it Salesbury urged the Welsh people to petition the king that they should have the Bible in their own language. The death of Henry VIII, and the issue by Edward VI of the first Prayer Book, made the work of translation still more urgent. Hitherto the service had been in Latin. If the new service in English appeared to the people of Devon and Cornwall to be 'like a Christmas game,' how much more strange must it have appeared to the monoglot Welsh? It is unlikely that the Prayer Book was much used in Wales, for but few even of the priests knew English, and they were, they said, 'too old to go to school again.' So Salesbury undertook the task of translating into Welsh the epistles and gospels appointed to be read in the communion service on Sundays and Holy Days throughout the year, and these appeared in 1551 with the title of *Kynniver Llith a Ban*.

The accession of Mary brought with it the return of Roman catholicism, and it was Sir Edward Carne of Ewenny whom she deputed to present her realm's submission to the pope. Sir James Croft's attempt to raise Wales in support of Wyatt's rebellion proved a complete failure. Some advanced protestants now withdrew to the continent. Among them was Richard Davies and his wife, who settled in Frankfort. Davies was the son of the priest of Gyffin in the Conway valley, and had become a protestant at Oxford. Another exile was Thomas Young of Hodgeston in Pembrokeshire. He had been principal of one of the Oxford colleges, and was precentor at St. David's, where the precentor acted as head of the chapter, for there was no dean. But the number of exiles from Wales was very small, certainly not more than a dozen.

Even more significant is the fact that there were only three martyrs in Wales in Mary's reign. Of these the first to be burnt was Robert Ferrar, bishop of St. David's. In Edward VI's reign he had fallen foul of his chapter, especially of its masterful precentor, Thomas Young, and they had secured his imprisonment. When Mary ascended the throne he was still in prison in London. He refused to accept the return to Roman catholicism, and was tried and condemned to death. He was sent to Carmarthen to suffer the sentence, and there was burnt in March 1555. His successor at St. David's was Henry Morgan, the chancellor of Llandaff who had been mainly responsible for despoiling St. Teilo's shrine. The next to die was Rawlins White, a poor fisherman of Cardiff. He was condemned by Anthony Kitchen, who had been made bishop of Llandaff by Henry VIII, had accepted the church settlement of Edward VI, had returned to Roman catholicism under Mary and was to be the only one of Mary's bishops to take the oath accepting Elizabeth's supremacy. The third martyr was William Nichol of Haverfordwest, but he is nothing but a name. A mile or so away from the scene of Nichol's martyrdom lived Sir John Perrot of Haroldston, the reputed son of Henry VIII. He was accused of heresy as early as 1554, and three years later was detained in the Fleet prison on the charge of harbouring heretics. But he was released, apparently on the intervention of the queen, who showed her favour to him by granting him the castle and lordship of Carew out of the confiscated patrimony of Rhys ap Griffith. Her martyrs in Wales were drawn from the ranks of less eminent men.

There was thus but little resistance in Wales to the religious changes of Henry VIII and Edward VI, and even less to the restoration of Roman catholicism under Mary. Partly this may have been due to the fact that some of the changes, the suppression of the monasteries for example, had coincided with the stern repressive measures of Rowland Lee. Partly it was because the significance of each change was not realised at the time. Monasteries had been dissolved before, and even now it was the lesser ones which went first. When the Reformation gathered momentum it was too late to resist. Besides the gentry, whatever their religious beliefs, profited by the changes, and no one was forthcoming to lead any resistance. Moreover no leaders arose from among the higher dignitaries of the church. They, also, had enriched themselves, and became more and more divorced from the lower clergy. But most striking of all was the indifference of the people, and this, one must conclude, was because their religious life had decayed. For it has been truly said that men will abandon so lightly only what they lightly hold.

CHAPTER V

THE REFORMATION SETTLEMENT

THE first decade of Elizabeth's reign was a period of toleration. Despite the martyrdoms of the previous reign, the protestants took no revenge, and for over ten years no Roman catholic died for his faith in England or in Wales. The transition was therefore a peaceful one. In Wales it was made easier by the state of the episcopate. The see of St. Asaph was vacant as Bishop Goldwell had already been transferred to Oxford before Mary died. He had been a chaplain to Cardinal Pole, and was allowed by Elizabeth to pronounce the cardinal's funeral oration before withdrawing to the continent. Bangor, also, was vacant through the death of its bishop. In Llandaff, Kitchen accepted the oath of Supremacy, the only one of Mary's bishops to do so. Henry Morgan of St. David's alone was deprived, and he died within the year.

The field was therefore open for the appointment of new men. Richard Davies returned from his exile to be made bishop of St. Asaph, and Thomas Young to occupy the martyred Ferrar's throne at St. David's. But Young soon became archbishop of York, and Richard Davies succeeded him at St. David's, to be followed at St. Asaph by Thomas Davies. Bangor was granted to Roland Meyrick, another of Ferrar's opponents within the chapter at St. David's in Edward VI's reign. All four were Welshmen, as was Hugh Jones who succeeded Kitchen in 1566. It is noteworthy that of the sixteen bishops appointed in Wales in Elizabeth's reign, no less than thirteen were Welsh.

Among the lower clergy there is little evidence of deprivation, and very few went into exile. Morris Clynnog, once chaplain to Cardinal Pole, had held sinecure rectories in Wales in addition to several benefices in England and had become bishop-elect of Bangor just before Mary's death. He was given a passport to leave for Flanders. Griffith Robert, who had similarly been made archdeacon of Anglesey, also withdrew, probably in Morris Clynnog's company. To Flanders, also, went Morgan Phillips, precentor of St. David's and former principal of an Oxford college, together with his distinguished pupil, the Englishman, William Allen. Most important of all the Welshmen in this small group was Owen Lewis, a young fellow of New College, Oxford, who was destined to become the leader of the Welsh exiles.

The accession of Elizabeth threw the Welsh gentry into grave perplexity, and most of them temporised. Sir Edward Carne, Mary's ambassador at Rome, did not wish to return, but realised that a refusal would mean the confiscation of the Benedictine lands which he had acquired at the dissolution. He therefore persuaded the pope to pretend to hold him against his will, and when Elizabeth sought the intercession of King Philip of Spain to secure his release the position had to be explained to the Spanish government by the pope's secretaries. Carne's cousin, Sir Thomas Stradling of St. Donat's, had been active in suppressing heresy in Mary's reign. On the accession of Elizabeth he avoided open resistance. Nevertheless two years later he was imprisoned because of the renown which had come to St. Donat's through the discovery in the trunk of an ash tree, brought down by a storm, of a figure of the Cross. He was released after two years and was not further molested. Although he still refused to accept the Act of Uniformity, he attended church services conducted according to the order in the Book of Common Prayer. The Bulkeleys of Beaumaris had profited by the dissolution, but Richard Bulkeley was reported to have abstained from anglican communion services for sixteen years. The gentry thus wavered, then fell into habits of partial conformity, into compromise and acquiescence, and, as the dissolution and the breach with Rome receded into the past, a generation grew up which was ignorant of the old faith.

Catholic practices continued everywhere among the people. Bishop Nicholas Robinson of Bangor reported in 1567 that images and altars stood undefaced in churches, and that vigils were held and pilgrimages made in honour of the saints. Bishop Davies reported similar practices in his diocese. He attributed their continuance to ignorance and 'superstition' rather than to the persistence of Roman catholic beliefs.

His precentor, Thomas Huet, found that the sexton had concealed a number of 'ungodly popish books,' hoping for the return of the old religion, and Huet burnt them in 1571 in the cathedral vestry, thereby no doubt destroying many a beautiful illuminated manuscript. Even Middleton, Bishop Davies's successor, still found Roman catholic ceremonies continuing everywhere, the host being elevated in the communion service, crosses placed on graves, holy days observed, prayers said for the dead, and rood lofts and altars still not pulled down. A letter of 1589 describes similar conditions in Caernarvonshire. The writer reported that people crossed themselves on all occasions. They carried beads openly, and 'made such clappings with them in the church that a man could hardly hear the minister for the noise thereof.' A writer of a few years later describes how people in north Wales would go barefoot on pilgrimages and hold vigils at places where they had always been accustomed to do so, even though the images themselves had now been pulled down. So it was that age-long practices continued not only throughout Elizabeth's reign, but well into the seventeenth and eighteenth centuries. In time the vigil on the eve of the saint's day came to be less and less observed, but the patronal feast itself continued with its customary games, trials of strength and of agility, dancing and drinking, until they, too, died out with the spread of non-conformity.

These practices could only have persisted with the connivance of the clergy. Many priests had retained their cures through all the changes from Henry VIII to Elizabeth. They conformed outwardly because the changes in doctrine had little meaning for most of them, but they kept to their old practices and way of life. Reports from the four bishoprics all tell the same story. The great majority of priests were resident, though there was some non-residence (livings being sometimes given to students who had not yet taken orders) and some pluralism. Very few in any diocese were of sufficient education to be licensed as preachers, and of these some were Romanist in doctrine, so that they could not be trusted. The Book of Homilies was not translated until the next reign; divine worship therefore consisted in administering the sacraments and in the reading of the church services. Bishop Davies complained bitterly of the effects of lay impropriation. The tithe owners, he said, would not 'give competent wages, but shift with a priest that shall come galloping thither from another parish, and for such pains shall have forty shillings a year.' Some church buildings had fallen into ruin through neglect, and some had disappeared altogether.

The cathedral records show that there was considerable slackness even in the cathedral chapters. The vicars choral of St. David's were of poor education. Some were found 'insufficient in reading'; others were dismissed for misdemeanours, and two were severely admonished for keeping taverns within the cathedral precincts. When the Thirty-Nine Articles were approved by parliament in 1571 and ordered to be read by all priests, they were not listened to with much interest. The clerk to the St. David's chapter reports that when it came to the turn of the treasurer, Dr. Hugh Price, to read them 'the people thronged out of the church, it being toward dinner time,' and the clerk himself 'tarried not to hear anything read, because it was dinner time.' Possibly religion in Wales reached its lowest ebb in these years in the attempt to force the reprobate, Ellis Price, on the diocese of Bangor on the death of Meyrick in 1565. He was not even in holy orders (though he held several rectories), but he was the protégé of the earls of Pembroke and of Leicester. Richard Davies supported the claims of his own precentor, Thomas Huet, against Price, but Archbishop Parker obtained the nomination of Nicholas Robinson, a Welshman from the Conway valley, and he remained bishop of Bangor for nearly twenty years.

There is therefore little evidence of response to the Reformation in the first decade of Elizabeth's reign. To the people of Wales it had not presented itself as a spiritual force. But in Europe generally opinion on both sides in the religious struggle was becoming solidified. Calvin's views were securely entrenched in several countries, and in 1562 Bishop Jewel's *Apology or Defence of the English Church* gave a reasoned definition of the anglican standpoint. Elizabeth's strong and vigorous government, also, was becoming firmly established. On the other side the Roman catholic church had been reorganised in doctrine, in morals and in fighting efficiency. The Jesuit order had been founded in 1534, and in 1563 the Council of Trent had ended its work. The hispanised form of catholicism, which emerged from the Council, was as alien to the old Welsh religious tradition as was the Calvinism of Geneva. In the struggle between the opposing forces, Wales, like Ireland, was therefore neutral at first, but while the Counter Reformation triumphed in Ireland, the outcome in Wales proved to be otherwise.

The first move in the struggle went to the reformers. The authorities had always recognised the need to instruct the people in the only language they could understand, whether it be Cornish or Welsh. But the first definite information of this being done in Wales comes from the instructions of Bishop Thomas Davies to the clergy of St. Asaph in 1561. After the gospel and epistle had been read in English they were to be read 'aptly and distinctly' in Welsh, while the Catechism was to be read and 'declared' (that is explained) in Welsh once every Sunday. How far this was done it is impossible to say. The only translation available to the clergy was that contained in Salesbury's *Kynniver Llith a Ban*, and his peculiarities as a translator had made this text virtually unusable. He was a scholar of the Renaissance, and he deliberately latinised his vocabulary in order to emphasise the etymology of words. Besides, under the false impression that it simplified their meaning, he omitted the mutation of consonants at the beginning of words, assuming that the reader would introduce them himself. These two idiosyncrasies made it difficult, without much practice, to read aloud his version of the gospels and epistles, so that it can hardly have been extensively used.

The need for a full translation of the scriptures was a pressing one. Therefore, in 1563, an act was introduced into parliament to provide for the translation both of the Bible and of the Book of Common Prayer. The bishops of Bangor, Llandaff, St. Asaph, St. David's and Hereford were to see that this was done, and that one copy, at least, was placed in each church by March 1, 1567, under penalty of forty pounds for each bishop. From that day onwards the service was to be in Welsh 'where that tongue is commonly spoken or used.' Meanwhile the gospel and the epistle of the day should be read and 'declared' in Welsh at every communion service, and, once each week, the Lord's Prayer, the Articles, the Ten Commandments and the Litany were also to be read and 'declared' in Welsh. Finally a copy of the Bible and of the Book of Common

Prayer in English were to be placed in each church together with the Welsh versions so that those reading them might 'by conferring both tongues together the sooner attain to the knowledge of the English tongue.'

The time allowed was short for the translation of the whole Bible, but it was probably known that Salesbury already had much of it in hand. He proceeded to Abergwili, where Bishop Richard Davies and he worked in collaboration. In 1567 there appeared first the Book of Common Prayer and then the New Testament, published 'at the costs' of a Carmarthen merchant named Humphrey Toy. The Prayer Book was probably the work of Salesbury, though the translation of the gospels and epistles in it differs from that of the same passages both in *Kynniver Llith a Ban* and in the New Testament. Salesbury was responsible also for most of the New Testament, for Bishop Davies's share was restricted to the First Epistle to Timothy, the Hebrews, the First and Second Epistles of Peter, and the Epistle of James. The Book of Revelation was translated by Thomas Huet. Bishop Davies added a prefatory letter to the Welsh people (*Epistol at y Cembru*), in which he sought to prove that the protestant church was merely a return to primitive Christianity in the pure form in which it had existed before corrupt practices had entered the Celtic church from Rome.

The peculiarities which had marred Salesbury's earlier work were also present in the new translation. They made it impossible for the great majority of Welsh people to read it. Bishop Davies, indeed, prepared in manuscript his own translation of the pastoral epistles which was free from these blemishes. It was probably Salesbury's stubbornness which prevented the two men from proceeding with the translation of the Old Testament. Both were good Hebrew scholars. In fact, in 1568, there appeared the Bishops' Bible in English, in which Richard Davies was responsible for revising the translation of the Books of Joshua, Judges, Ruth and the First and Second Books of Samuel. Sir John Wynn states that they quarrelled over the translation of one word. It is much more probable that they disagreed over Salesbury's theories of translation which now met with much hostile criticism. However this may be, Wales had to wait twenty years for its translation of the whole Bible.

While the translation of the New Testament was being prepared, the Roman catholic exiles were actively working for the reconquest of England and Wales for the old faith. As early as 1561, Morris Clynnog urged that Elizabeth be overthrown by foreign invasion. It was better, he said, for his fellow-countrymen 'to attain eternal blessedness under a foreign lord than to be cast into the nethermost hell.' Soon he and Griffith Robert moved to Italy, and Griffith Robert entered the service of Carlo Borromeo, the saintly cardinal-archbishop of Milan, who was the central figure of the Counter Reformation. Here in Milan, under the influence of Renaissance scholarship and impelled by an exile's love of the land of his birth and of its language, he wrote his Welsh grammar (*Gramadeg Cymraeg*), and published it on St. David's Day, 1567. In the next year there appeared in Rome Morris Clynnog's *Athravaeth Gristnogavl* (Christian Doctrine), a brief digest of the Roman catholic faith. But more important than either publication was the establishment, also in 1568, of a seminary at Douai to train priests for the re-conversion of England and Wales. The need for them was urgent. Most priests in England and Wales had conformed; the faithful few were dying one by one, for it was nearly a decade since Elizabeth had ascended the throne, and the faith was withering away for lack of priests. So William Allen, with the assistance of Morgan Phillips and Owen Lewis, established the Douai seminary to train priests for the 'English' mission. Phillips generously supported it with financial aid, and bequeathed all his property to it when he died.

Rome, Milan and Douai thus became the three centres of Counter Reformation activity in respect of Wales. The three methods by which its re-conversion was to be effected, that is, by foreign invasion, by the provision of religious literature in Welsh and by a steady flow of seminary priests, had also become defined. This development coincided in time with the publication of the Book of Common Prayer and the New Testament in Welsh by the protestants. The first moves had now been played by both sides.

These, however, coincided also with the first crisis of Elizabeth's reign. Mary, Queen of Scots, fled to England in 1568 and became the centre of plots by Roman catholics against Elizabeth. Her flight was followed in 1569 by the revolt

Y DRYCH CRISTIA NOGAWL:

YN YR HWN Y DICHON POB CRISTIAWN
GANFOD GWREIDHIN A DECHREVAD
pob daioni fprydawl:

SEF GWYBOD MODH I WASANA
ethu Duw, drwy ei garu ai ofni yn fwy
na dim, ag i daflu ymaith beth byn-
nag a r a fo rwyftr i hynny.

Y RHANN GYNTAF
yn peri gwafanaethu Duw
drwy ei garu.

Conuertimini ad me, & conuertar ad vos,
ait Dominus exercituum. 3. Malach. 7.

Dymchwelwch chwi ataw ff, a mineu a
dhymchwelaf ataw chwitheu, med
Arglwyd y lhuoed.

Rhotomagi apud hæredes
Iathroi Fauonis.

1585

Y DRYCH CRISTIANOGAWL, 1585
Attributed to Griffith Robert. The above title page states that it was printed in
Rouen, but it is probable that this is fictitious, and that it was printed in a cave
in north Wales.

THE TITLE PAGE OF THE FIRST WELSH BIBLE, 1588

of the northern earls. This showed that the outlying areas were still unreconciled to the religious changes, and it was put down in blood. A much more important event was to follow. Pope Pius V had realised that, despite the revolt of the earls, England and Wales were drifting away from the faith. Habits of partial conformity were undermining the hold of the old religion on men who salved their consciences by the assurance that no subjects had the right to rebel against their sovereign. Time alone might have sufficed to establish protestantism. Pope Pius therefore decided to bring matters to a head. He instituted a 'process' in Rome in December 1569, and examined numerous witnesses, among them Goldwell and Morris Clynnog, and in February 1570 he excommunicated Elizabeth and deprived her of her 'pretended right' to the throne. Roman catholics would therefore be relieved of their allegiance to her. The papal Bull, however, now presented them with the stern alternatives of faith and disloyalty on the one hand or of conformity and eternal damnation on the other. Indecision was no longer possible. The attitude of the government also hardened. The revolt of the earls, and the assassination plots which followed the Bull, made strong measures necessary, and the massacre of St. Bartholomew in 1572 gave English protestants a gruesome object-lesson from across the Channel. The period of toleration came to an end, and Roman catholics were once more executed, though ostensibly it was on grounds of treason. But the faith which had withered in a decade of tolerance now blossomed anew.

The first consequence of the papal Bull was the Ridolfi plot to assassinate Elizabeth in 1571. Among those implicated in it was Hugh Owen of Plas Du, near Pwllheli. He came from a part of the country which, because of its remoteness, was hardly touched by the new religion, and, although his elder brother had been sheriff of Caernarvonshire, a younger brother was a student at Douai. Hugh Owen fled abroad, and during forty years of wandering in Flanders and in Spain was an active conspirator high in the favour of the Spanish government. Thomas Morgan of Llantarnam, a member of one of the branches of the great house of Tredegar, was arrested for complicity in the same plot. He had gained the confidence of Mary, Queen of Scots, and it was he who arranged the conveying of her letters in cipher to her supporters. His release from the Tower made him suspect to his fellow conspirators, for no one could be completely trusted in their difficult work, but Mary sent him secretly to Paris, and there he remained in exile managing her affairs as queen-dowager of France.

Hugh Owen's emissaries kept him in touch with his friends in Wales, and there is some evidence of the activity of the seminary priests in these years. In 1578, ten years after the establishment of the college at Douai, it was decided to open another in Rome. There was already an English 'hospital' in Rome, an ancient foundation whose purpose was to look after pilgrims from Britain, and both Sir Edward Carne and Bishop Goldwell had acted as wardens of it. Morris Clynnog became warden in 1577. In the next year, Owen Lewis, who was now archdeacon of Hainault but who lived in Rome, succeeded in obtaining the establishment there of a new English College with Morris Clynnog as rector, assisted by three Jesuit teachers. Of the forty-two students in the college in 1579, thirty-three were English and nine were Welsh. But Morris Clynnog proved 'insufficient' for the task. It may well be that the Jesuits were anxious to get control of the college from the start. However this may be, the warden was accused of favouring his fellow-countrymen, especially his own nephew and the nephew of Owen Lewis. William Allen also had a relative in the college, and Allen appears to have taken the opposite side in this quarrel. There was constant strife between the English and the Welsh students, so that finally the pope had to intervene, and Morris Clynnog was deprived of the rectorship. Soon afterwards he left Rome for France. Within a short time he appears to have been drowned when on a voyage from Rouen to Spain.

The centre of Welsh catholicism on the continent then moved to Milan, where Griffith Robert was confessor to St. Charles Borromeo for fifteen years, and a canon of the cathedral. In 1580 Owen Lewis became one of the archbishop's vicars-general, that is, he deputised for him in his absence. But the affairs of Wales were lost sight of in the great throng of business in the archbishop's court. The forces of the Counter Reformation were themselves divided into a Spanish faction, supported by the Jesuits, and an anti-Spanish faction of which Owen Lewis and his associates formed a relatively unimportant group. Besides, in 1584, St. Charles died, in the arms of his friend, Owen Lewis, and the Welsh exiles thereby lost their greatest patron. Griffith Robert was soon afterwards induced to give up his canonry. Though it was nearly thirty years since he had seen his native land, he continued to issue the remaining parts of his Welsh grammar, and in 1585 there was published a tract on the Christian life, called *Y Drych Cristianogawl* (The Christian Mirror) which was attributed to him. The title page states that it was printed in Rouen, but, writing of it the next year, the puritan, John Penry, says that it was 'printed in an obscure cave in North Wales,' and it is certain that the seminary priests had a printing press in a cave at the foot of the Little Orme. Little is known of Griffith Robert's subsequent life, but his letters show that he retained to the end his dislike of the Jesuits.

An intercepted letter from another of these exiles, Thomas Morgan, to Mary, Queen of Scots, led to the arrest and execution of Francis Throckmorton in 1583. In the autumn of the same year, Morgan was visited by William Parry, a native of Northop in Flintshire. Like most of the conspirators, Parry's life was obscure and involved. In his many journeys on the continent he had acted as one of Cecil's spies, but had apparently become a catholic, although he kept this a secret. When he returned to England he had several interviews with the queen herself. He was arrested in mysterious circumstances, but was pardoned and left again for the continent. Although he still wrote to Cecil, he was now in touch with Morgan. Yet, when he returned to England in January 1584 he became a member of parliament. He was arrested again, and was again released on Elizabeth's intervention, but soon afterwards was accused of having planned to assassinate her. Under torture he confessed to this and implicated Morgan, but later he withdrew his confession. This withdrawal did not save his life and in March 1585 he was executed for treason. Whether he was guilty or not is a problem which is never likely to be solved. Certainly he had had unusual opportunities to assassinate the queen had he wished to do so.

The queen's ministers now made great efforts to extradite Morgan, and the French government concurred to the extent of placing him in the Bastille. He still corresponded both with

Mary, Queen of Scots, and with his fellow conspirators, who had taken new heart at their success in assassinating William of Orange. It was Morgan who introduced Anthony Babington to Mary, but his letters were intercepted by Walsingham, who uncovered the new plot. This was the last attempt to rescue Mary, and involved in it were Hugh Owen, William Allen and the great Jesuit missionary, Parsons. It was to have important repercussions in Wales, because of the part played in it by two young Denbighshire squires, Thomas Salusbury of Llewenni and Edward Jones of Plas Cadwgan. Thomas Salusbury was the son, by her first husband, of Catherine of Berain, who was herself a great-granddaughter of Henry VII. His friend, Edward Jones, was known to be a recusant, but the head of the great house of Llewenni seems to have become a Roman catholic only during his stay in London. There the two young men embraced the cause of the captive queen. They fled to Wales when the plot was discovered, but were caught and executed in September 1586. This disaster to one of the greatest families in Wales shook the Welsh gentry, and terrified many of them into finally abandoning their lingering attachment to the Roman catholic faith.

The execution of Mary, Queen of Scots, which followed Babington's plot, removed an obstacle to King Philip's plans for the Spanish conquest of England. Preparations for the Armada were hastened, and when William Allen was made cardinal in 1587 this was regarded as significant of an immediate attack on England, for it was understood that Allen would be the new archbishop of Canterbury. Owen Lewis also was consecrated bishop of Cassano in the state of Naples. He was named as a future archbishop of York, but the Spanish faction objected to this, and it is more probable that he would have become bishop of St. David's had the Armada succeeded. The hopes of both men were shattered by the disaster which overtook Spain in the defeat of the Armada.

As the danger from foreign invasion had increased, so had the severity of the measures taken by the government to suppress recusants and seminary priests. The attention of the Council of Wales was drawn to them, and Henry Sydney was said to be out of favour with the queen because of his tolerant attitude in applying these measures. It was possibly on this account that John Whitgift, who became bishop of Worcester in 1577, was, in the same year, in Sydney's absence, made vice-president of the Council. He was a resolute and resourceful man, and for two years he actively governed Wales. The returns which the four bishops were asked to make in 1577 reveal only a few recusants, all of whom were in the diocese of Llandaff, and almost all living near the English border in Monmouthshire. This area, it is true, remained the chief centre of Roman catholicism in Wales for three centuries, but it is certain that at that date there were recusants in other parts of Wales. Many of them were gentry, and were protected by influential friends, so that their names were omitted from these lists. Whitgift enquired particularly into the activities of John Edwards of Chirk, who, with his son and grandson of the same name, did much to preserve the old faith in east Denbighshire, although the family derived its wealth from the sequestered lands of Valle Crucis. Flintshire, also, especially around Holywell, was a centre of recusancy, as was Oswestry across the border.

In 1579 'evil disposed persons' were reported to have 'crept among Her Highness's subjects' in Wales, and the Council was instructed to deal with them. The great Jesuit missionaries, Campion and Parsons, were said to be on the borders of Wales in the summer of the following year, and it was their activities which led to the harsh penal act of 1581, by which non-attendance at church was punished by a fine of £20 a month, and the hearing of the mass by imprisonment. It was not until 1582 that the first seminary priest was arrested in Wales, one John Bennet of Holywell, who had been educated at Douai. He was caught as he was passing Sir Thomas Mostyn's house at Gloddaith, and was imprisoned and condemned to death, though this sentence was changed to banishment for life in 1585. In exile be became a Jesuit, and, despite his sentence, returned in 1590 to Holywell where he ministered until his death thirty-five years later.

The first catholic martyr to suffer in Wales was Richard White or Gwyn, a native of Llanidloes and a schoolmaster at various places in Flintshire. He was arrested as early as July 1580, was brought repeatedly before the assizes and moved from one gaol to another. He received much harsh treatment, though it must be said that his own language and demeanour were violent also. He suffered the gruesome death of a traitor at Wrexham in October 1584. He was a poet of merit, and some of his verse survives. A poem exulting in the death of William of Orange is not now attributed to him. It reflects, however, the bitterness of an unknown Roman catholic, and his own poems are very harsh in tone.

Each succeeding return made by the bishops shows an increase in the number of recusants. This was no doubt due partly to the success of the seminary priests in strengthening the adherence of those who had hitherto wavered in their faith, and partly to the insistence of the government that the laws against recusancy should be more rigidly applied. Nevertheless there was much evasion. Many recusants were of good family, and justices of the peace, who had themselves temporised, sheltered them when they could. When James Powell, the chief seminarist in Wales, who was known as 'the bishop of Llandaff,' was arrested in 1588 and imprisoned in Monmouth gaol, his friends managed in some way to secure his escape, and there is no record that any of them were afterwards punished for it.

The same slackness appears in the behaviour of the clergy. When Bishop Blethyn came to Llandaff in 1575 he found the diocese in a deplorable state. Its spoliation had continued throughout the long administration of Kitchen, 'the calamity of his see,' as a later writer was to call him, until it had become the poorest diocese in Wales. Buildings had been pulled down, said Blethyn, manors and farms granted away, and books and treasures lost. Above all he had to combat the 'contempt' of the clergy. Bishop Richard Davies drew a dark picture of his own diocese four years later. He claimed that he excommunicated five hundred persons annually for various moral delinquencies, a statement which would hardly be credible were it not made by the bishop himself. It was not unusual for a bishop to accuse his predecessor of misdemeanours, and Davies's successor, Middleton, claimed that the great bishop had never bestowed a living except for a consideration, his defence being the extreme poverty of the see. But Middleton, himself, despite his early reforming zeal, was later brought before the Court of High Commission and deprived of his see, ostensibly for forgery, but actually for the simony with which he had charged his predecessor.

An even darker picture of Wales emerges from the writings of the puritan, John Penry. He was born in Breconshire, almost certainly in 1563. There is no evidence as to his birthplace, but it was probably at Cefnbrith, in the parish of Llangamarch. He was educated at Cambridge, and afterwards at Oxford, and while a student became convinced that presbyterianism should be substituted for episcopacy as the system of church government. It was probably on this account that he did not take orders. Soon after leaving Oxford he published, in the spring of 1587, a *Treatise containing the Aequity of an Humble Supplication* to draw the attention of the queen and of parliament to the state of his native land. He was concerned at the persistence of superstitious beliefs and practices, but his main attack was on the clergy. For he was convinced that a 'saving knowledge' of the gospel was necessary for salvation, and that this 'saving knowledge' could only be obtained through hearing the gospel preached. But he claimed that this was not done in one out of twenty of the parishes of Wales. The sacramental view of religion, which holds that salvation can come through participating in the services of the church, he condemned outright, and he was bitter in his attack on the 'dumb ministers' who did not preach. He urged that the universities should be encouraged to send out preachers. If there were insufficient clergymen who could preach in Welsh, those who could do so, but who held livings in England, should be encouraged to return to Wales. If this should not prove adequate then 'private men,' that is, laymen, should be allowed to preach. He urged also that the whole of the Bible should be translated, for in some places passages from the Old Testament were read in English to people who understood not one word of that language.

The *Treatise* was submitted to parliament by two of its members, but Penry soon found himself arrested and brought before the Court of High Commission. Archbishop Whitgift maintained that Penry's doctrine that preaching was necessary for salvation constituted heresy. Nevertheless Penry was released after a month's imprisonment. He then published, early in 1588, an *Exhortation unto the governours and people of Wales*, addressed to the Council of Wales, in which he repeated his arguments, and once more begged that the whole Bible be translated. Even Salesbury's New Testament, he claimed, 'was not understood by one in ten of the hearers.' He had heard, however, that a new translation was about to appear.

This new translation was the work of William Morgan, the vicar of Llanrhaeadr ym Mochnant. He was a native of Penmachno in Caernarvonshire, and was educated at Cambridge, where he was taught Hebrew by Tremellius. It is probable that he was assisted in the work of translation by Dr. David Powell of Ruabon, by Richard Vaughan who later became bishop of Bangor, and by Edmund Prys, archdeacon of Merioneth, who had been his fellow student at Cambridge. Prys was a poet of outstanding merit, and it was possibly through his influence that the idiom of the new translation was so pure. Morgan also revised the translation of the New Testament, eliminating Salesbury's idiosyncrasies. The new work appeared in 1588, and the privy council ordered that a copy should be placed in every church before Christmas. Seven years later Morgan became bishop of Llandaff, but in 1601 he was transferred to what was now the wealthier see of St. Asaph, and remained there for the last three years of his life. His translation was once more revised after the authorised English version had appeared in 1611. This revision was the work of Richard Parry, Morgan's successor at St. Asaph, and of Dr. John Davies of Mallwyd, the greatest Welsh scholar of the day. It appeared in 1620. The edition was still intended for use in churches only. It was not till 1630 that the 'little Bible' (*y Beibl Bach*), was issued for general distribution.

The appearance of the Bible in Welsh coincided with the defeat of the Spanish Armada. The danger from foreign invasion was lessened, and Whitgift was able to turn his attention to the puritans, those protestants who were of the opinion that the Elizabethan religious settlement had not gone far enough in doctrine, in ceremony or in church government. There was hardly a trace of puritanism in Wales, but among those who suffered for it was John Penry. He had been associated with the secret press which had published a series of attacks on the bishops, called the *Martin Marprelate Tracts*. Penry had therefore fled to Scotland, where he remained for three years. But in Scotland, the home of presbyterianism, he came to be of the opinion that the ecclesiastical system should be neither episcopal nor presbyterian. The church, he thought, should have no connection with the state, but should be only a gathered community of believers. He therefore returned to London, and joined a group of separatists, but he was soon arrested, and, in May 1593, when he had barely reached the age of thirty, he was hanged.

Two months later, at Beaumaris, died William Davies, the second Roman catholic martyr to be executed in Wales. He was a native of Denbighshire and was educated at Rheims. When he returned on his mission in 1585 he spent most of his time in Anglesey, where he was arrested early in 1592 and executed in the following year. Although the Armada had been defeated the government still feared the possibility of foreign invasion, as is shown by its concern with coastal defence. It was equally concerned about the education abroad, at Rome, Valladolid and elsewhere, of the sons of the Welsh gentry. Moreover the work of the seminary priests was strengthened at the end of the century by the revival of the Benedictine order. This revival arose mainly out of the Spanish colleges, and to Valladolid went John Leander Jones, a native of Llanfrynach in Breconshire, and John Roberts of Trawsfynydd in Merioneth, both of whom had been William Laud's fellow students at St. John's College, Oxford. They returned to England from Spain, and John Roberts paid the supreme penalty on Tyburn in December 1610.

It is certain that the number of recusants had increased under persecution, but they remained few. A return of 1603 numbers 11 men and 21 women in the diocese of Bangor, 100 men and 150 women in the diocese of St. Asaph, 145 men and women in the diocese of St. David's, and 381 men and women in the diocese of Llandaff. These figures are so uncertain that they cannot be taken to indicate the full extent of Roman catholicism in Wales at the end of the sixteenth century, but they may indicate its distribution. Catholicism was to be found not so much in the remote and mountainous areas as in the fertile land along the English border in Flintshire and Monmouthshire. It persisted, not because of isolation, but through the patronage of local magnates. Even so the number of Roman catholics was small, for the return of 1603 gives the communi-

cants in Wales as over 200,000. If these figures are correct
the 808 catholics formed less than half of one per cent of the
population.

Wales, therefore, had followed England in accepting the
Reformation. Everything points to the fact that it had done so
not through enthusiasm for the new religious changes, but
through lack of leadership in resisting them, through indifference and through the passage of time. Towards the end of the
century with the publication, in 1595, by Morris Kyffin of a
translation of Bishop Jewel's *Apology*, under the title of *Deffyn-
niad Ffydd Eglwys Loegr*, an attempt was made to explain to
the Welsh people the nature of the Elizabethan religious settlement and to win them to its support. There is little indication
that it had any effect. Yet despite the lukewarmness of the
Welsh, the influence of the Reformation on their development
as a nation was as profound as anything in their history. In
Ireland, the victory of Roman catholicism established a difference in religion between the Irish and the English people which
proved to be the chief element in the growth of Irish national
sentiment. This difference in religion was sufficiently strong to
counteract the anglicisation of the Irish people through the
disappearance of their own language. In Wales, on the other
hand, the Reformation forged yet another link between Wales
and England. The Welsh clergy, subject to the control of Canterbury and closely associated with their English counterparts,
were a medium through which English influences came into
Wales. But this anglicising element was more than counteracted by the deep influence of the translation into Welsh of the
Bible and of the Book of Common Prayer. Together they form
the greatest contribution of the Reformation to Wales. The
translation was grounded in the best Welsh literary tradition,
so that in the Church services the Welsh people became accustomed to hearing good Welsh continually, and this familiarity
with the Bible prevented the Welsh language from degenerating
into a number of dialects and gradually disappearing. In view
of the smallness in number of the Welsh people and their close
proximity to England, it is doubtful if, without this difference
in language, the consciousness of a separate Welsh nationality
would have endured.

CHAPTER VI

ELIZABETHAN AND JACOBEAN WALES

The union with England and the religious changes were scarcely more important in the history of Wales in the sixteenth century than the emergence into power of a class of gentry which was to dominate the life of Wales for three centuries. This development was already far advanced when Henry VII ascended the throne, and it would have continued even if the Acts of Union had never appeared on the statute book. The gentry, as we have seen, had come into being through the disruption of tribalism and of manorialism in the later middle ages. The commutation of dues and services into money payments and the letting out of the lords' own demesne to individual tenants were the two chief factors in this disruption. As the lords tended more and more to become non-resident, much of their power passed to their stewards, many of whom established new families. The growth of trade in the boroughs, small though it was, led to some accumulation of wealth, and this was frequently invested in land. Pestilence and war hastened the development which had already begun. The poor became poorer, and surrendered their rights to the land, while those more fortunately placed were taking advantage of the social turmoil to enrich themselves. They were helped by the fact that many members of the greater nobility were eliminated in the wars or were ruined by their own extravagance in maintaining immense households. Thus it was that a class of lesser gentry became securely established.

The rivalry between the new families was as intense as was their oppression of their poorer neighbours. Rhys ap Thomas accumulated so vast an estate that he became the greatest magnate in west Wales. Ellis Griffith, a Flintshire soldier who spent the greater part of his life in the garrison at Calais, reflects the opinion of Rhys's contemporaries when he says that no man's land was safe from him. 'For I heard many people from that part of the country say,' he writes, 'that within twenty miles around the place where old Sir Rhys ap Thomas dwelt there was not in the possession of the poor yeomen any land which, if he fancied it, he did not obtain . . . without consulting the owners, who without doubt heaved oft against him heavy sighs, which, in the opinion of many, fell on his grandson. Thus do we see the truth of the proverbs exemplified: The children of the unjust are uprooted; After haughtiness a long death.' In this way does Ellis Griffith account for the disaster which later overtook Rhys ap Griffith, and express the dissatisfaction of ordinary people with the rapacity of his family.

This development reached its highest point in the sixteenth century, which saw greater redistribution of land in Wales than any period since the Norman Conquest. Henry VII's accession to the throne contributed to it. He had been supported by several of the new families, and his success consolidated the fortunes of many. Rhys ap Meredith, for example, who was Henry's standard bearer at Bosworth, firmly laid the foundations of the family of Plas Iolyn in Denbighshire. His grandson, the notorious Ellis Price, succeeded in becoming sheriff of Merioneth, Caernarvon and Anglesey and member of parliament for Merioneth. He greatly extended his lands through sycophancy to the earl of Leicester, and both he and his son, Thomas Prys, the poet and pirate, amassed wealth by dubious means which brought them to the attention of the Court of Star Chamber. Henry's success also enabled many Welshmen to settle in London at a time when the rapidly expanding city was acting as a magnet on men from all the outlying parts of both England and Wales. Many became merchant tailors, haberdashers, cloth workers, bakers, spinners and tradesmen of every type. Morgan Williams of Glamorgan set up in trade as an ale brewer in Putney. He prospered and married the sister of his neighbour, Thomas Cromwell. His son, Richard (who leased the lands of Neath Abbey), assumed the name of Cromwell and became a landowner in Huntingdonshire. The Lord Protector, Oliver Cromwell, was Morgan Williams's great-great-grandson. At the same time as Welshmen flourished in trade, Welsh lawyers teemed at the courts at Westminster, where their natural eloquence won them success. Among them was John Price, who married Morgan Williams's niece and was the author of *Yny lhyvyr hwnn*. Another Welsh lawyer, William Owen of Henllys in Pembrokeshire, published in 1521 an *Abridgement of the Common Law* which was the first book by a Welshman to be printed. He acquired sufficient wealth to purchase the lordship of Cemaes in Pembrokeshire from the Audley family, which had fallen on evil days, and, in his turn he, also, established a 'county family.'

The Acts of Union did not start this development, but they contributed to it. By the removal of any restrictions which remained on the participation of Welshmen in the commerce of the towns, the acts enabled them to accumulate wealth, which was generally invested in land. The acts also gave recognition to the disappearance of gavelkind and its replacement by primogeniture. This had long been the general practice, and the gentry were anxious that it should be legally recognised, for continual sub-division among male heirs had prevented the consolidation of their estates. The introduction of English land law not only legalised mortgage and the free buying and selling of land, but also permitted entail, so that, if it were desired, a successor to an estate could be prevented from disposing of it at pleasure. These provisions, taken together, facilitated the acquisition of land and, at the same time, contributed to the growth and preservation of large estates. But the most important consequence of this radical change in land tenure was the confusion and uncertainty which prevailed for half a century. The new gentry took advantage of this confusion to get possession of the land of the peasants by chicanery and subterfuge. They used much ingenuity in searching for flaws in titles to land. Where they could they turned copyhold into leases. Generally they let out land on short leases and raised the rents on their expiration. They secured mortgages and foreclosed whenever an opportunity presented itself. They put forward spurious claims, and frequently used physical violence to maintain them. Often the threat of litigation would be sufficient to intimidate their victims, especially in view of the ruinous expense entailed in a journey to London to defend such cases.

Moreover, the Acts of Union arranged for the representation of Wales in parliament. This brought knights of the shire from various parts of Wales into contact with one another and with their English counterparts, and produced greater social cohesion within the gentry as a class. As the century progressed these contacts became closer, for the sessions of parliament became

longer, and the members and their families had better opportunities to become acquainted with one another. There was
much intermarriage between the Welsh families, and between
them and the English gentry, especially when it became fashionable to have London houses and to live in them during the
'season.' Many Welsh squires sought English wives, and many
English squires married Welsh heiresses. There was a greater
tendency also for English gentry to settle in Wales as the country
became less isolated. Alban Stepneth, for example, moved from
Hertfordshire to Pembrokeshire, and afterwards married suc-
cesively two Welsh heiresses, thereby founding the family in
west Wales which bears his name.

The dissolution of the monasteries presented this class with a
rare opportunity to increase their estates, and they took full
advantage of it, irrespective of their religious beliefs. The monasteries had, in fact, become closely knit into the social fabric of
the countryside around them. Their abbots were drawn from the
ranks of the local gentry, and neighbouring magnates took an
active part in their internal affairs. As the monasteries ceased to
cultivate their land, much of it was let out on lease to the local
gentry. The remainder was generally managed by stewards
drawn from the same social class, and they were in a favourable
position to obtain monastic land on lease during the dissolution,
when a vast amount of land came suddenly on the market,
greatly increasing the social turmoil which prevailed. It is difficult to say whether the new landlords were better or worse than
the old. In many cases they were to all practical purposes the
same, where the land passed into the hands of the stewards
under whose management it had been. Other land, it is true,
went to absentee speculators, who regarded their property
merely as a source of wealth. These, no doubt, exploited their
tenants more than the monks had done. But, in general, it was
the great families, such as the Morgans at Llantarnam and the
Bulkeleys at Penmon, who profited by the dissolution. There
was intense litigation among them, especially in Elizabeth's
reign over the question of 'concealed' land, that is, over land
which, it was claimed, had rightfully belonged to a monastic
house or collegiate church, but had been 'concealed,' generally
through having been leased by the monastery or church in
question some time before the dissolution.

The new gentry were active in Elizabeth's reign in enclosing the waste lands and commons. It is true that the conversion of arable land into pasture, and its enclosure in large sheepwalks, did not take place to any great extent in Wales. Moreover, much of the land had already been enclosed into separate fields, which were held as compact farms. Rice Merrick, writing his description of Glamorgan in 1578, says that old men had told him that they remembered in their youth how cattle would run for want of shade from the main road traversing the Vale of Glamorgan to Barry, some four miles distant, without any hedges to prevent them. These hedges, he said, were made, for the most part, in the early years of the century. When George Owen, writing of his own part of the country in the last decade of Elizabeth, says that 'most of it is champion (that is, open country) and without enclosures so that they till in the open fields in many and several pieces, and keep their cattle in summer by herds amongst the pieces and fields of corn,' it is only to stress the inconvenience which this caused, and the many actions for trespass which arose out of it. It is probable that he exaggerated its extent in order to emphasise this point, and that much of the land was already enclosed in separate fields. The government, fully aware of the dangers arising from a decrease in the production of grain, more than once instructed the Council of Wales to enquire into decayed tillage, as well as into the enclosure of the commons. Moreover, Elizabeth's act of 1598 for the maintenance of husbandry, which ordered that land formerly used for tillage, but now converted to sheep pastures, must be restored to its former uses by the May of the following year, singles out 'Pembroke in South Wales,' in addition to the Midland shires where the practice had become general. Despite this, however, we find surprisingly little evidence of the enclosure of arable land.

That arable land was not used in Wales for the rearing of sheep was due in part to the existence of waste lands and of open moorlands which were ample for this purpose. In the past, it is true, crofters had frequently encroached on the waste, appropriating small 'parcels' of land which amounted to anything from two to forty acres. But vast areas remained, and with the beginning of the industrial development of Wales, these lands were becoming far more important, for they were frequently rich in mineral deposits, and their woods provided the timber necessary for smelting. The enclosure of the waste and of the commons was therefore carried out with increasing rapidity towards the end of the century. It was a matter of great importance to the small freeholders, who were largely dependent on the waste for grazing their cattle and sheep. Sometimes the enclosure was peacefully arranged, the lord of the manor obtaining a certain proportion, and the remainder being divided among the other claimants. More often there was disagreement, and there were frequent appeals to the Council of Wales, and much litigation. Riots occurred in various parts of the country, especially in the early seventeenth century, and many cases were brought before the Court of Star Chamber. These riots were small in scale, but were very widespread, and their leaders were often responsible men.

The activities of the earl of Leicester attracted great attention. In 1563 the queen had granted him the lordship of Denbigh. He immediately proceeded to raise the rents of his tenants and to enclose waste land. This led to disturbances, when hedges were pulled down, and two youths, related to the Salusburys of Llewenni, were hanged for their share in the riots. Leicester was also made chief ranger of the queen's forest of Snowdon. He tried to extend its limits into Merioneth and even into Anglesey, and sought to bring freeholders within the jurisdiction of its courts. He established commissions to enquire into any encroachments of the forest, and by intimidation and the packing of juries sought to get verdicts in his favour. He was supported by Ellis Price of Plas Iolyn, but met with strong opposition from the gentry, notably from Sir Richard Bulkeley of Beaumaris, who used his influence with the queen to thwart the earl's designs. Bitter hostility continued between Leicester and the north Wales gentry until his death.

The lands of the crown were, in fact, rapidly passing into private hands. The continual rise in prices in the sixteenth century made it necessary for the crown to dispose of much of its lands in order to obtain money. Elizabeth did this on a large scale in England and in Wales. Frequently she 'farmed' crown lands out to individuals, and they caused much discontent by proceeding to enquire minutely into the titles of persons suspected of encroaching on these lands, and bringing their cases before the Court of Exchequer. This practice continued under James I and Charles I, when the crown became almost bankrupt in the years before the Civil War. In the period when he ruled without a parliament, Charles I sold to citizens of London, in return for sums of ready money, large tracts of land in every shire in Wales except Glamorgan, and these were resold to the Welsh gentry.

The age of Elizabeth also saw a tremendous expansion in foreign trade, and great fortunes were made thereby. The most spectacular of all careers in her reign was that of Richard Clough. He was the son of a Denbigh glover, and was apprenticed to the Mercers' Company in London, where he became an associate of Sir Thomas Gresham and one of the founders of the Royal Exchange. He lived most of his brief life in Antwerp (he was only forty when he died), and the wealth which he accumulated there became proverbial. Some of it he used to lease crown lands in Caernarvonshire and Flintshire. He had married as her second husband the famous Catherine of Berain, and of their two daughters, one married a Salusbury of Llewenni and the other a Wynn related to the house of Gwydir. Clough's great wealth, therefore, helped to enrich the gentry of north Wales. Catherine's own matrimonial career knit these families closely together. She was married first to John Salusbury of Llewenni, then to Richard Clough, afterwards to Morris Wynn of Gwydir and lastly to Edward Thelwall of Plas y Ward. By her first three husbands she had offspring, and by their marriages as well as her own the majority of north Wales squires became interrelated.

Foreign commerce gave opportunities to the younger sons of the gentry who, through the adoption of primogeniture, were forced to seek their own livelihood away from home. Among them was Thomas Middleton, the fourth son of the governor of Denbigh castle. He became a member of the Grocers' Company of London, and amassed wealth which enabled him in 1595 to purchase Chirk castle and lordship, and establish a family there. Very soon there were complaints to the Council of Wales that he had enclosed 'sundry great parcels of commons and waste.' The matter was referred to the Court of Star Chamber, but Middleton claimed that his enclosures had been carried out solely in the interests of agriculture. Middleton obtained his wealth through the eastern trade, and was one of the founders of the East India Company. In 1613 he became lord mayor of London.

In these different ways great estates were consolidated. Some proved to be temporary, while others have lasted for centuries. In Pembrokeshire Sir John Perrot of Haroldston built up a vast estate largely out of the sequestered lands of Rhys ap Griffith. Perrot was a commissioner for 'concealed lands,' and his rapacity in evicting his tenants and encroaching on the domains of his neighbours kept Pembrokeshire in constant turmoil. Queen Elizabeth entrusted to him the thankless task of Lord Deputy in Ireland, but he was an imperious man, and he quarrelled with 'that fiddling woman,' as he called his half-sister, the queen. He was arrested on the charge of having conspired with the King of Spain to make himself an independent ruler of Wales, the same charge as had been brought against Rhys ap Griffith, out of whose ruin his own fortunes had sprung. He died in the Tower in 1592. His son was allowed to succeed to his lands, but he, however, left no heir, and the estate dissolved.

Far different was the destiny of the house of Gwydir, the prototype of all the gentry of Wales. The family rose to importance as the fortunes of the neighbouring houses of Penrhyn and Cochwillan declined. The greatest of his line was Sir John Wynn. He extended his estate with ruthless determination, being constantly at law with his neighbours, and he was prepared to bribe officials to gain his own ends. So severely did he oppress his tenants that he was censured and fined by the Council of Wales. He lived like a tribal chieftain, and owned vast herds of cattle, but he was also a man of great business ability, interested in developing the mineral wealth of his estate. He was a scholar, too, imbued with the Renaissance love of beauty as his house at Gwydir showed. Gwydir had been bought by his great-grandfather, and tradition had it that the Wynns were but an illegitimate branch of the house of Cochwillan. But Sir John Wynn wrote his *History of the Gwydir Family* to trace his ancestry back to the princes of North Wales. 'For a great temporal blessing it is,' he said, 'and a great heart's ease, to a man to find that he is well descended.' Other families also sought to make their wealth venerable by inventing pedigrees. George Owen, for example, whose father had bought the lordship of

Cemaes, sought to prove his right to it by descent from its Norman founder through one Alice, who is otherwise unknown to
history, while Sir Edward Stradling of St. Donat's gave currency
to the myth of the twelve knights who supported Fitz Hamon
in the conquest of Glamorgan, among whom he included one of
his ancestors.

The new gentry were a turbulent lot, and were frequently at
strife among themselves. In 1557 Sir George Herbert of Swansea
marched in battle array against the castle of his enemy, Sir
Rice Mansel, at Oxwich, and in 1576 there was a bloody affray
in the streets of Cowbridge between the Bassets of Bewper and
the Turbervilles of Penllin and their respective followers. When
they did not engage in actual fighting the gentry were frequently
at law with one another. The records of the Court of Star Chamber show that they were as often guilty of trickery at the expense
of each other as they were of oppressing their tenants. Nevertheless they were the instruments used by the Tudors for local
government and administration.

As the century wore on the gentry showed a tendency to
become anglicised in speech. This was not a sudden development; far less was it the result of deliberate policy either on
the part of the government or of the gentry themselves. In fact
some of the most oppressive of the squires and some of the richest
of the new commercial families were among the patrons of
Welsh letters in the late sixteenth and early seventeenth centuries. Sir John Wynn, Sir Edward Stradling and George Owen
all wrote in English, but they were patrons of the local bards,
and Stradling made possible the publication of Dr. Siôn Dafydd
Rhys's Welsh grammar. The enormous expense of publishing
the popular version of the Welsh Bible in 1630 was borne by
Thomas Middleton and by Rowland Heylin, a Montgomeryshire merchant who had become sheriff of London. Yet the tendency was for the Welsh language to disappear among them, due
to their contacts with the English gentry. Sir John Wynn's
letters show that when Welsh squires married English wives,
they expected them to learn Welsh, and some English parents
objected to such marriages on that account and because of the
remoteness of Wales. But these English wives introduced the
English speech into their households. Even more serious was the
fact that many a Welsh house ended in an heiress married to an

Englishman, thus becoming entirely anglicised. Very frequently the gentry took to living outside Wales for the greater part of the year.

The influence of education tended in the same direction. Sir John Wynn's great-grandfather, the founder of his house, had been sent to school at Caernarvon 'where he learnt the English tongue, to read and write and understand Latin, a matter of great moment in those days.' Sir John sent his own sons to Eton, to Bedford, to Westminster, and to St. Albans. Shrewsbury school also attracted the sons of the Welsh gentry at this time. The monastic schools had disappeared with the dissolution, while schools where the bards had taught the Welsh language and the mysteries of their craft were becoming rare, although Griffith Hiraethog still had pupils towards the middle of the century. Their place was taken by a number of Tudor foundations, or refoundations, when the endowments of the monasteries or collegiate churches were used in a few cases to establish schools. In this way schools came into existence at Abergavenny, at Brecon, at Bangor, at Carmarthen, at Cowbridge, at Ruthin and elsewhere. In their counterparts in England the pupils were forbidden to speak English, in order that they might learn more effectively to use Latin and Greek. In the Welsh schools, the senior pupils conversed in Latin and Greek, but the junior pupils were allowed to speak in English. Needless to say, no Welsh was to be spoken. Furthermore, in 1571, Queen Elizabeth granted a charter on the petition of Dr. Hugh Price of Brecon, the treasurer of St. David's, for the establishment of Jesus College, Oxford, the first protestant foundation in the university. A connection with Wales did not form part of the original legal constitution of the college, but there is no doubt that this was the intention of the founder. Very soon, Jesus College developed spontaneously into a college for the principality, and this connection was strengthened by the work and generosity of its 'second founder,' Sir Eubule Thelwall, its principal from 1611 to 1630, who obtained for it a new charter in 1622. The Welsh connection received legal sanction from an indenture between the college and its greatest benefactor, Sir Leoline Jenkins in 1686. Thus the sons of the magnates came to be educated in the great English public schools, and those of the lesser gentry in the grammar schools of Wales, while a great number of the clergy went to Jesus College. The atmosphere in all these places was English. This was through no contempt for things Welsh, but merely because the object of Tudor education was to teach 'civility,' that is, the manners of towns and of courts, and a knowledge of English had become a necessity for a cultured man. The schools, and even more so Jesus College, fostered an intense interest in Welsh antiquities, but in a cultivation of the Welsh language they took no part at all.

There thus came about the dichotomy which has marred so much of Welsh life. On the one hand was the Welsh-speaking peasantry, inarticulate but for its bards, who themselves became few through lack of patrons. On the other hand, were the 'natural leaders' of the people who became English in speech, and to this difference in class and in speech there was added, in succeeding centuries, a difference in religion. The position in Wales came to resemble that in Ireland, except that the Welsh gentry were of the same race as their tenantry, whereas in Ireland they were of English descent. Very different was the position in Scotland, where the laird spoke the same language as the crofter, worshipped in the same church and frequently sent his sons to the same school.

The changes which took place in the social life of Wales in the century before the Civil War were, therefore, changes in landownership rather than in the means of production. Welsh life remained almost entirely rural. Farming for subsistence only (in so far as this had ever existed in a strict sense), was, it is true, giving way to commercial farming. It is certain that new land was being brought under corn, and in the second half of the sixteenth century corn was exported from Glamorgan and Pembrokeshire as far afield as London, and even, if George Owen is to be believed, to Venice and other places abroad. Both George Owen and Rice Merrick attribute the superiority of their shires in this respect to the presence of ample supplies of lime. At the same time methods of cultivation were being improved. But not all squires were progressive; many had neither the ability nor the capital to develop their estates. Cattle rearing, the traditional occupation of the Welsh tribesmen, remained their chief source of income. The cattle trade with England had increased when the March was pacified and reduced to shire ground. It became increasingly important with the rapid growth of London and the need to feed its expanding population. Welsh drovers and their herds therefore became familiar sights on the roads of England. Archbishop John Williams called the drovers 'the Spanish fleet of north Wales, which brings hither that little gold and silver we have.' The Civil War interrupted the trade for a time, and brought disaster to the squires who relied on the sale of their cattle to meet their cash payments. For example, parliamentary soldiers at the siege of Gloucester seized nine hundred beasts which were in the charge of eighteen drovers. So, early in the war, the gentry of north Wales were forced to petition the king for a safe conduct for their herds. 'The sale of your petitioners' cattle and Welsh cottons,' they said, 'being the most considerable commodities of these countries, cottons mostly vented in Shrewsbury, and our cattle driven and sold in most parts of England, hath been and is the only support of your petitioners' being and livelihood, among whom there be many thousand families in the mountainous part of this country who, sowing little or no corn at all, trust merely to the sale of their cattle, wool and Welsh cottons for provision of bread.'

The Welsh 'cottons' referred to in this petition were a coarse woollen cloth. Sheep rearing had not been of much importance in mediaeval Wales, and Welsh wool had been of little account. But, stimulated by the rising prices of the sixteenth century, the wool trade had developed. 'I judge there is now twice as much wool shorn in Pembrokeshire,' wrote George Owen, 'as was forty years past.' The wool was spun and woven on the farms themselves, so that it was of the coarsest texture. Gild life had never been strong in Wales, but in Elizabeth's reign, gilds of weavers and tuckers appeared in Carmarthen, in Brecon, in Haverfordwest and elsewhere. But Welsh cloth still remained poor in quality, and there were complaints that it was discrediting English cloth when it was sold abroad at Rouen and other places. In consequence there was a tendency for the wool to be bought by English merchants, of Bristol and of Barnstaple, to be made up elsewhere. The Welsh cloth of north Wales was also 'finished' in England. The natural centre of this trade was Oswestry where, in 1619, goods to the value of £2,000 were said to change hands in the weekly market. Shrewsbury merchants bought cloth there in large quantities and transferred it to their own town and to London in wagons. There ensued a bitter struggle, and the Drapers' Company of Shrewsbury succeeded in having the market itself held at Shrewsbury. Both towns, however, made common cause against London interlopers and against the agents of French merchants who were buying cloth in north Wales and shipping it direct to France from Aberdovey.

Wool and hides, (the by-products of sheep and cattle rearing), also formed the chief items in both the foreign and the coastal export trade of Wales in the early sixteenth century. This period saw the beginning of modern British commerce, and the Welsh, with their newly acquired privileges of citizenship, were able to participate in it. Tudor mercantilist policy encouraged the expansion of shipping and foreign trade. Greater attention was paid to harbours and creeks, and together with this went an attempt to suppress piracy. This was a matter of difficulty as both the townspeople of the ports and the local gentry were in league with the pirates. Thomas Lewis of the Van, near Caerphilly, for example, stored his town house at Cardiff and his country manors with spoils brought by pirates into the roadstead at Penarth. John Callice, the chief pirate operating in the Bristol Channel and the Irish Sea, had the closest association with the Glamorgan gentry, and among his friends was the comptroller of customs at Cardiff. He was entertained at Haverfordwest by Sir John Perrot's agent, and was aided and abetted by the townsfolk of Pembroke. So serious did this matter become that the government in 1575 entrusted the work of suppressing piracy to a commission composed of Sir John Perrot and four others (among whom was Bishop Richard Davies), but they were not successful, partly because of Perrot's violent quarrels with Richard Vaughan, the vice-admiral of south Wales, and partly because it was clear that Perrot himself had profited from the activities of the pirates. Piracy did eventually die out, but this was not through the efficiency of the Tudor government. It disappeared through the general pacification of the country, through the loss of trade in pirated Spanish goods when peace with Spain was restored, and through the ruin of some of the families who connived at it, including that of Sir John Perrot.

The foreign trade of the south Wales ports was mostly with France, especially with Brittany. Salt and wine were imported, and cloth and hides exported. Towards the end of the century these were entirely surpassed in importance by the export of coal from west Glamorgan and Carmarthenshire. Meanwhile Beaumaris and all the little ports along the coast to Milford Haven traded with Ireland, slates being exported from north Wales and coal and culm from Pembrokeshire. Among the imports were timber for the small shipbuilding industry which throve in many places, and Irish live stock. The coastal trade was in wool, butter, cheese and general merchandise, while herring fishing was carried on in Cardigan Bay, and barrels of salted herring were sent to English ports and to Dublin. Welsh commerce remained on a small scale, but it provided a school of seamanship for Welsh sailors, and started a tradition in the small coastal towns where, for generations, sons have followed the occupations of their fathers and gone down to the sea in ships.

The Tudor period also saw the beginnings of industrial development in Wales, stimulated by the growth of capital through trade and the exploitation of the New World. Here again the commercial policy of the Tudors in developing a self-sufficing state assisted the growing industries. There was a careful exploration of the country's mineral resources, and both technical skill and capital were imported from abroad. Moreover the constant wars led to an increase in the demand for ordnance and the encouragement of the brass industry. Naturally the attention of the government was directed to Wales because of its ample woodlands, its mineral deposits and its water supply.

The right to search for copper and precious metals in Wales and other places was granted to Daniel Hochstetter, a German, who, together with English associates, formed in 1568 the Society of the Mines Royal. In the same year another German, Christopher Shutz, launched a company called the Society of Mineral and Battery Works, with the sole right of making brass and wire. Of these two joint-stock companies it was the latter which first paid attention to Wales, by establishing a brass foundry and a wire making factory at Tintern. The brass foundry did not show much progress, but the wire-works was very successful, mainly because of the increased demand for wire for use in carding wool. Later the Mines Royal Society, which had extensive copper mines in Cornwall, and was in search of suitable sites for smelting, turned its attention to Neath, attracted there by an abundant supply of wood and coal in close proximity to the sea, and by the ease with which copper ore could be transported there from Cornwall. A smelting furnace was started at Neath in 1584 under the management of Ulrich Frosse. It did not, however, remain in operation for very long, but the connection of Neath with copper smelting was later to be revived.

At the same time the Society of Mines Royal became interested in the exploitation of the lead deposits in Cardiganshire. Operations were started in Elizabeth's reign, but these did not attain any importance until a lease of all mines between the Dovey and the Ystwyth was granted in 1617 to Sir Hugh Middleton on payment of £400 a year. Sir Hugh was a younger brother of Sir Thomas Middleton, and four years previously he had completed a great scheme which provided London with its first adequate water supply. From his Cardiganshire mines he was reputed to have made a profit of £2,000 a month. After his death the lease was taken over by Thomas Bushell, who introduced new methods of extracting silver from the ore, and who obtained permission in 1637 to mint coins in the castle at Aberystwyth. The outbreak of the Civil War five years later brought this to an end. Bushell was a royalist, and is said to have raised a regiment on the king's side, but his mining enterprises sank into the general ruin brought about by the war.

The coal industry alone was the product of local initiative. Coal had been used long before this, but the industry itself did not arise until the decline in the country's wood supply, which coincided with an increased demand for timber for the navy, made it necessary to obtain other fuel. While the crown had always reserved its right to mine all metals, the right to dig coal had always belonged to the owner of the soil. The first pits were therefore shallow holes made by the farmers themselves, but the sinking of shafts required more capital. These were generally located in the areas where coal was found near the sea coast, in west Glamorgan, in Pembrokeshire and in Flintshire, and much of the coal raised was exported to France and to Ireland.

The social turmoil of the sixteenth century which had produced the great families had also, by the same process, deprived the poor of their rights to the land. There had thus grown up a class of wage earners, many of whom found occupation in the new industries. But many were reduced to destitution. Pauperism had existed in England and Wales, and legislation had been enacted to deal with it, well before the dissolution of the monasteries. It is not probable that the dissolution contributed much to its growth. But as the century advanced the number of vagrants increased. Soldiers, who had been mustered in Wales to suppress the troubles in Ireland, frequently returned incapacitated. Also Irish immigrants, refugees from the frequent rebellions, provided west Wales with a difficult problem throughout the sixteenth and well into the seventeenth century. Whole parishes in Pembrokeshire, says George Owen, were inhabited by the Irish. They made aqua vitae in great abundance, and sold it around the country on horseback. A writer of the next century congratulates the county on being rid of the 'Hibernian swarm,' but deplores the taste for whisky they had left behind. Welsh vagabonds had an unenviable reputation in England, and Elizabethan literature has frequent references to their 'cozening.' Throughout the century the Council of Wales was concerned with the excessive number of alehouses in Wales, often 'in desert and secret places, as woods, commons, waste grounds and mountains.' The Council regarded them as breeding grounds of disturbances, and considered the unlawful games practised in them to be harmful to the 'maintenance of artillery,' that is of archery, for the bow still remained an important weapon of the Elizabethan militia. Elizabethan legislation tried to distinguish between the 'valiant' beggars and the worthy poor, and to relieve the latter by voluntary and assessed contributions. After the act of 1572, Welsh local records have frequent references to vagabonds, both male and female, being burned by a hot iron through the gristle of the right ear and whipped. The great act of 1601 provided for the nomination by the justices of the peace in each parish of two or three overseers who were empowered to raise the amount necessary for the relief of the poor. This was supplemented by the severe law of settlement of 1662 which provided for the return of new arrivals in a parish to their old homes. These acts together formed the basis of the poor law until the nineteenth century.

CHAPTER VII

THE CIVIL WAR

RICHARD BAXTER, the eminent puritan divine, classified the supporters of king and parliament in the Civil War in the following way. 'A very great part of the knights and gentlemen of England,' he wrote, 'adhered to the king, and most of the tenants of those gentlemen, and also most of the poorest of the people, whom the others called the rabble, did follow the gentry and were for the king. On the parliament's side were the smaller part of the gentry in most of the counties, and the greatest part of the tradesmen and freeholders and the middle sort of men, especially in those corporations and counties which depend on clothing and such manufactures.' This economic factor was, in fact, of supreme importance in the struggle. The great rise in prices in the sixteenth century had both impoverished the crown, which was dependent for much of its revenue on fixed rents, and given a stimulus to industrial activity. Therefore, while the crown was becoming bankrupt, a wealthy middle class was rapidly expanding. It is said that in the parliament of 1621 the members of the house of commons could have bought up the king and the lords three times over. The new class did not pay anything like its fair share in taxation, but it strongly resisted attempts made by the crown to increase revenue through such devices as the granting of monopolies in the manufacture of goods and by attempting to revive obsolete feudal dues. The Civil War was a struggle for power between the middle class on the one hand and the king and the landed aristocracy on the other.

These considerations determined the attitude of Wales. In Wales there were very few of the 'middle sort of men'; the whole trend of the previous century had been towards the rise of the gentry and the consolidation of their estates. The gentry had been intensely loyal to the Tudors through gratitude for past favours and, still more, through a lively expectation of favours to come. This loyalty was transferred to the house of Stuart for the same reason. When James ascended the throne the Scottish unicorn replaced the Tudor dragon as a supporter of the royal arms, and his Scottish followers obtained offices at court, where they were as unpopular in their turn as Welshmen were in Henry VII's day. But Welsh courtiers still continued to receive royal favour. For James had reason to be grateful for Welsh support. When his succession had been doubtful, the second earl of Essex (great-grandson of Walter Devereux, Lord Ferrers, the opponent of Rhys ap Griffith) had sought by a *coup d'état* to make the queen declare for James. Essex was a great landowner on the Welsh border in Herefordshire, in Breconshire, in Glamorgan and in Pembrokeshire, and he drew his main support from his Welsh estates. His chief agent in the plot was Sir Gelly Meyrick (son of Roland Meyrick, bishop of Bangor) who perished with Essex on the scaffold. Even the Welsh catholic exiles had favoured the Scottish succession against the Spaniards, for they continued to hope for James's conversion, though Hugh Owen still belonged to the Spanish faction, and was soon deep in Guy Fawkes's plot. When Ben Jonson's masque *For the Honour of Wales*, was performed before the king in 1618, James listened with approval to a panegyric of the Welsh nation. 'Where hath the crown at all times better servitors, more liberal of their lives and fortunes?' asked the epilogue. Moreover, when James, in pursuance of his unpopular Spanish policy, sent Prince Charles and Buckingham to Madrid to woo the infanta, the prince was joined there by several Welshmen, among them Sir John Vaughan of Golden Grove (son-in-law to Sir Gelly Meyrick), as comptroller of the prince's household, his son Richard Vaughan, and Richard Wynn, son of Sir John Wynn of Gwydir.

Among those who gained advancement at the court of James I was John Williams of Conway, the most eminent Welshman of the seventeenth century. He was descended from the ancient houses of Penrhyn and Cochwillan, now in decline, and was god-son to Sir John Wynn. After leaving Cambridge he obtained rapid preferment, becoming dean of Westminster in 1620 and bishop of Lincoln in the following year. He was high in the favour of Buckingham and of James, who made him lord keeper when he was thirty-nine years of age. In all but name he was lord chancellor of England, and he was the only protestant prelate who ever held the great seal. He amassed great wealth, and his household was thronged with the indigent sons of Welsh families who expected him to provide for them either in his own service or elsewhere. He was both a scholar and a patron of scholars. Despite his overweening ambition, his craft and hot temper, he was generous and had the moderation of a statesman. After the death of James his influence declined, and through the enmity of Laud, who pursued him with a vindictiveness strangely out of keeping with Laud's saintly character, Williams lost the office of lord keeper, and was brought to trial and imprisoned in the Tower. The Long Parliament set him free, and King Charles in his last extremity, called on Williams's support and made him archbishop of York. It is the opinion of Gardiner, the greatest historian of the struggle, that if Charles had trusted Williams instead of Laud, 'there would have been no Civil War and no dethronement.'

Welsh politics in the seventeenth century depended upon loyalty to persons rather than to principles. The Welsh gentry, with some exceptions, were loyal to the king; their tenantry were loyal to them. Neither class was greatly interested in the constitutional struggle. There was no opposition to government policy in Wales as there was to the English plantations in Ireland or to the attempt to impose the English liturgy in Scotland. Of the hundreds of pamphlets which appeared during the struggle not one sought to explain the parliamentary standpoint in the Welsh language. The peasantry had no means of deciding on the questions at issue. Nor was puritanism of much importance in Wales at this time. There were a few sectaries along the border, on both the English and the Welsh sides, but their numbers were insignificant. The re-issue of the Book of Sports in 1633, which roused such opposition in England, caused little disturbance in Wales. As events proceeded towards a crisis there was, it is true, considerable hesitation on the part of many squires. Neither did they respond readily to the extraordinary taxation levied by the king. In each succeeding year there was difficulty about the payment of ship money, and in 1638 Montgomeryshire and Carmarthenshire defaulted altogether. Breconshire and Cardiganshire did so the following year, while Carmarthenshire, Caernarvonshire, Denbighshire, Flintshire, Montgomeryshire, Pembrokeshire and Monmouthshire were seriously in arrear, and not one shire paid in full. There was also some natural reluctance on the part of the peasantry to serve in the king's levies, and there was much evasion and desertion. Yet the country in general was loyal to the crown.

Among the magnates who supported parliament, two had great influence in Wales. The earl of Pembroke owned Cardiff castle and much land in Glamorgan. He was a man of violent and unstable temper and his opposition to the king was mainly due to personal pique. His son sat for Glamorgan in the Long Parliament and took the same side as his father. The earl of Essex, who had succeeded to his father's estates despite the latter's attainder, was of finer quality. Unlike Elizabeth's dashing favourite he was a man of strong principles, and was punctilious in his sense of duty. He was made commander-in-chief of the parliamentary forces, and Sir John Meyrick (nephew to Sir Gelly Meyrick) became one of his chief subordinates. Their influence was partly responsible for the parliamentarian-ism of south Pembrokeshire, and for the important part played by this area in the war. But by no means all the south Pembroke-shire squires supported parliament. Many wavered, and many came out for the king. Indeed the nucleus of parliamentary strength there lay, not in the squires, but in the towns of Pem-broke, Tenby and Haverfordwest, which were held by the local trained bands. Here the main influence was that of John Poyer, the mayor of Pembroke, a prosperous merchant, trading with the parliamentary city of Bristol. He realised at an early date the importance of Milford Haven as a possible landing place for troops from Ireland, and, six months before the outbreak of hostilities, he was already warning parliament of this danger. The only other pocket of parliamentary resistance in Wales was Wrexham. This town had long been affected by the puritanism of Cheshire, and this was strengthened by the influence of the Middletons of Chirk. The family, as we have seen, had amassed great wealth through trade in the city of London. Sir Thomas Middleton, son of the lord mayor who had partly borne the expense of publishing the Bible of 1630, sat for Denbighshire in the Long Parliament. It was through association with Wrexham, and possibly with Sir Thomas Middleton himself, that John Jones emerged as a parliamentary leader, born though he was in remote and royalist Merioneth.

The loyalty of Wales was of great service to the king. It was within easy reach of his headquarters at Oxford, and provided an admirable base for the supply of men and provisions. A contemporary called it the 'nursery of the king's infantry.' From the outbreak of war onwards, repeated commissions of array were issued to Welsh leaders to recruit men for the king's army, and in all campaigns a considerable proportion of his infantry came from Wales. The Welsh royalist commanders, on the other hand, though men of high rank, were of no ability, with the exception of Sir John Owen of Clenennau, a poverty-stricken cavalier from wind-swept Eifionydd, and a man of great valour. Equally important for the king was the proximity of Wales to Ireland, whence men and supplies could be brought through Chester or Beaumaris or Milford Haven. Moreover Wales provided the king with a safe region beyond the line of the Severn into which to withdraw his forces and recuperate. As Wales remained clear of the main parliamentary armies until the last stages of the war, many eminent royalists sought refuge there, notably Jeremy Taylor at Golden Grove, Archbishop Ussher of Armagh at Cardiff and St. Donat's, and the future archbishop of Canterbury, Gilbert Sheldon, at Llantrithyd.

When the Long Parliament met in 1640, the great majority of the Welsh members were for the king. After it had assembled relations between Charles and his opponents rapidly grew worse. The prerogative courts of Star Chamber and High Commission were abolished and the authority of the Council of Wales was curtailed. After the outbreak of the Irish rebellion in October 1641 events moved swiftly to a crisis, and in August 1642 war broke out.

The campaigns of the Civil War in Wales can only be understood as part of the general strategy of the war. In the early stages the king was on the offensive; his objective was London, the centre of parliamentary resistance. When he had raised his standard at Nottingham on August 22 he marched to Shrewsbury to collect the Welsh infantry recruited by his commissioners of array. He was joined there by a considerable force, led by Sir Edward Stradling of St. Donat's and William Herbert of Cogan, the member of Parliament for Cardiff, who had taken the opposite side to his relative, the earl of Pembroke. The king

then marched on London, but he was intercepted by the earl of·
Essex at Edgehill on October 23. It was an indecisive battle,
but many of the Welsh including William Herbert were slain,
and Stradling was taken prisoner. Meanwhile the marquis of
Hertford had been made lieutenant-general of the western
counties including the whole of south Wales. He had hoped to
hold the south-west of England for the king, but his reception
there was so hostile that he and his following were forced to
escape in coal boats from Minehead and made for Cardiff, where
he arrived on October 3. There he proceeded to raise an army.
The greatest landowner in Monmouthshire was the marquis of
Worcester. He was a Roman catholic, and could hope for
nothing from a parliamentary victory, so he spent his wealth
lavishly for the king. But Charles dared not prejudice his own
position by granting a commission either to Worcester or to his
son, Edward Somerset (who bore the courtesy title of Lord
Herbert of Raglan), on account of their religious beliefs. They,
on the other hand, regarded Hertford as an interloper, and this
jealousy did much harm to the royalist cause. Hertford left
Cardiff on November 4 to join the king at Oxford. As both
Gloucester and Hereford were held for parliament, he proceeded by way of Tewkesbury, where he was attacked, and his
inexperienced Welsh levies put to flight. He managed to reassemble them, and with about two thousand men took Hereford and joined the king before Christmas. The campaign of
1642 had thus ended without a decision.

In 1643 the initiative still remained with the king. He
planned a threefold attack on London, from the centre, from the
south-west and from the north. The success of his plan depended
on the capture of the three great strongholds of Gloucester,
Bristol and Hull. Gloucester was of supreme importance as its
capture would give the king full command of the Severn and
clear the road to Wales. Lord Herbert of Raglan raised an army
to lay siege to it, but he was completely taken by surprise at
Highnam in the Forest of Dean on March 24, and the greater
part of his force, including many of the Welsh gentry, was either
killed or captured. The royalist historian, Clarendon, was bitterly critical of Lord Herbert's inefficiency. Clarendon was of
the opinion that if the money spent on this force had been
brought to the king, the war might have been ended that sum-

Vera effigies Clariss: Do.ⁿⁱ Iohānis Wynn de Gwedur in Com Carnarvon Equitis et Baronetti &c. Obijt primo die Martij. 1626. Ætat: 73.

Honoris ipsius causa   Ro Vaughan sculp   Proiique D.D:

SIR JOHN WYNN OF GWYDIR

PEMBROKE CASTLE

mer. Nevertheless the king made Lord Herbert his lieutenant-general in Herefordshire and south-east Wales. The king himself then proceeded to besiege Gloucester, but the city was relieved by Essex, and this campaign ended in the indecisive first battle of Newbury on 20 September.

The royalists had met with more success in the south-west. On July 26, the city of Bristol was taken almost by assault, by a force under Prince Rupert. It included a large contingent of Welsh troops under the command of Sir John Owen of Clenennau, who was severely wounded in the engagement. The loss of this puritan city, the greatest seaport of the west, was a serious blow to parliament. Moreover its fall released the royalist fleet and greatly encouraged the king's supporters in south Wales. Richard Vaughan of Golden Grove, who had succeeded his father as second earl of Carbery, had been made lieutenant-general in west Wales, and he now decided to attack south Pembrokeshire. Two royalist ships which appeared in Milford Haven were soon captured by the parliamentarians, but on land the royalists met with little resistance. Carbery advanced into Pembrokeshire in August; Tenby surrendered almost immediately and Haverfordwest was occupied. Most of the Pembrokeshire squires who had wavered declared openly for the king, with fateful consequences later on. The town of Pembroke alone held out.

The king's attack had thus been repulsed in the centre but had been successful in the south-west. In the north his armies were defeated and had to abandon the siege of Hull. The total result was a stalemate, and in consequence both sides looked for allies. In September parliament signed a Solemn League and Covenant with the Scots, who promised military support on the understanding that presbyterianism should be introduced. The king turned to Ireland, and in the same month agreed to a truce with the Irish rebels which would release his troops for service in England. These troops were, in fact, English, but the opinion gained currency that they were Irish catholics who were being brought over to exterminate protestantism. The king's decision focussed attention on north Wales which was on the main route to Ireland. Archbishop John Williams had returned to Conway early in the war, and, at his own expense, had fortified his native town, for it commanded the road along the coast, and was the gateway into Anglesey and Snowdonia. He had soon opened communication with Ormonde, who commanded the king's forces in Ireland. Thomas Bulkeley, who was now created a viscount, fortified Beaumaris, another key position in the transit of men and materials from Ireland. The parliamentary leader was the puritan, Sir Thomas Middleton of Chirk, serving under the supreme command of Sir William Brereton. In order to forestall the arrival of the regiments from Ireland, Middleton decided to attack. He crossed the Dee in November at Holt, and quickly took Wrexham, Hawarden, Flint, Mostyn, Mold and Holywell. Denbigh alone held out, under its governor, Colonel Salusbury, who was popularly known as 'Blue Stockings' (Hosanau Gleision). But, on November 18, Middleton just as quickly abandoned his conquests, for the 'Irish' army landed both in Anglesey and on his flank in Flintshire and was placed under the command of Lord Byron, one of Prince Rupert's ablest lieutenants. Middleton thought that his militia would be no match for these seasoned troops, who were however, in fact, so badly demoralised that Ormonde had feared they would not fight. The archbishop exerted himself to provide them with clothes and food, at Conway and at Chester. Byron then advanced into Cheshire, only to be routed by Fairfax at Nantwich on January 29, 1644.

The Irish truce gave a wider significance to the local campaign in Pembrokeshire also, for to gain control of Milford Haven would be a great asset to the king. However, throughout the war, parliament retained command of the sea, a fact of the greatest importance in understanding the course of events in Pembrokeshire, and the parliamentary fleet arrived in time to save Pembroke. Pembrokeshire also provided parliament with a young and energetic leader in Rowland Laugharne, who had been a page in the earl of Essex's household, and whose father was a cousin to Sir John Meyrick. He proved more than a match for Carbery, who had mistakenly dispersed his forces in small garrisons. These Laugharne took one by one. By a combined land and sea assault he captured the fortress which the royalists were constructing to dominate the Haven at Pill (within the present-day town of Milford). He occupied Haverfordwest. The royalist garrison in Tenby offered strong resistance, but the town fell on March 9, 1644, and Laugharne advanced and occupied Carmarthen. Carbery's power was broken. He was bitterly criticised for his inefficiency, and was even suspected of treachery, and it is at least noteworthy that his estates escaped sequestration. To save theirs the Pembrokeshire gentry again changed sides, and the bitter recrimination among them continued.

By the early months of 1644 the king had lost the initiative. It was necessary to reorganise his forces, and Prince Rupert seems to have been given supreme command in Wales. His adjutant in north Wales was Lord Byron, and, in south Wales, Lord Carbery was replaced by Sir Charles Gerard, a very able professional soldier. A vigorous recruiting campaign was undertaken once again. Gerard then proceeded to reduce west Wales. With some two thousand five hundred horse and foot he crossed into Wales at Chepstow, and advanced to meet Laugharne. He marched rapidly through Cardiff, took Kidwelly, which was then an important haven, and, on June 18, occupied Carmarthen. He then quickly reduced Cardigan and Newcastle Emlyn, as well as the castles at Laugharne and Roch, and on August 22 took Haverfordwest. By the end of the month he was besieging Pembroke and threatening Tenby. Laugharne, despite his ability, was completely outgeneralled by him, but already, on July 2, Cromwell, with the aid of the Scots, had defeated the king at Marston Moor, and Gerard was recalled with his work unfinished.

Meanwhile Middleton from his base in Cheshire had consolidated his position in north-east Wales. He raised the siege of Oswestry in July and made raids into Montgomeryshire, capturing Newtown on September 4. Montgomery castle, a key position on the Welsh border, was surrendered to him without any resistance by its owner, Edward Lord Herbert of Cherbury, the philosopher and historian. Outside the town of Montgomery the parliamentary forces were repulsed, but they rallied, and, on September 14, there took place at Montgomery the most considerable battle fought in Wales during the first Civil War. Brereton and Middleton commanded on one side and Byron on the other, and their whole strength was assembled. The battle was fought with desperation, but it ended in a complete victory for parliament. The power of the king in north Wales had been destroyed.

The battle of Marston Moor had lost for the king the whole of the north of England. The disaster which overtook Essex's army in Cornwall however retrieved the balance to some measure, and led Cromwell and others, who were dissatisfied with the prosecution of the war, to obtain the passing by parliament in April 1645 of the Self-denying Ordinance, by which members of both houses of parliament resigned their military commands. Fairfax became commander-in-chief, and in north Wales, Sir Thomas Middleton was replaced by his brother-in-law, Thomas Mytton. On the king's side, Archbishop John Williams, also, lost command at Conway. He had displeased the royalists by resisting their endless demands for money, and he was evidently moving towards neutrality in the struggle. Sir John Owen, between whom and the archbishop there was the traditional antipathy which exists between the men of north and south Caernarvonshire, had moved secretively into the town, and, on May 9, 1645, he took possession of the castle as if it were in the hands of the enemy. He also seized the valuables which the local gentry had placed there in the archbishop's safe-keeping.

The recall of Gerard by the king had allowed Laugharne to recover all his losses in west Wales, but early in 1645 Gerard returned. From Chester he marched through mid Wales, by way of Llanidloes, ravaging as he went, and on April 23 he encountered Laugharne at Newcastle Emlyn and completely defeated him. Laugharne hurriedly fell back on his bases in south Pembrokeshire; Cardigan and Haverfordwest were evacuated; Picton castle, which stoutly resisted Gerard, was taken by assault; Carew also fell, and once more Pembroke and Tenby, which could be provisioned from the sea, alone held out. But once more, also, the king's requirements in the greater theatre of war proved the salvation of the parliamentarians in Pembrokeshire. In view of the impending battle, which was fought at Naseby on June 14, Gerard was again recalled. Laugharne, though no match for Gerard, was far superior in ability to the local royalist leaders, and he defeated them with great loss on August 1, at Colby Moor, some three miles from Haverfordwest. He quickly cleared the royalists out of Pembrokeshire, and was now in a position to go further afield. By October 12 he had occupied Carmarthen. He then advanced into Glamorgan, and in November he reached Brecon. By the close of the year his forces were besieging Aberystwyth. The king's power had been irretrievably broken at Naseby, so that this time Laugharne was able to hold his conquests.

The battle of Naseby had cost Charles half his forces, including a large body of Welsh foot. Once more he turned to Wales and to Ireland for reinforcements. With Gerard he retired to Raglan Castle, which became his headquarters for some weeks. On July 16 he met his commissioners of array in Cardiff. But he found the greatest difficulty in raising a new army. One Welsh levy after another had perished in the struggle, and the people did all they could to resist enlistment. The gentry also were dissatisfied with the way they had been treated, in being superseded by English commanders. Even more important was the discontent caused by the behaviour of the king's armies in Wales. The word plunder, which had become current in Germany during the Thirty Years' War, was now introduced into the English language, and Rupert and his professional commanders made the people familiar with its meaning. The Welsh made it clear that they would move only if officered by their own men, and Charles was forced to comply. He had, in the meantime, already sent Lord Herbert of Raglan, who had now become earl of Glamorgan, to Ireland on a mysterious mission to raise two regiments of Irish soldiers. On August 25, Lord Herbert signed with his co-religionists in Ireland a 'Treaty of Glamorgan,' which Charles found it politic to disavow. Lord Herbert still hoped to bring an Irish force to relieve the king at Chester, where he had retired with Gerard. But there was no time to recruit an army, for on September 10 Rupert surrendered Bristol, a crushing blow to the king's cause, and on September 24, the king himself, from the walls of Chester, saw his last army defeated at Rowton Heath.

From this time onwards the war became a matter of sieges, as the last pockets of resistance were captured one by one. In west Wales Colonel Rice Powell, one of Laugharne's lieutenants, took Aberystwyth in April 1646. In the south-east parliament used the services of Thomas Morgan, the governor of Gloucester. He was scarcely bigger than a dwarf, but he had seen service in the Thirty Years' War, and had a European reputation in the conduct of siege operations. Before the end of 1645 he had taken Chepstow and Monmouth, and in August 1646, Raglan fell to him. In north Wales, Mytton took Ruthin in April. He then by-passed Conway and captured Caernarvon in June after a long siege. The parliamentary forces then crossed into Anglesey, and Beaumaris fell on June 14 to Colonel John Jones, who negotiated the surrender of the island. Conway town was taken in August, and Archbishop John Williams, who had failed to obtain redress from the king, actively assisted Mytton in the reduction of the castle, which held out till November. By this time Denbigh had fallen, held to the last by its redoubtable governor, Hosanau Gleision. Finally Harlech, which was ably defended by William Owen of Brogyntyn, brother of Sir John Owen, fell on March 15, 1647, the last of the king's fortresses in England and Wales to surrender.

The uneasy peace which followed the end of the first Civil War did not last long. In the heat of the struggle opinions had become more pronounced. Parliament and the city of London remained presbyterian. They wished to substitute presbyterianism for episcopacy as the established form of church government, and were entirely intolerant of religious differences. But in the army there had grown up sects who disbelieved in an established church of any kind, and who demanded both religious and political liberty. They felt that Providence had given the victory to them, showing, by wager of battle, its approval of their cause. They had a special grievance in the proposal to disband the army without making up its arrears in pay. They therefore marched on London, seized the king's person and expelled the presbyterian leaders from parliament. The king, however, escaped and entered into a treaty with the Scots, by which he agreed to establish presbyterianism for three years in return for Scottish support. So deep was his loathing of presbyterianism that he cannot have intended to keep his word.

It was events in Pembrokeshire which precipitated the second Civil War. These events arose out of the mutual recriminations of Laugharne and Poyer on the one hand, and, on the other, those 'subtle ambidexters,' as Poyer called them, the gentry who had changed sides with the ebb and flow of the parliamentary fortunes. Laugharne and Poyer had been obliged to levy contributions from them, and they accused the two leaders of misappropriating public money. Richard Baxter emphasises that both Laugharne and Poyer were episcopalians; they had little regard for the presbyterians, and still less for the sects. (Poyer had, indeed, presented a chalice inscribed with his name to St. Mary's, Pembroke, in 1645, while the war was still on.) Laugharne's patron, the earl of Essex, had himself become lukewarm in the parliamentary cause, and was now dead. As late as June 1647, Laugharne had suppressed a royalist rising in the Vale of Glamorgan, but it is evident that the king's agents were in touch with him, and he was called to London to answer to parliament for charges made against him. Poyer was a complex character. He was violent and impulsive, and in his boastful moods was prepared to measure himself up against Cromwell himself. When commissioners were sent to demobilise the troops, the parliamentary forces in west Wales were included in the order. Poyer was displaced by Colonel Fleming as governor of Pembroke, but he refused to surrender the castle, and on March 8, 1648, impetuously fired on the part of the town where Fleming's troops were billeted. Rice Powell's men were also dissatisfied and threw in their lot with Poyer. When the revolt had started the leaders were led to welcome royalist aid, and declared for the king.

Colonel Horton was sent down by Cromwell to suppress the rising. He advanced up the river Usk and across to the vale of Towy. There was much skirmishing with Rice Powell, in which Fleming was killed, and Horton was forced to retire to Brecon. Powell then decided to take the offensive and advance along the coastal route. He passed through Swansea and Neath, and negotiated with the royalists of the Vale of Glamorgan and the governor of Cardiff Castle. It was important to Horton that Powell should not be allowed to establish himself in Cardiff, and Horton made forced marches southward to intercept him. Meanwhile Laugharne had slipped away from London and joined Powell on May 4. Four days later the two armies met at St. Fagans, outside Cardiff. Laugharne and Powell had eight thousand horse and foot, and Horton only three thousand. But Horton's soldiers were highly trained men, and after fierce fighting for two hours they won the day. Laugharne and Powell retired hastily to south Pembrokeshire.

Trouble had also broken out in north Wales, where Colonel John Jones was commissioner for the disbanding of troops. There were disturbances in Anglesey, and Sir John Owen seized this opportunity to attack Caernarvon with a small force of four hundred men. His attempt to establish contact with south Wales was foiled. Mytton, operating out of Caernarvon castle, quickly engaged him, and in a skirmish at Llandegai, near Bangor, on June 5, defeated him and took him prisoner. The revolt in Anglesey was even more futile. Lord Byron was hastily sent to take charge of the rising, but he had a bad reputation for plunder, and the local landowners resented his interference. He had to withdraw to the Isle of Man, and Richard Bulkeley, the son of Lord Bulkeley, took command. Bulkeley was as incompetent as he was vain. He allowed Mytton to cross the straits unmolested, was then routed by him, and retreated hastily to Beaumaris leaving his horses, most of his arms and the whole island to Mytton. On October 2, Beaumaris surrendered. For its contumacy the island had to pay £7,000.

By this time the war in Pembrokeshire, also, had come to an end. Rice Powell had installed himself in Tenby and Laugharne and Poyer in Pembroke. Their success in the previous war had been due, above all, to the parliamentary command of the sea. Moreover they were now matched against a man of greater ability even than Gerard, for Cromwell himself decided to take charge. He reached Cardiff a week after the battle of St. Fagans; three days later he was in Swansea, and leaving Horton to besiege Tenby (which surrendered on May 31) he advanced on Pembroke. There the siege dragged on from week to week. Cromwell had to rely on starving the garrison, though his own troops lacked supplies, for the countryside was hostile. He had heavy guns brought by sea, and Laugharne and Poyer, realising that no help would come from Prince Rupert's navy, surrendered on July 11, after a siege of forty-eight days. For its part in the second Civil War, a fine of £20,000 was imposed on south Wales.

Sir John Owen was condemned to death, but was reprieved, it is said, through Ireton's intervention. Laugharne, Powell and Poyer were also condemned. Cromwell was severe on them, as they 'had sinned against so much light,' having supported parliament in the first war. But Fairfax decided that one alone should die. The choice was left to Providence through the puritan device of drawing lots, and this fell on Poyer. He was shot at

Covent Garden on April 25, 1649, and died with exemplary
bravery. Three months earlier Charles I had died at Whitehall.
Among those who signed his death warrant were Colonel John
Jones, and Thomas Wogan, the member of parliament for the
Cardigan boroughs. To the parliamentarians Charles was 'that
man of blood' whose word no one could trust; to his followers he
was a saintly martyr, and the scholarly cavalier, Rowland
Vaughan of Caergai, who had fought at Naseby, hastened to
translate the *Eikon Basilike* into Welsh, so that his fellow-countrymen should be acquainted with the king's last meditations, for,
as the translator claimed in his dedication to Sir John Owen,
no author or book outside Holy Writ was more worthy of
devotion.

CHAPTER VIII

THE GROWTH OF PURITANISM

PURITANISM, like the Reformation, was introduced into Wales from England; it was in no way an indigenous growth. The religious settlement in England and in Wales had, in fact, been largely the work of Queen Elizabeth herself. Many of her advisers, including even Archbishops Parker and Grindal, wanted to depart further than she did from the practices and system of the Roman catholic church, while Archbishop Whitgift wished to abandon the Thirty-nine Articles of belief of the church of England, and adopt others which were more Calvinistic. Some churchmen embraced a far more extreme standpoint. There remained, therefore, within the church of England a body of opinion which desired further changes of varying degrees in the ceremonies, the doctrine and the government of the church. Some insisted that there was no scriptural justification for episcopacy, and wished to substitute for it a presbyterian system on the Scottish model, while still retaining the closest association between church and state. Generally speaking, those who advocated these changes were marked by a greater seriousness in their conduct and attitude of mind than were those who did not, and in consequence were often objects of dislike and of ridicule. It was to this desire for radical change, and to this new way of life, that the term puritanism came loosely to be applied.

These varying opinions were reflected in Wales. Thus Lewis Bayly, a native of Carmarthen, published early in the seventeenth century, while a clergyman in England, a celebrated work called *The Practice of Piety*. Its fame, and his repute as a preacher, secured for him in 1616 the bishopric of Bangor. His book was to become the devotional reading of generations of puritans, and had a profound influence on John Bunyan. No less than seventy editions appeared in English in two centuries, while it was also translated into French, German, Polish, Romansh and one of the languages of the American Indians.

In 1630, in the author's lifetime, there appeared a translation into Welsh, *Yr Ymarfer o Dduwioldeb*, by the cavalier squire, Rowland Vaughan of Caergai, who was later to translate the *Eikon Basilike*. Bayly thus illustrates the difficulty involved in deciding who should be called a puritan. The way of life which he taught was characteristic of extreme puritanism, yet he remained a bishop. Moreover he was himself guilty of the abuses common in his day. He held six livings in addition to his bishopric, gave ten livings within his diocese to his son and others to his son-in-law, while his opponents brought against him charges of an even more serious nature.

Still more difficult is it to decide in the case of Rhys Prichard, 'the old Vicar.' He was born at Llandovery in 1579, and after being educated at Jesus College, Oxford, returned as vicar to his native parish. Soon he became chaplain to the earl of Essex, the future leader of the parliamentary forces, and through his patronage obtained the living of Llanedy and a prebend in the collegiate church of Brecon. William Laud, the future archbishop, held the see of St. David's from 1621 to 1626, and between him and Prichard there can have been little sympathy, for Laud was an Arminian, and Prichard a Calvinist, but on Laud's departure Prichard became chancellor of the diocese and vicar of Llawhaden. He was thus an inveterate pluralist. Yet he gained a wide reputation as an eloquent preacher against the evils of his time. Moreover, realising the delight which his parishioners took in singing carols, he composed for them a vast quantity of rough, popular verse. This was not published in his lifetime, but the work of collecting it was undertaken after his death by a puritan minister, Stephen Hughes, and it appeared in parts in 1659, 1670 and 1672. A collected edition was published in 1681, and for this the puritan editor adopted the celebrated name of *Canwyll y Cymru* ('The Welshmen's Candle').

Prichard was deeply influenced by Bayly's *Practice of Piety*, and much of his work is little more than a versifying of this book. He upheld episcopacy, and taught that the sacraments should be accepted even at the hands of unworthy priests. But he sternly condemned non-preaching clergymen, and encouraged their parishioners to seek religious instruction outside their own parishes. He was a bitter opponent of Roman catholic doctrine, particularly of the belief in purgatory and in prayers for the dead, and he adopted an extreme form of Calvinism, which teaches not only that the elect alone are saved but also that once saved they cannot afterwards fall from grace. Yet his main interest was not in dogma but in conduct. He drew a dark picture of the life of his time, of the luxury-loving gentry, and of the drunkenness, vice and superstitious practices of the people. His own demeanour was austere and puritanical.

Rhys Prichard died in 1644. On the outbreak of war two years earlier he had taken the side opposite to that of his patron and had supported the king. He thus remained loyal to both church and state. In this, as in his admiration for *The Practice of Piety*, his great popularity as a preacher, his extreme Calvinism and condemnation of Roman catholicism, as well as in his bitter castigation of the morals of his age, he bore a close resemblance to the early methodist leaders of the eighteenth century.

There thus remained within the church a body of opinion which may well be called puritan. Its adherents sought to remedy matters in various ways. One was to buy up the impropriated tithes of various parishes, and use the revenue to provide salaried preachers, more especially in the towns. This scheme, which was put into operation in 1625, is of peculiar interest to Wales, for among its twelve authors were John White, a member of a distinguished Tenby family, and Rowland Heylin, who, with Sir Thomas Middleton, was to bear the cost of publishing the Bible of 1630, while the largest purchase made was of the living of Presteign. But the government soon intervened, and the trustees were brought to trial in the Court of Exchequer and their funds confiscated.

Towards the end of Elizabeth's reign there had arisen in England a new conception of the nature of the church. Its exponents abandoned any idea of a comprehensive church embracing all persons within the state. They held that membership should be restricted to those who had personally experienced religious conversion. It was one of these 'gathered churches' that John Penry joined in London in the last few months of his life, and it was as a separatist that he died. But Penry had no influence whatsoever in the land of his birth. Nevertheless, early in the sixteen-thirties a group of separatists makes its appearance in the Olchon valley, in the Welsh-speaking area of west Herefordshire. Its members disbelieved in the baptism of infants, and therefore belonged to the baptist denomination which had a short time previously come into existence in London. The origin of the Olchon baptists still remains a mystery, but their security they owed to the isolation of this remote valley among the Black Mountains. It was within the diocese of St. David's, but was far away from the administrative centre of the see at Abergwili. Moreover it was near the frontier of both Monmouthshire and Breconshire, a factor of importance to those who wished to escape arrest in days when a sheriff's authority was limited to his own shire.

In 1633 William Laud became archbishop of Canterbury. He immediately revived the Court of High Commission, and infused life and vigour into its activities. Two years later there was summoned to appear before it the aged rector of Llanvaches in Monmouthshire, William Wroth. He was a saintly character, devout and earnest in his preaching of a simple evangelical creed, and he was in close contact with the puritans of the neighbouring city of Bristol. Together with him there appeared before the court, William Erbery, the young vicar of St. Mary's in Cardiff. Erbery was a contentious, strong-minded man, and the previous year the bishop of Llandaff had admonished him for his irregular practices and had deprived his curate of his licence. This curate was Walter Cradock, a native of Usk, and a 'bold, ignorant young fellow,' in the bishop's opinion. Cradock had then gone to Wrexham, for this town was strongly influenced by the puritanism of Cheshire. There he converted Morgan Llwyd, a native of Cynfal in Merioneth, who was then a schoolboy in the town. Within two years Cradock was forced to leave Wrexham. He sought refuge at Brampton Bryan in Herefordshire, the seat of Sir Robert Harley, a puritan landowner who offered protection to several puritan preachers. Here he converted Vavasor Powell, a youth who had been born a few miles away at Knucklas in Radnorshire but who was then assisting his uncle, the vicar of Clun, across the Shropshire border.

Meanwhile the cases against Wroth and Erbery dragged on until 1638. Erbery was then forced to resign his living, but Wroth submitted. Nevertheless, in November 1639, the pastor of the first independent church in London was sent by his congregation 'to help old Mr. Wroth, Mr. Cradock and others' (among them probably both Morgan Llwyd and Vavasor Powell) to 'gather' a church at Llanvaches. It was this historic meeting which founded the first 'gathered' church within the borders of Wales. Its adherents were drawn together solely by their need for a deeper spiritual life. It is unlikely that they intended to break away from the church, and there is no evidence to show that Wroth was deprived of his living before his death a year or so later. But the uncompromising attitude of Laud and the outbreak of the Civil War made any half measures impossible.

These were the faint beginnings of nonconformity in Wales. It is noteworthy that they were all associated with the border counties. Puritanism had spread from London along the main trade routes to Bristol and Chester, and thence into Wales. The interior of the country, inaccessible geographically and isolated by its language, remained entirely untouched by the new movement. Even in the early years of the war, since the king's armies were in control of Wales, puritanism had little opportunity to secure a foothold anywhere.

With the outbreak of war the Welsh puritans had fled to Bristol, and after the fall of Bristol to London. Their goods were seized by the royalists, and a Committee of Plundered Ministers was set up by parliament to look after the welfare of these refugees. Its leading member was John White of Tenby. By the time the king was defeated this Committee had absorbed the functions of other committees and became all-powerful in Wales as in England, for it had the great wealth of the church at its disposal. It proceeded to expel the royalist clergy from their livings, some for 'malignancy,' that is for active support of the king, some for pluralism, others for scandal in their private lives. It 'approved' others, and, in fact, the great majority of the clergy remained in their livings, many of them taking the initiative in seeking certificates of approval. As there were few puritans in Wales to take the place of those who were expelled, parliament had, immediately after Naseby, struck upon the novel idea of sending Walter Cradock and two others as itinerant preachers to south Wales, although they did not commence their duties till the autumn of 1646. They were allowed £100 each out of the revenues of the church. In 1648, the Committee sent Morgan Llwyd, Vavasor Powell and one other person on a similar mission to north Wales, Llwyd receiving £120 and Powell £100. But the itinerants met with little success. Moreover the central committee in London was forced to work through county committees, and with the triumph of the parliamentary forces many time-servers found a place on these and used them for their own selfish ends. There was, in consequence, much corruption and profiteering.

The puritans within Wales were independents, that is to say, their churches were autonomous bodies with little association between them. There was no presbyterian movement in Wales in these years. But, in 1649, John Miles, after having been baptised by immersion at a baptist church in London, returned to Wales to establish a similar church at Ilston in Gower. Soon there were other like churches at Llanharan, Hay, Carmarthen and Abergavenny. These baptist churches were effectively supervised by Miles and formed together a close organisation, which constituted the nearest approach to a presbyterian system in Wales.

The slow progress of puritanism continued to attract the attention of the government. Cromwell's chief lieutenant in Wales was Colonel Thomas Harrison, one of his best cavalry officers, and through his influence parliament passed in February 1650 an Act for the Propagation of the Gospel in Wales. This act delegated authority in Wales to Harrison and seventy other Commissioners, and is noteworthy since it constitutes the only attempt made throughout the centuries to grant Wales a measure of self-government. The leading Commissioner was Colonel Philip Jones of Llangyfelach, who had distinguished himself in Cromwell's army. Among the others was the regicide, Colonel John Jones. Some of the old Welsh families were represented, for example by Sir Erasmus Philipps of Picton, but they were few, and the majority of the Commissioners were English. Any five of them, acting together, could examine ministers, and, if they thought fit, eject them from their livings. Within three years they had ejected 278 persons in all, of whom 82 were from north Wales, 151 from south Wales (53 of these were from Pembrokeshire alone) and 45 from Monmouthshire. Those ejected for pluralism were generally allowed to keep one living. Among the reasons given for the ejection of others were an inability to preach in Welsh, the use of the Book of Common

Prayer and drunkenness or scandal in their private lives. The act allowed for the payment of one-fifth of the revenue of a parish to the wife and children of the ejected clergyman, but the lot of these was frequently very hard. The striking fact, however, is the large number of clergymen who survived these ejections and remained in charge of their parishes.

To appoint successors for the ejected ministers, the act nominated twenty-five Approvers, 'godly and painful men,' among whom were Cradock, Miles, Llwyd and Vavasor Powell. Any five of these could 'approve' preachers, who would receive a salary of £100 a year, and could also appoint school-masters at a salary of £40. The funds for both purposes were, in fact, to be drawn from the sequestered revenues of the church, yet, in the history of Great Britain, this was the first provision for education ever made by the state. Fifty-nine schools were established. They were free and open to both sexes. Latin and Greek were taught in some of them, but the stress was on English, and there is no evidence that any attention was paid to Welsh.

The Approvers were less successful in their religious than in their educational work, for puritan ministers were hard to find. They had, therefore, to fall back on itinerant preachers. Of these the most remarkable was Vavasor Powell, himself. He frequently travelled a hundred miles in a week, preaching in two or three places every day. But the itinerants were often uneducated men, craftsmen, old soldiers and the like. They were frequently English in their speech and fantastic in their views. Hence they were disliked, abused and even assaulted. Petitions from both north and south Wales complained that parishes were left for two years without services, and it soon became evident that the system under the Propagation Act had failed.

The act had been passed for three years only; it was therefore due to lapse in 1653. In that year, also, Cromwell expelled the Long Parliament and declared himself Lord Protector. This won for him the bitterest hostility of the extreme puritans. Some of these expected the imminent coming of Christ, which would establish in a Fifth Monarchy (the successor of the empires of Assyria, Persia, Greece and Rome), an era of peace and goodwill when the saints should reign. They now believed

Sir John Philipps of Picton

LLANDAFF CATHEDRAL
The nave in ruins before restoration in the nineteenth century

that Cromwell stood in the way. Prominent among them were Thomas Harrison, Vavasor Powell and Morgan Llwyd. Powell preached in London in December 1653 a sermon in which he publicly called the Protector 'the dissemblingest perjured villain,' and then fled to Wales where he was said to be enlisting troops for a rising. Because of the disturbed state of the country, Cromwell was forced to entrust its government to twelve major-generals, Wales forming part of the territory allocated to Major General James Berry. Berry was a fair-minded and conscientious man, and was much concerned about the spiritual welfare of those whom he governed. 'If some course be not taken,' he wrote, 'these people will some of them become as heathens.' But the agitation of the Fifth Monarchists continued, and in 1655 there appeared a violent attack on Cromwell, entitled *A Word for God . . . against wickedness in High Places* which was evidently the work of Vavasor Powell. In opposition to him Walter Cradock organised a loyal address to the Protector, yet rumours of proposed risings in Wales still continued to spread.

The confusion was increased by a welter of strange beliefs. In addition to his apocalyptic calculations, based on the books of Daniel and of Revelation, concerning the coming of the Fifth Monarchy, Morgan Llwyd taught that Christ dwelt mystically in the hearts of men. His occult ideas he derived from the writings of the German, Jacob Boehme, and he incorporated them in 1653 in his *Llyfr y Tri Aderyn*. In that year, also, he heard of the teaching of George Fox, the quaker, whose belief in the guidance of an inner light resembled his own. Llwyd, therefore, sent John ap John, of Ruabon, to Fox to enquire about this new faith. His envoy returned as a convert, becoming the first quaker missionary in Wales. Fox, himself, came to Wales in 1657 on a great missionary tour, and had marked success in the English parts of Radnorshire, Montgomeryshire and south Pembrokeshire. Meanwhile the baptists had spread in Radnorshire, along the upper Wye Valley. But these differed from the followers of John Miles in that they rejected Calvinism; furthermore, both the Calvinistic and the Arminian baptists were divided among themselves on the question of the admission to their sacraments of other Christians. Finally, in a restricted area in English Flintshire, Philip Henry, the most saintly of all the Welsh puritan leaders, successfully established presbyterianism.

The itinerant system came to an end when the Propagation Act lapsed, for there was afterwards no financial provision to maintain it. Some itinerants became settled in particular parishes, as, for example, Morgan Llwyd at Wrexham and Walter Cradock at Usk. The place of the Commissioners was taken by a body generally known as the Triers. They were more moderate men, but they found the country in a state of religious chaos. Churches were closed and were falling into ruin, and in many parishes no services were held. The attempt to reorganise the church during a period of upheaval had caused a financial muddle, in which the tithes had been left uncollected. Furthermore, puritan preachers were few, and the position became worse with the passing of the first generation of puritan leaders, for Erbery had died in 1654, full of strange, unorthodox ideas, and Llwyd and Cradock both died in 1659. Consequently it was even suggested that a college should be set up in Wales to train ministers, but this came to nothing. Yet among the younger generation the Triers did find in these years some outstanding men, notably Stephen Hughes, who held the living of Mydrim, and Samuel Jones who held that of Llangynwyd. Their success, however, was small, and the remarkable persistence of anglicanism became evident when the crisis came in the months which followed Cromwell's death.

The year 1660 saw, therefore, not the coming of Christ as Morgan Llwyd had calculated, but the return of the merry monarch, Charles II. This was welcomed with acclamation in Wales, where royalist sympathies had always remained strong, and it was celebrated in verse by Huw Morus of Pontymeibion, the most considerable poet of his day. The puritan leaders were immediately overthrown. Thomas Harrison was executed, as was Colonel John Jones, who, four years previously, had married the Protector's sister and had served with distinction in the government of Ireland. He died with great courage and dignity. The other Welsh regicide, Thomas Wogan, succeeded in leaving the country, thus saving his life. In strange contrast were the fortunes of Colonel Philip Jones. He had served in Cromwell's upper house as Philip, Lord Jones, and had accumulated a large estate. He succeeded not only in making his peace with Charles II's government but in legalising his landed acquisitions. Four years later he purchased Fonmon Castle, where he lived for the remainder of his life, becoming in 1671 high sheriff of Glamorgan.

The Restoration was the work of presbyterians who had remained hostile to Cromwell and his army. In England, where the presbyterians were strong, there was in consequence some attempt at compromise between them and the royalists, but in Wales the presbyterians were few, and there the full force of reaction was immediately felt by the puritans. Vavasor Powell was soon arrested, and, apart from a brief interval of a few months, he remained in prison until his death in 1670. There he wrote his best known work, an account of puritan sufferings entitled *The Bird in the Cage, Chirping*. Bigoted and fanatical though he was, he was also a man of great fortitude and amazing versatility. It would be hard to deny him the title of being the most remarkable Welshman of his day. John Miles, with most of his congregation, left for America, where he founded the town of Swanzey, Massachusetts. Other puritan clergymen were now removed to make room for the former incumbents of the parishes which they occupied, or for the fresh nominees of the king or of the other patrons of livings. In 1660 and 1661, ninety-three were ejected for these reasons. By 1662 it was evident that the attempt at compromise had failed even in England, and all who refused to accept the Act of Uniformity and the Prayer Book were now forced to leave the church. But whereas, in England, by far the greater number of ejections of puritan ministers by the government of Charles II followed this act of 1662, in Wales these numbered only twenty-five, in contrast with the ninety-three ejections in the previous two years. This difference reflects the relative weakness of the presbyterians in Wales, as compared with the baptists and the independents, on whom the oppression of the royalists had fallen earliest, though among those now ejected was the saintly presbyterian, Philip Henry.

It had therefore become evident by this time that religious unity, for which moderate men on both sides had striven, was no longer possible. Dissent could not be reconciled with the established church by persuasion; the government made another attempt to destroy it by persecution. Memories of the time of Cromwell caused the dissenters to be regarded as seditious, and it was natural that their political power should be eliminated. But they were deprived also of their privileges as citizens in the towns; they were denied the right of public worship; they were excluded from the universities, and an attempt was made to prevent them from educating their children in the principles of their own faith. This persecution varied considerably from time to time and from place to place. It fell most heavily on the quakers, and the prisons were soon full of them. Richard Davies, of Cloddiau Cochion, the second great apostle of the quaker faith in Wales, spent most of his time in prison. The other denominations, in common with the quakers, were subjected to heavy fines, and their goods were distrained upon and sold at ridiculously low prices to pay these fines. They were refused burial in consecrated ground, and in some cases bodies were exhumed and buried at the cross-roads. Mild though this persecution was in comparison with the dragonnades of contemporary France, it left a lasting tradition of bitterness.

In this persecution the timeservers who had attached themselves to the parliamentary cause while it was triumphant fell away. The differing sects, also, joined forces, and worshipped together in private houses and in out of the way places. But the foundations of puritanism had, by now, been soundly laid, and it was strong enough even to start new churches in these difficult years. For in 1668 some thirty baptists formed a church on the borders of Carmarthenshire and Pembrokeshire, aided by two representatives from the baptists in the Olchon valley. The new church, which became located at Rhydwilym, replaced Ilston as the centre of that denomination in west Wales.

The harshness of the persecution was tempered by the fact that Charles II, for all his faults, was no persecutor. He wished, in particular, to mitigate the condition of the Roman catholics, and in 1672 he issued a Declaration of Indulgence, relieving both Roman catholics and dissenters from the penalties of the Clarendon Code. Licences to preach were granted to individuals in respect of certain places. In all 185 such licences were granted in Wales from April 22, 1672 to February 3, 1673, of which 49 went to north Wales and 136 to south Wales. But Charles's need for money soon led him to reassemble parliament, and this not only compelled him to withdraw the indulgence but proceeded to pass the Test Act of 1673.   In his determination to root out both Roman catholicism and dissent, Archbishop Sheldon went further, and decided to ascertain the precise extent of the problem by obtaining statistics from every parish. The returns for Wales are not complete, and they involve many insoluble problems, but it has been estimated that while anglican conformists in the four Welsh dioceses numbered 153,046, the Roman catholics numbered 1,072 and the dissenters 4,193.

The indulgences of 1672 and the religious census of 1676 taken together enable us to see the extent of nonconformity in Wales in these years. It is true that both sources imply that the dissenters were fewer in number than they actually were. (The baptists of Rhydwilym, for example, did not apply for a licence, and there were no returns in 1676 of any dissenters in the neighbouring parishes.) Even so, it can safely be said that dissent accounted for less than five per cent of the population. Some one-third of these dissenters were baptists, and the remainder were independents, for there were very few presbyterians, except in Flintshire, though in some cases it is difficult to distinguish between the independents and the presbyterians. Geographically, the dissenters were far more numerous in south than in north Wales. North Wales, as we have seen, accounted for only 49 licences. Not one of these went to Anglesey, and when the duke of Beaufort went on progress through Wales in 1684 it was said that 'there were not three sectaries in the whole isle.' The dissenters were weak also in Caernarvonshire and Merioneth, despite the efforts of Hugh Owen of Bronclydwr, though the quakers were numerous in the neighbourhood of Dolgelley. Wrexham was a strong centre of dissent, but this was so only because the influence of the English border counties was felt there. In south Wales, dissent had infiltrated from the border into the uplands of Radnorshire; otherwise it was strongest in the lowland areas, especially in 'pockets' where such men as Stephen Hughes or Samuel Jones were active. Of the four thousand dissenters in the whole of Wales, over half lived in the three south-eastern shires of Brecon, Glamorgan and Monmouth.

The Test Act of 1673 was directed primarily against the Roman catholics, who were now to suffer their severest persecution. In Wales their numbers had remained reasonably constant, and of the thousand Roman catholics returned in the census of 1676 one-half lived in Monmouthshire, while the remainder were about equally divided between Breconshire and Flintshire. Across the Herefordshire border, on the lands of the earl of Worcester, at Cwm in the parish of Llanrothal, there had been founded in 1622 a Jesuit 'college,' a group of priests whose members served their co-religionists in south-east Wales. The 'college' continued in existence even throughout the Civil War and the Cromwellian period, so powerful was the patronage of the earl of Worcester. In the reaction which followed Charles II's indulgence, the attention of the house of commons was, on more than one occasion, drawn to the activities of these priests. So, when Titus Oates's libellous fabrications spread a wave of hysteria throughout the country in the autumn of 1678, the house at Cwm was raided, the priests imprisoned, and their books and valuables confiscated. Some priests died in gaol. Of the others, Philip Evans of the Society of Jesus was hanged at Cardiff in July 1679, and with him John Lloyd, a secular priest. A month later John Kemble, a secular priest from the Welsh part of Herefordshire, was hanged at Hereford, and five days later David Lewis of the Society of Jesus, a native of Abergavenny, was hanged at Usk. Truly may they be called martyrs, for they died for their faith, and for their faith alone. This was the severest blow which Roman catholicism had suffered in Wales since the Reformation, and from it the faith never fully recovered. Here and there, traces of the old religion persisted, but its adherents were few. When Roman catholicism revived in Wales in the nineteenth century this was due to the influx of Irish workers into the great industries.

A welcome change in this tale of persecution is provided by the co-operation of moderate puritans and anglicans during these years in providing Wales with a system of schools. Thomas Gouge, an ejected puritan minister in London, became concerned about the moral state of Wales about 1672, and started to found schools there. He formed a Welsh Trust some two years later to extend the work, and secured the help of the future bishops, Tillotson and Stillingfleet. He co-operated also with Stephen Hughes, who, in the face of great difficulties, encouraged though he was by William Thomas, who was to become bishop of St. David's in 1678, was endeavouring to provide Wales with devotional books. The printing of these books was supervised in

London by yet a third ejected minister, Charles Edwards, author of *Hanes y Ffydd Ddiffuant*. The climax of their work was the issue in 1678 of a new edition of the Bible in Welsh, of which the Trust distributed a thousand copies free to the poor. But the primary object of the Trust was to establish schools. It is impossible to say how many were set up, nor how long each course lasted, but Tillotson estimated that between 1,600 and 2,000 children were taught each year. Although the Trust aided the publication and distribution of Welsh books, its schools were conducted entirely in English, and this may be one reason for their failure. Moreover they met with bitter opposition from some quarters, notably from Bishop Humphrey Lloyd of Bangor. Also the relaxation in persecution, which alone had made possible the work of the Trust, ended about 1680, when the king was prepared to sacrifice the dissenters in his search for political allies against the Whigs, who were seeking to exclude his brother from the throne. This coincided with the death in 1681 of Gouge, the only man who could preserve unity among his associates. The Trust was therefore dissolved, and the schools came to an end.

Despite the fact that the Five Mile Act forbade ejected ministers to hold schools, many tried to do so in order to earn a livelihood. One such school was opened in these years at his home at Brynllywarch by Samuel Jones, the ejected minister of Llangynwyd. He had been a fellow of Jesus College, Oxford, and was a scholar of repute. His school therefore became well known. In time (though there is definite evidence of this only after the Revolution of 1688), he had students of mature age who were preparing for the dissenting ministry. The school thus became a Dissenting Academy, and its teaching was held in such high esteem that sons of the local gentry are said to have been educated there.

Charles II's dependence upon his Tory, high church supporters in his struggle against the Whigs, had, as we have seen, brought a period of comparative toleration to an end, and the remainder of his reign saw a return to the conditions of the early years. As always, persecution fell most heavily on the quakers, who, at the Court of Great Sessions at Bala in 1677, were even threatened with burning. They had become numerous in Montgomeryshire and in Merioneth through the efforts of

Richard Davies, among whose converts was Charles Lloyd, the squire of Dolobran, near Llanfyllin, who, despite his social prominence, was soon in prison at Welshpool. So severe was this renewed persecution that the quakers determined to emigrate, and when William Penn obtained the grant of Pennsylvania from the king in 1681, Welsh quakers bought from him 40,000 acres of land. They left for America in 1682. In the next year they were joined by Thomas Lloyd, brother of Charles Lloyd, and it was he who acted as deputy-governor for William Penn in his absence. The Welsh quakers played a large part in the affairs of Pennsylvania in its early days. In Wales, on the other hand, their community fell into decay. This was no doubt hastened by the loss of its more vigorous elements through emigration, yet the final disappearance of quakerism in Wales came later, when it was absorbed into the other denominations after the passing of the Toleration Act.

The Arminian baptists of Radnorshire also emigrated in 1683, and their sect likewise disappeared from Wales. They settled on the outskirts of Philadelphia. Later on they were joined, in 1701, by Calvinistic baptists from west Wales, but even in America the two bodies found it difficult to agree, and the latter bought 30,000 acres of land lower down the Delaware River. So numerous were the Welsh of Pennsylvania in the early eighteenth century that it was sufficiently profitable to publish books in Welsh in America for their benefit.

The other denominations also suffered in the last years of Charles II. Philip Henry's goods were distrained upon, and warrants were issued for the arrest of both Stephen Hughes and Samuel Jones. Some bishops once more sought to reconcile the dissenters by argument. Bishop William Thomas, the friend of Stephen Hughes, had conferences with them at Carmarthen and St. David's, and the learned and devout Bishop William Lloyd of St. Asaph held lengthy public debates at Oswestry and at Wrexham. Bishop Lloyd ensured the attendance of the dissenters by having writs issued against them. Despite this compulsion he felt certain that he had convinced them in their hearts, but in order to be doubly sure he solicited the help of Judge Jeffreys in getting the penal laws rigorously applied.

The accession of James II to the throne introduced a new factor. He was a convert to Roman catholicism, and in August

1686 came on pilgrimage to St. Winifred's Well at Holywell, the last royal pilgrimage in these islands. He tried to improve the position of his fellow-believers by claiming the power to dispense with the penal laws. At first he sought the co-operation of the anglicans. When this failed, he returned in April 1687 to his brother's policy, and issued a Declaration of Indulgence. But, two years previously, his cousin, Louis XIV, had revoked the edict of Nantes, and there was scarcely a town in England or Wales which did not contain some Huguenots who had fled from the terror. James II's promises, sincere though they may have been, were therefore regarded with suspicion, and by none more so than by the dissenters whom they were intended to conciliate. When the king ordered the indulgence to be read in all churches, seven bishops petitioned against this, and were consigned to the Tower. Among them was Archbishop Sancroft, but their leading member was none other than Bishop William Lloyd of St. Asaph, who took the chief part in the discussions which followed. They were acquitted amid great popular enthusiasm, and the archbishop, in his turn, sought to reconcile the dissenters. He issued articles to his clergy, enjoining them 'to have a very tender regard to our bretheren, the protestant dissenters,' and 'on occasion to visit them at their houses, and receive them kindly at their own.' Therefore, when James II was driven from the throne, it was natural that the Revolution of 1688 should be followed by the Toleration Act of 1689.

The dissenters of England and Wales were to live for a century and a half under the system set up by this Toleration Act. They were allowed freedom of worship, provided their meeting houses were licensed, and their services held with unlocked doors. Roman catholics and unitarians were, however, excluded from toleration. Moreover the Test and Corporation Acts still debarred all those who did not receive the sacraments according to the rites of the Church of England from municipal offices and from the service of the crown. It had thus become evident both that it was impossible to absorb dissent into the church by agreement, and that the attempt to destroy it by persecution had failed. But the position was still one of toleration and not of equality. It was a compromise which seemed revolutionary to the high church party, but which left the dissenters unsatisfied and determined upon further efforts to gain religious and political liberty. Their numbers in Wales remained for a time extremely small. Yet they were to exercise an influence on our national development entirely disproportionate to their numbers. This was due to a moral earnestness and resolution which triumphed over difficulties, and gave them an ascendancy over their less active neighbours. In time the dissenters came to comprise the majority of the people of Wales.

CHAPTER IX

CHURCH AND STATE: 1660–1760

THE Revolution of 1688, while it brought toleration to the dissenters, entirely consolidated the position of the anglican church. The alliance between the gentry and the clergy was never again to be shaken, and together they dominated the life of Wales. In the towns of England rich dissenters might still associate with the aristocracy on terms approaching equality; in Wales the social division was far more clearly marked. It is true, there were few really poor people among the Welsh dissenters. They were mainly yeomen farmers whose economic position gave them some independence. But there were few squires within their ranks. Besides, the dissenters were remarkably few in number. The course of Welsh history was therefore determined for a period by the character of the anglican church and its relations with the state.

It was natural that Charles II, on his Restoration, should give preferment to those who had distinguished themselves in the service of the house of Stuart. But he began thereby the practice of granting high office in the church, especially in Wales, as a reward for political support, to the great detriment of the religious life of the people. The Restoration bishops were far less eminent men than those of Elizabethan Wales. They may not have been more guilty of abuses than their predecessors, and many of these abuses were but lightly regarded at the time, yet the long period of neglect which now ensued, though it was relieved in some exceptional cases, was destined to have grave consequences. Among Charles's bishops, William Lucy, who immediately succeeded to St. David's, had, at least, the merit of residing in his see. But he gave many benefices to non-residents, and his nepotism in respect of his numerous sons was unashamed. Much of his relatively long episcopate was taken up with an unedifying struggle against the neighbouring bishop of Gloucester. Henry Glemham, who, with his brother, had fought with distinction in the Civil War, was appointed to St. Asaph through the influence of his niece, Lady Castlemaine, the king's mistress. He was 'a drunken, swearing rascal' according to Pepys, who was certainly no puritan. The most remarkable appointment of all was that of William Beaw to the bishopric of Llandaff. He, also, had been a soldier in the king's army, and in exile had become 'lieutenant-colonel of horse under the czar of Mosco.' Later he entered the service of the king of Sweden in his wars in Poland, but at the Restoration he returned, and, despite his age, took orders in the hope of immediate preferment. 'A little bishoprick' was offered him, and this he took, he says, 'in the expectation of a sudden remove.' This was in 1679, but at Llandaff he was destined to stay for the remaining twenty-six years of his life. He complained bitterly that this lengthy episcopate in Wales was 'a disease which none of his predecessors were suffered to labour under so long,' and at the age of eighty-three he was still importuning the archbishop for translation to the wealthier see of St. Asaph. He had heard on this occasion that 'it had been buzzed in the queen's ear (i.e. Queen Mary) that a Welsh bishop should be a Welshman,' but he held this to be a groundless objection. He died in 1706 at the advanced age of ninety-seven, having neglected his bishopric for a quarter of a century.

James II's policy threw the Welsh royalists into perplexity. The few Roman catholics in Wales naturally supported him. The marquis of Worcester (son of Charles I's earl of Glamorgan) had become a protestant, so that the leadership of the Roman catholics had passed to his brother-in-law, whom James made marquis of Powis. He accompanied his royal master into exile and held high office in his court at St. Germain. But James's patronage of the Roman catholics sharply divided the anglican clergy. Bishop William Lloyd of St. Asaph, as we have seen, took a leading part in opposing the king, and was rewarded soon after the Revolution by being transferred to Lichfield. The great majority of the clergy also opposed the king, so that of the 'nonjurors', who refused to swear allegiance to King William III on account of their belief in non-resistance and the divine right of kings, only eighteen held benefices in Wales. Two of the leading nonjurors were, nevertheless, Welsh. One of these was Bishop William Lloyd of Norwich, who had been Beaw's predecessor at Llandaff. He was a man of great distinction and piety, and to him the nonjuring archbishop, Sancroft, delegated his powers in spiritual matters. The other was Bishop William Thomas of Worcester, who had encouraged Stephen Hughes, and had for five years held the see of St. David's.

As with the clergy, the great majority of the people, also, were alienated by James's Roman catholicism. Huw Morus of Pontymeibion, who had welcomed the Restoration of Charles II in eloquent verse, now celebrated the victory of La Hogue which destroyed any hope of the return of his brother. There were, indeed, a few signs, here and there, of opposition to the Revolution. The town of Abergavenny lost its charter, apparently because of disaffection, and, in Cardiff, one Edward Llewellyn of Newton Nottage was prosecuted for calling William III a fool. But when repeated attempts to assassinate the king led to the formation in 1696 of the National Association for his protection, this body was welcomed with much enthusiasm in Wales, and the Welsh gentry hastened to join. The roll for the shire of Glamorgan alone contains 760 names, and among them is that of Edward Llewellyn of Newton Nottage.

Loyalty to King William, however, did not mean subservience, as one famous episode showed. In 1695, the king had proposed to grant the lordships of Denbigh and Bromfield and Yale to the Dutch statesman, William Bentinck, his trusted adviser, whom he made earl of Portland. The lordships formed part of the hereditary domains of the crown, and were valued at over £100,000. This proposal was strongly resisted by Robert Price of Pentrefoelas, member of parliament for Weobley. The Dutch followers of the king were highly unpopular, and Price, in a resounding speech, induced the house of commons in 1696 to accept unanimously an address to the king opposing the grant. This caused a sensation, and William wisely gave way.

The Revolution marked the triumph of the Whig party over their Tory opponents. They made the most of their victory, and their wrath fell particularly on James's sole nominee to a Welsh bishopric, Thomas Watson, bishop of St. David's. He consistently opposed the new government and also fell foul of his cathedral clergy, notably of his registrar, a son of the former bishop, William Lucy. Charges of simony were brought against Watson, and the controversy which followed was conducted with extreme bitterness. In time he was tried in the ecclesiastical courts and found guilty. Not only was he therefore removed from his see in 1699, but he was also excommunicated and denied Christian burial when he died eighteen years later. He was the second bishop of St. David's since the Reformation to be deprived for gross misconduct. In strange contrast was the treatment of Edward Jones who was appointed to the see of St. Asaph in the reign of William and Mary. He was charged with the same offence as Watson and signed a confession of guilt, but through the protection of the court party was sentenced only to suspension from his office for six months.

The triumph of the Whigs enabled the dissenters to disregard with impunity the penal restrictions still imposed upon them. The practice of 'occasional conformity' grew up, that is of taking the sacrament in order to qualify for office in municipal corporations while continuing to frequent dissenting places of worship. Matters were brought to a head by Sir Humphrey Edwin, a rich London wool-merchant who had become possessed of the estate of Llanmihangel, near Cowbridge, and of much land in the Vale of Glamorgan. In 1697 he became lord mayor of London. On election he took the sacrament in church as the law required, but then proceeded on a Sunday afternoon in full regalia to a presbyterian meeting house, compelling his sword bearer to accompany him, and locking him up in a pew when he sought to depart. This scandalised even moderate anglicans, and when Queen Anne ascended the throne, four and a half years later, bills against occasional conformity were introduced into parliament. For Anne, unlike William III and her sister, Mary, adhered to the high church party. She reconciled the great body of the clergy to the Revolution by her grant, soon after her accession to the throne, of Queen Anne's Bounty. This transferred moneys originally paid to the pope, but appropriated by the crown at the Reformation, to the church for the purpose of increasing stipends in the poorer parishes. Bills imposing severe penalties for occasional conformity were therefore passed by the commons, but, despite the efforts of the queen, were thrown out by the lords.

Passions were soon afterwards greatly inflamed by the affair of Dr. Sacheverell. Although his grandfather and two granduncles had been ejected puritan ministers, Sacheverell represented the extreme wing of the high church party. He gained notoriety by preaching a series of violent sermons, vituperating the Revolution, the Whigs and the dissenters. For this the government decided in 1710 to impeach him. The Whig administration had by this time become extremely unpopular, and although the lords found him guilty they merely suspended him from preaching for three years. So light was this sentence that it was regarded as an acquittal. The event was therefore celebrated throughout the country. Bonfires were lit in Wrexham, and processions marched through the town smashing the windows of the dissenters' homes and of their two meeting houses. A well-wisher then bestowed on Sacheverell the living of Selattyn in the diocese of St. Asaph, across the Shropshire border, and his journey there almost resembled a royal progress, so great were the crowds which came to meet him. In Shrewsbury he was welcomed by fifty thousand people. This gave a clear indication of the strength of the high church party on the Welsh border, and the affair precipitated the fall of the Whigs in the same year. Their place was taken by the Tory government of Harley and St. John. Both ministers had been brought up under presbyterian influences, and Harley, who sat for Radnor, was the grandson of the protector of Walter Cradock and Vavasor Powell. Yet both now stood for high church principles, and, in 1711, they secured the passing of an Occasional Conformity Act. The house of lords agreed to it only with difficulty, and, even so, the penalties certainly were lighter than in the earlier bills.

There ensued a bitter struggle for power between Harley (now Lord Oxford) and St. John (now Lord Bolingbroke), and a return of the exiled Stuart claimant seemed possible in the event of the queen's death. To compromise Oxford, who remained the more moderate of the two, Bolingbroke, with the strong support of the queen, induced parliament to pass the Schism Act of June 1714. Under the threat of severe penalties, this act prohibited anyone from teaching without a licence from a bishop. Its purpose was to destroy the dissenting schools, and cause the children of dissenters to be compulsorily educated as churchmen. It was an iniquitous measure, and it showed clearly that Bolingbroke, if he obtained sole control of the government, would seek to repeal the Toleration Act. As the dissenters were now securely entrenched, this would undoubtedly have led to resistance on their part, and possibly to a renewal of civil war. But Bolingbroke was frustrated in his designs, for he obtained the dismissal of Oxford only five days before the sudden death of the queen on August 1, 1714. Dissenters throughout the country held services of thanksgiving for this deliverance, and the baptists of west Wales have continued to this day to observe the first Sunday in August as a day of prayer and thanksgiving, though, naturally, not now for the original reason. A deputation of dissenters waited on the new king to express their loyalty. Its leader was Dr. Daniel Williams of Wrexham, the most eminent presbyterian of his day in England, whose name is remembered because of his remarkable benefactions to education and because of his gift to the nation of the library which still bears his name.

In view of these events the nature of the anglican church in the reigns of George I and George II was determined by political considerations. To make the protestant succession secure, and with it the Toleration Act, it was necessary to control the episcopate. For the bishops, in addition to their wide ecclesiastical and religious authority, were important members of the house of lords at a time when the upper house retained its powers. Party alignment in the state had become more definite, and until the final defeat of Jacobitism a deliberate choice was made of Whig bishops. This political subservience was demoralising, but the alternative was a possible overthrow of the Revolution settlement. Unfortunately the country clergy in Wales, few though the nonjurors had been, belonged predominantly to the high church party, so that there arose an entire lack of sympathy between the bishops and their clergy.

It was the practice of the government to appoint bishops in the first instance to the poorer sees. The hope of advancement would then ensure their continued support, and any independence could be punished by long rustication. It was the misfortune of Wales that its bishoprics were the poorest in the kingdom, so that translation to richer sees was almost an universal rule. In consequence, during these two reigns, nine bishops were appointed to Bangor, of whom eight were transferred; six to Llandaff of whom four were transferred; six to St. Asaph, of whom five were transferred, and in St. David's, also, six appointments were made with five transfers. One bishop of St. Asaph (not included in this reckoning) was transferred before he was consecrated. Another bishop, this time of Bangor, unsuccessfully importuned the archbishop for the same concession 'to avoid such a long journey.' A bishop of St. David's succeeded in getting his release within a year, while, even in the reign of George III, one bishop held the same see for only three months. Sometimes it was only with difficulty that men could be induced to accept the Welsh sees, so remote were they considered, and the expense involved in consecration often exceeded the total first year's revenue of a Welsh diocese.

In the circumstances there was little inducement for a bishop to visit his see. Many were advanced in years or in indifferent health, and recoiled from the arduous and expensive journey. There was little provision, either, for their residence. Thus, Bishop Beaw had allowed his palace at Mathern to fall into such dilapidation that no bishop of Llandaff resided in the see from his day until 1821. The bishops' political duties as members of the house of lords involved a stay in London of six months in each year whether they wished it or not. Hoadly, bishop of Bangor, is said never to have visited Wales. He was one of the most distinguished of the political bishops, and during the five years of his episcopate he engaged in a dispute with the nonjurors, over non-resistance and the divine right of kings, which is known as the Bangorian Controversy. His important political services led to his appointment to the successively more opulent sees of Hereford, Salisbury and Winchester. But he was a cripple; he could not stand to administer the sacraments, nor could he preach except when kneeling. Neither could he ride on horseback, so that his appointment to the difficult and mountainous diocese of Bangor was an impropriety.

There were some bishops who attended to their duties with devotion. George Bull, whom Anne appointed to St. David's in 1705, has been called 'one of the glories of anglican scholarship,' so great was his knowledge of the early fathers. He assiduously traversed his wide diocese to confirm his people, and this despite his advanced age, for he was seventy when he was made a bishop. Bishop Herring of Bangor (later archbishop of York) also rode 'intrepidly' through his mountains, accompanied by his chancellor, chaplain and secretary, together with two or three friends and their servants. But they were exceptions. Non-residence and the ever present hope of removal seriously affected the efficiency of the bishops in Wales. They neglected their episcopal visitations and their periodical meetings with their clergy. Young persons were left unconfirmed for years. The archbishop was forced to ask the bishop of St. Asaph to confirm in the diocese of Bangor during Hoadly's absence. Nor was there a single ordination in Bangor in Hoadly's episcopate or in that of his successor, who, indeed, stayed for only two years. Candidates had therefore to go across the border in search of a bishop who would ordain them. Such a one was 'the little Welsh deacon,' who was the sole candidate to present himself to the bishop of Gloucester in 1769, and 'who flew hither from his native mountains by accident, like a woodcock in a mist.' In addition there was much pluralism and nepotism, though neither would be regarded as much of an abuse at the time. The poverty of the bishops justified their holding livings and ecclesiastical offices *in commendam*, for otherwise they could not meet their expenses, and the general attitude towards nepotism is expressed by the curate who wrote to his archbishop in 1724: 'I do not presume to find fault with the bishop for preferring his nephew. I only wish it were my good fortune to be a bishop's nephew too.'

The gulf between the diocesans and their clergy was widened by the fact that few of the former were Welsh. This had not been true of Elizabeth's bishops, and even among Charles II's appointments, Bishop Robert Morgan of Bangor preached with eloquence in both languages, while his son-in-law, Humphrey Humphreys, who was appointed in William III's reign to the same see, was one of the best Welsh scholars of his age. But from the accession of George I to 1870 no person able to preach in Welsh was appointed to a Welsh see. The attitudes of the bishops towards their clergy in this matter of language differed widely; some saw the impropriety of giving preferment to monoglot Englishmen in parishes where the people could not understand them, while others, such as Bishop Drummond of St. Asaph, thought it desirable to eradicate the Welsh language as quickly as possible. In any case the bishops were in no position to appreciate the eminence of some of their clergy. Neither Goronwy Owen, the greatest Welsh poet of his day, nor Ieuan Brydydd Hir, the greatest Welsh scholar, ever obtained better preferment than a curacy, and the latter's writings are full of bitter complaints against the English bishops, yr Esgyb Eingl, as he called them. Nor could there be much sympathy between the bishops and their clergy in more spiritual matters. The Hanoverian bishops had the virtues of tolerance and charity. But they disparaged the supernatural aspects in religion, and in the eyes of their clergy their tolerance dangerously resembled indifference. For their part, the bishops regarded with suspicion any unwonted earnestness in the parish priests, for this might be a cloak for subversive Jacobite activity.

No easy generalisation is possible with regard to the condition of religion in Wales in the early years of the eighteenth century. The church had taken some time to recover from the Civil War and the sixteen years of puritan rule, but the Restoration, also, had brought with it a return to some of the old abuses. Many of the clergy were well-connected and obtained their livings through family influence. There was, in consequence, much absenteeism, since incumbents of Welsh parishes would often in addition be chaplains to great noblemen or hold curacies in fashionable churches in and around London. Frequently they might plead that there was no adequate provision for residence in their parishes, for their rectories were often little better than cottages. Many also were pluralists, and regarded their livings as sinecures. Furthermore the incumbents of purely Welsh parishes were often English in speech. Later on in the century, in 1773, the churchwardens of Trefdraeth in Anglesey brought the case of their vicar before the ecclesiastical courts, for he spoke no Welsh and his parishioners understood no English, but the authorities ruled that an ignorance of Welsh did not justify deprivation.

The standard of education of the clergy was, as might be expected of their social position, remarkably high. There was a large proportion of graduates among them. Besides, they produced a considerable body of doctrinal and devotional literature in these years. Some of this was original work, but most of it consisted of translations. Its quantity presupposes a reading public for such books, for otherwise it is unlikely that they would have continued to appear. Moreover it proves that many of the clergy were not indifferent to the spiritual aspects of their religion. Literary composition does not, of course, in itself refute the charge that the clergy neglected their parochial duties, and the greatest literary figure of his age in Wales, Ellis Wynne, author of *Gweledigaetheu y Bardd Cwsc*, was, justly or unjustly, cited before the bishop's court on exactly this charge. Yet the letters and diaries of the time show that on the whole, services were regularly held in most parishes. As the century advanced there was a marked decline in the number of the sons of the gentry, and hence of graduates, who entered the church. The standard of education among the clergy fell, and soon, a year or two at a grammar school, or even at a dissenting academy, was all that separated the plough from the pulpit for most clergymen.

The underlying cause of all the defects from which the church suffered in Wales was poverty, and this poverty was due, above all else, to the fact that the tithes had passed in so many parishes into the hands of lay owners, and were not applied to religious purposes. Valuable light is thrown on this subject by a small book, entitled *A view of the state of Religion in the Diocese of St. David's*, published by Erasmus Saunders in 1721. Saunders shows that the tithes were impropriated in over three-quarters of the livings in this diocese. The revenues of the church thus passed into private hands, and out of them the lay owners paid only the most pitifully small stipends to the vicars whom they employed to conduct the services for them. The tithes of Llanddewi Brefi amounted to the considerable sum of £400 a year, but of this the incumbent received only £8. Towards the middle of the century John Rowland held the parishes of Llangeitho, Nantcwnlle and Llanbadarn Odwyn, in addition to that of Llanddewi Brefi, so that, if he conducted services in all four, he would have to travel eighteen miles each Sunday, and for this obtained a stipend of £46 a year. There were at least two hundred livings in the diocese where the stipend was under £50 a year. Such poverty naturally led to pluralism, for a clergyman could not otherwise live, and pluralism, of necessity, involved non-residence.

The unbeneficed clergy, the curates, were in a still worse position. Seldom, if ever, would they receive more than £10 a year. In consequence they would have to serve three or four churches to make a living. These would often be miles apart, and the services would therefore be held only when the curate arrived on horseback, and would be hurried through so that he could proceed elsewhere. Since the curate's income was scarcely more than that of the lowest paid of his parishioners, it would be unreasonable to have expected him to be highly educated, and poverty often brought with it demoralisation and apathy. Of him, at least, it would not be true to say that he wasted his time drinking port with the squire, for he would seldom penetrate beyond the kitchen if he visited the hall at all, but he would often join his parishioners in the alehouse after the service. The sexton, says Erasmus Saunders, 'to get a sorry maintenance was allowed the privilege of selling ale by the churchyard side.' This was sometimes true even of the clergy, and one, if his indignant archdeacon is to be believed, was known to stop the service when there were customers.

The rapacity of the lay impropriators accounted also for the neglect of the church buildings. These were often made of clay and would easily fall into decay unless cared for. Some, says Erasmus Saunders, had their windows boarded up because they were without glass, and had their seats removed by the impropriators. Others were in ruins, 'the solitary habitations of owls and jackdaws,' while one was let out to the dissenters. It was very seldom that they were paved; their floors being merely hardened earth, covered with rushes which were changed six times a year. The practice of burial within the churches rendered them both untidy and insanitary. When Dr. Johnson visited Wales later in the century he found the church buildings 'mean and neglected to a degree scarcely imaginable.' 'They have no pavement,' he added, 'and the earth is full of holes.'

If the church in Wales suffered from grave defects, there is no evidence that it was on that account unpopular with the nation. The people were gay and carefree, given to superstition, but greatly addicted to singing hymns and carols, and to such practices as placing torches on graves at cockcrow on the feast of the Nativity. Their religion was not the all-absorbing concern which it afterwards became, and sabbatarianism, too, was a later development. Yet they were capable of great devotion. Despite the gloomy picture which he draws, Erasmus Saunders pays them an eloquent tribute. 'There is,' he says, 'I believe, no part of the nation more inclined to be religious, and to be delighted with it, than the poor inhabitants of these mountains. They don't think it too much, when neither ways nor weather are inviting, over cold and bleak hills to travel three or four miles, or more, on foot, to attend the public prayers, and some times as many more to hear a sermon, and they seldom grudge many times for several hours to gather in their damp and cold churches to wait the coming of their minister, who, by occasional duties in his other curacies, or by other accidents, may be obliged to disappoint them or to be often variable in his hours of prayer.'

CHAPTER X

RELIGIOUS EDUCATION AND REVIVAL

DESPITE all that may be said of worldly prelates, of apathetic and even dissolute clergy, despite also the prevailing spirit of rationalism, the century after the Restoration was a period of great religious activity. This generally took the form of practical charity, of the relief of suffering and concern for the welfare of the poor, but there were, as well, many unexpected examples of saintliness and of the practice of the Christian life. Men of like mind began to join together in groups for the deepening of their own spiritual life and for carrying out their charitable purposes. By the end of the seventeenth century there were nearly forty of these groups in and around London, and their history appeared in 1697 in a booklet by Dr. Josiah Woodward, entitled, *An Account of the Religious Societies in the City of London, and of their Endeavours for the Reformation of Manners*. As this title shows, they were more concerned with 'manners,' that is, with conduct, than with dogma or religious belief. They were appalled by the vice and profanity of the age and by the desecration of the Sabbath. There were laws on the statute book against these evils, but they were not enforced. The groups therefore formed themselves into 'Societies for the Reformation of Manners' which collected funds, employed lawyers, hired informers and witnesses, and brought thousands of cases before the courts.

One of the most active members of these London societies was Sir John Philipps of Picton Castle in Pembrokeshire. He was the son of Sir Erasmus Philipps, one of the Commissioners under the Act for the Propagation of the Gospel in Wales, and was a descendant of Sir John Perrot. A man of considerable wealth himself, he had married the heiress of an East Indian merchant, a 'nabob,' and therefore was enormously rich. This wealth he used for a variety of charitable purposes, and most of his life was spent in planning and directing the activities financed by him. He was a member of parliament for the Pembroke boroughs and later for Haverfordwest. In this capacity, though still a young man, he introduced bills against profanity and debauchery. His reforming zeal was not much appreciated by the foul-mouthed and hard-drinking squires who were his fellow-members, and one of them was led to write to a friend: 'Can you contrive no way on earth to rid the House of this ghostly authority?' Soon societies similar to those in London were formed in many counties, and through Sir John Philipps's influence they were very active in Carmarthenshire and Pembrokeshire.

Simultaneously there had grown up in Germany a similar movement, known as the pietist movement, which was to be the source of many of the religious ideas of the eighteenth century. Its celebrated founder was Philipp Jacob Spener, a Frankfort pastor who was deeply influenced by Lewis Bayly's *Practice of Piety*. Spener stressed the need for personal piety and redemption, but his religion was an eminently practical one, finding its expression in an absorption in good works. He organised groups for prayer, meditation and the study of the Bible. These were called 'collegia pietatis,' and resembled the societies described by Woodward. Spener strongly emphasised the importance of the study of the scriptures, and his influence was felt in the establishment in 1694 of a new university at Halle, where his most famous pupil, August Hermann Francke, became professor. Like Spener, Francke believed in a practical theology, in the care of the poor, and the provision of orphanages, schools and colleges. So widespread was his renown that his advice was sought by the London reformers, and led, in 1699, to the foundation of the Society for the Promotion of Christian Knowledge.

The founder of the S.P.C.K. was Dr. Thomas Bray, who was born across the border from Welshpool and educated at Oswestry Grammar School. Of the four laymen who were associated with him in this work, one was Sir Humphrey Mackworth, an industrialist who, through marriage, had become possessed of coal mines and smelting works at Neath and had recently acquired an interest in the Cardiganshire lead mines. Within a month three other men were asked to join the group, one being Sir John Philipps, who became the most active and liberal benefactor of the society. Thus the S.P.C.K. had close associations with Wales from the start. Its foundation is evidence of a marked continuity in religious and educational work in Wales. Through it the influence of Bishop Bayly returned to the land of his birth; Sir Erasmus Philipps, also, provided a link between it and the schools of the Commonwealth; and, further, although it was under the influence of the pietists that the London reformers decided that penal action in the law courts alone was insufficient to reform manners without the aid of religious education, they were quite conscious that they were but continuing the work of Thomas Gouge's Welsh Trust. The work, wrote an early historian of the Society, 'began divers years ago in north and south Wales.' But in one important respect the S.P.C.K. differed from the Welsh Trust: it was confined to members of the church of England.

In the opening years of the eighteenth century, the S.P.C.K. gave evidence of remarkable activity in Wales. It arranged for religious societies of clergy and laymen throughout the country. It distributed, either free or at a cheap price, thousands of devotional books and tracts in Welsh and English, and sponsored two editions of the Welsh Bible. It was particularly disturbed because the poverty of the clergy made it impossible for them to buy books, and therefore it established four diocesan libraries, at Cowbridge, Carmarthen, Bangor and St. Asaph respectively, and presented each library with books to the value of sixty pounds. Smaller libraries, with books to the value of twenty pounds, were established in some ten other places. But most important of all was the foundation between 1699 and 1737, under the auspices of the S.P.C.K., of 96 charity schools in addition to over sixty other schools which were privately endowed in these years.

The motive behind the charity schools in Wales was purely a religious one: it was to save the souls of the children, and for this a knowledge of the scriptures was held to be essential. The methods of the schools were determined by this motive. They did not seek to instruct children in useful trades, as did the English charity schools, but devoted nearly all their attention to teaching them to read the scriptures and to catechising them so that they would reject the dogmas of nonconformity and of the church of Rome. The schools recognised that Welsh children could be taught only in Welsh, and no attempt was made in them to suppress the Welsh language. They won the support of many eminent churchmen in Wales, both laymen such as John Vaughan of Derllys, and prelates such as the saintly Bishop Bull of St. David's, Bishop Humphrey Humphreys of Bangor and his successor Bishop John Evans. But the greatest of their Welsh patrons were Dr. John Jones, dean of Bangor, and Edmund Meyricke, treasurer of St. David's, who gave the schools active support and left them important endowments. Despite all this the work of the S.P.C.K. was not successful in Wales, for the movement, although it provided Welsh books and teaching in Welsh, was directed from England. It arose from no spontaneous desire on the part of the people themselves, and the greatest difficulty was encountered in inducing the children to attend school. Besides, the schools became involved in the bitter sectarian controversies which arose at the end of the reign of Anne. They were first attacked by the high church party, who later obtained such complete control of them that they were suspected of Jacobitism. To avoid political divisions within itself the Society largely abandoned its interest in the schools and concentrated on its other activities. So, for the last twenty years of his life, Sir John Philipps withdrew from the charity school movement.

We have seen that the S.P.C.K., unlike Gouge's Welsh Trust, was exclusively anglican. The nonconformists in Wales were very few, and were relatively well-to-do. They were, moreover, not concerned with people outside their own fold, so that the number of charity schools set up by them was small. Yet some were established in these years, notably under the will of Dr. Daniel Williams of Wrexham, who died in 1716. The opposition of the local clergy was strong enough to prevent the setting up of Dr. Williams's schools at Flint, Conway and Beaumaris, but others were founded at Wrexham, Denbigh, Newmarket, Montgomery, Llanuwchllyn, Caernarvon and Pwllheli.

The influence of the S.P.C.K. waned in the third decade of the eighteenth century, but it was then strongly reinforced by the appearance in London of Moravian missionaries. The Moravian church had suffered many persecutions, and in 1722 a number of its adherents fled from their home in Bohemia and found refuge across the border in Saxony on the estates of Count Zinzendorf, a disciple of Spener and Francke. Here, at Herrnhut, they founded a religious community which became the model for others elsewhere, and their patron acted as their bishop from 1737 until his death in 1760. The community soon became world famous for its missionary and educational work, and some of its missionaries appeared in London as early as 1728. The Moravians are primarily important because they reintroduced a mystical element into religion. They held that the practice of piety and of good works was not enough; each individual must become conscious of sin and experience religious salvation. In regenerating their spiritual life they paid great attention to congregational hymn singing. They did not, however, emphasise the importance of dogma, so that they had no desire to become a separate denomination. Their method was to form small religious groups which would be 'little churches within the church' (ecclesiolae in ecclesia). In England, therefore, they adhered to the anglican communion; they were not nonconformists.

Independently of the Moravians, John Wesley formed the 'Holy Club' in Oxford in 1729. He was the son of a Lincolnshire rector who had been active in the charity school movement, while his mother was a distant relative of Sir John Philipps. Among the early members of the club were his brother Charles, and John Gambold, the son of a Pembrokeshire rector. George Whitefield did not join them until 1735, the year from which he dated his conversion, but he became their leader in that same year, when the Wesleys departed on a missionary tour in Georgia; and in order that he might continue at Oxford, Sir John Philipps, though he had never met Whitefield, made him an allowance of thirty pounds a year. During their tour in Georgia, the Wesleys came into close contact with the Moravians, but it was not till after his return, at a little Moravian meeting in Aldersgate street on May 24, 1738, that John Wesley had the mystical experience which determined his whole life. 'About a quarter before nine,' he writes, 'I felt my heart strangely warmed, and felt I trusted in Christ alone for my salvation, and an assurance that he had taken away my sin.'

This was the climate of religious opinion which prevailed when Griffith Jones, the vicar of Llanddowror, wrote in 1731 to the S.P.C.K. a letter suggesting the establishment of a new type of school, the letter which marks the beginning of his educational work. He was then forty-eight years of age. He was brought up in humble circumstances, and early in life he had experienced religious salvation, which had determined him to take orders. He was successively curate at Laugharne and vicar of Llandeilo Abercywyn. The Christian missions to India, which were now beginning, greatly attracted him at first, and this was probably what brought him into touch with Sir John Philipps, but after much hesitation he decided to stay in Wales, because of 'the extremely miserable blindness of his own country.' Soon he was preaching the gospel with a zeal and conviction which brought him into difficulties with his fellow clergymen. They scoffed at his crudity and lack of university education, and in 1714 he was cited before the bishop's court at Carmarthen, charged with preaching in parishes other than his own, and also with preaching in unconsecrated places. But he found a strong supporter in Sir John Philipps, who maintained that Griffith Jones had never preached in a parish without being invited either by the incumbent or some other responsible person, and if he had preached outside the walls of a church it was only because 'the church was not large enough to contain the hearers, which sometimes amounted to three or four thousand people.' Sir John went further, and two years later presented him to the living of Llanddowror, where he stayed for the remaining forty-five years of his life, and in 1720 Griffith Jones married Margaret Philipps, the baronet's sister.

It was the outbreak of an epidemic which led Griffith Jones to write to the S.P.C.K. in 1731. He saw men dying around him and he passionately believed that those who died in ignorance of Christ went to everlasting damnation. His desire to teach them took on a furious urgency. He begged the S.P.C.K. to send him 'forty or fifty small Welsh Bibles' and announced his intention to start a school in which he proposed to teach reading only, and to do so not only to children but also to men and women of all ages, while yet there was time.

The methodist revival in Wales arose out of the same ferment of opinion. It can be dated from the conversion of Howell Harris upon hearing the vicar of Talgarth preach on Palm Sunday in 1735, the year which also saw the conversion of George Whitefield. Later in the same year Daniel Rowland was converted by hearing Griffith Jones preach in Llanddewi Brefi. He was twenty-three, a year older than Howell Harris, and was already in holy orders and a curate to his brother, John, at Llangeitho. Quite independently the two young men began evangelising in their native shires. In order to qualify for orders, Howell Harris matriculated at Oxford in November 1735, but he was back at his home in Trevecka within three days. In May 1736 he sought the advice of Griffith Jones, and visited him at Llanddowror. Griffith Jones, no doubt, encouraged him to take orders, for on no less than three occasions he applied to the bishop of St. David's for ordination, but without success. This refusal was probably due to his irregularities, for both he and Daniel Rowland, although they did not meet one another until late in 1737, had already begun to group their converts into 'private societies.' Howell Harris was to say later on that he did so 'in imitation of the societies which Dr. Woodward had given an account of in a little treatise on the subject.' He did not obtain a copy of this booklet until 1739, but Griffith Jones may well have spoken to him of these groups. However this may be, the characteristic Welsh methodist organisation, the *seiat*, a group meeting for devotional purposes at a fixed centre, had come into being. By 1739 Howell Harris had established nearly thirty of them in south Wales. As in the case of the pietists and the Moravians there was no intention of forming a separate denomination, but since a new organisation was being set up, parallel with the church, it is difficult to avoid the conclusion that the seeds of disruption were there from the start.

The beginning of Griffith Jones's educational work and of the methodist movement therefore coincided in point of time. Soon Griffith Jones decided to extend his work beyond his own parish. He was hampered by a scarcity of teachers, and therefore fell back on a suggestion, made as early as 1719 by Sir Humphrey Mackworth, of employing 'itinerant masters.' When he began to do this is not certain; possibly in 1737 in the year of Sir John Philipps's death. At any rate, in the winter of that year, thirty-seven classes were held. The plan adopted was simple enough. He first sought the support of the incumbent of a parish and the use of his vestry. Generally this was granted, but if not a private room was hired. An itinerant teacher would then arrive, and stay for about three months. This was considered long enough to teach reading. It was also as long as poor people could afford to attend, and the classes were usually held in the winter months when they could best spare the time, and when farm servants could find substitutes to do their work. Thereby Griffith Jones hoped to get at the mass of the people, for the charity schools had only touched the fringe of the problem. The itinerant masters taught only reading and the catechism, for these alone were thought necessary for salvation. It was considered equally important to teach the old as the young, and in some of the day schools two-thirds of the pupils were adults, while special provision was made for them in evening classes. Also it was realised that the people could be taught only in the language which they could understand, and so the schools were conducted in Welsh. Griffith Jones himself expressed considerable attachment to the Welsh language, 'grown old in years, but not decayed.' He hoped that it would continue till the end of time. But with its preservation 'abstractedly considered' he was not concerned; his purpose was purely the saving of souls. Yet the consequence of his work was the expansion of a reading public for Welsh books, and more than anyone else in his day he helped to keep the language alive.

Griffith Jones's schools met with a mixed reception. Two virulent pamphlets were published concerning him, one anonymously and the other by John Evans, the non-resident incumbent of the neighbouring parish of Eglwys Gymun. Griffith Jones's passionate evangelical appeal, or 'enthusiasm' as it would then be called, was repellent to the better clergy, who laid store by the dignity and orderliness of the church services, while he, for his part, did not hesitate to condemn what he considered to be their apathy. His teachers, humble men who were paid some three to four pounds a year, were therefore sometimes assaulted and frequently molested. Nevertheless he also received much assistance. From the first his chief supporter was Bridget Bevan of Laugharne, the daughter of John Vaughan of Derllys and wife of the member of parliament for Carmarthen boroughs. She was a fashionable woman, familiar with polite society at Bath and elsewhere, and the title 'Madam' seemed to attach itself naturally to her. She helped him to collect funds in order to train his teachers and keep his organisation going. To his subscribers he issued an annual report, characteristically called *Welch Piety*, which gives an accurate picture of the extraordinary proportions to which the movement attained. From 1737 to his death in 1761 no less than 3,495 classes were held, and 158,237 pupils passed through them, in addition to the unregistered adults who attended at nights. These adults numbered, according to Griffith Jones's estimate, twice or three times as many as the day pupils. Nor did the movement cease with his death; in fact it reached its high water mark two years later, under Madam Bevan's direction, when 279 classes were held. Griffith Jones left his fortune of £7,000 to her to carry on the work, but in time it declined, and on her death in 1779 it collapsed, for although she left £10,000 to the schools her will was contested, and her estate remained in Chancery for thirty years.

It would be difficult to exaggerate the greatness of Griffith Jones's work. His conception of education was admittedly narrow, but he should be judged only on the basis of his motive, which was to save men's souls. Nor did he show any great originality in ideas. His greatness lay in his remarkable powers of organisation and in his ability to translate his purpose into practical form on a grand scale. He helped to make the Welsh a literate nation, and his circulating schools were the most important experiment in religious education in the eighteenth century not only in Wales but in Britain and all the British dominions.

All the leaders of Welsh methodism came into close contact with Griffith Jones. His association with the two young evangelists, Howell Harris and Daniel Rowland, has already been described. In 1738, a third leader, William Williams, the son of dissenting parents, was converted on hearing Howell Harris preach in the churchyard at Talgarth. He thereupon decided to seek admission to holy orders, and was ordained a deacon, becoming curate to Theophilus Evans, the author of *Drych y Prif Oesoedd*. But his vicar was one of the chief opponents of methodism (he was the author of a *History of Modern Enthusiasm*), so Williams was soon dismissed. He married a companion of Griffith Jones's wife, and a friendship was formed between the two men. Howell Davies, who, also, was converted by Howell Harris in 1738, became curate to Griffith Jones himself before he settled in Pembrokeshire. Last among the great leaders of Welsh methodism was Peter Williams, who was converted by Whitefield at Carmarthen in 1743, and became curate to John Evans at Eglwys Gymun, the neighbouring parish to Llanddowror.

His vicar was Griffith Jones's bitter enemy, and so Peter Williams was dismissed, as might be expected. These were all very young men and they were greatly influenced by Griffith Jones, who was over thirty years their senior. Besides, he had undergone the same mystical experience as they had, and, like them, had been accused of irregularities, namely of intruding into other parishes and preaching in the open air. Moreover the early methodists had no more intention than he had of leaving the church; like Griffith Jones they were inspired by the new spirit in religion, the new 'enthusiasm,' and hoped for a revival within the church itself. Griffith Jones used many methodist exhorters as teachers in his schools. The connection between his work and methodism was therefore organic, and his enemies accused him in print of being the originator of the movement. Yet in successive numbers of *Welch Piety* he was at pains to defend his schools against the charge of methodism. He strictly enjoined his teachers not to exhort their pupils, but to attend only to catechising, a way of teaching which the methodists deplored. Soon he sharply criticised the methodist leaders themselves, notably Daniel Rowland, when the excesses of their congregations embarrassed him. But his chief objection was to lay-preachers; he held that ordination was essential for preaching the word of God. This placed the exhorters (most of whom were unordained) 'in great straits,' for they evidently set great store by his opinion. Yet there was no open breach between him and them. Howell Harris had left the methodist movement ten years before Griffith Jones died in 1761, but he had continued to write affectionately to the old man, while William Williams composed an elegy to him which is excessive in its praise. It is probable that Griffith Jones acted as a restraining influence on his young associates, and helped to keep them within the church of England.

Although methodism in Wales was but one aspect of a general religious revival, it was a spontaneous movement. Howell Harris may have heard of the Oxford methodists from Griffith Jones when he visited him in May 1736, but he does not mention them in his diary until October 1737. It was not until March 1739 that he met their leader, George Whitefield, who then took him to a Moravian meeting. Harris was greatly influenced by the Moravians, for their spiritual life and methods were like his own. Three months later he met John Wesley. But already a grave difference of opinion had arisen between Whitefield who was a Calvinist and Wesley who was an Arminian. This difference became a definite rift in 1741. The Welsh methodists sided with Whitefield, and thus began the very close association between them and his followers in England (who were known as 'Lady Huntingdon's connexion,' through the patronage of that lady, a friend of Madam Bevan). In spite of this cleavage relations between Howell Harris and John Wesley did not cease. Wesley paid, in all, forty-six visits to Wales, though he complained bitterly that 'the heavy curse of the confusion of tongues' hindered his work. In time he left Welsh Wales to Howell Harris, and they agreed not to attempt to proselytise 'each other's people,' but both preached by invitation to each other's followers, and Harris was invited by Wesley to attend his conferences, a considerable honour. This co-operation was largely due to the fact that both remained within the church of England, that both subordinated doctrine to the great work of the salvation of souls, and that the doctrinal differences between them were by no means as pronounced as they came to be between their followers.

Wesley's movement developed along episcopal lines, whereas, almost unknown to themselves, the Welsh methodists evolved a presbyterian organisation. In October 1740 some eight ministers of all denominations and eight laymen met at Glyn, Defynnog. But Howell Harris strongly objected to working with dissenters, and so the first purely methodist 'association' or *sasiwn*, took place in January 1742 at Dygoedydd, near Llandovery. This was a meeting of representatives from the methodist societies, and they decided that, in addition to ordained ministers, six public exhorters should devote all their time to the work of evangelising, while twelve others should also exhort, although at the same time following their own callings. But a far more important association met exactly a year later at the new congregational chapel of the Watford, near Caerphilly, for Whitefield himself was present at this meeting, and it was then that the Welsh methodists finally decided to throw in their lot with him rather than with Wesley. In time monthly and quarterly meetings came to be held, in addition to the 'society meetings' and the 'association.'

All five leaders of the movement were very young men. They furthered their cause by itinerant preaching and organising 'societies.' Howell Harris was possessed of immense energy and great physical endurance. He went on extended tours on horseback through the thirteen shires, travelling 150 miles a week and preaching twice or oftener every day, sometimes at midnight or early in the morning in out of the way places to avoid molestation. Their greatest orator was Daniel Rowland, who attracted crowds varying between two and four thousand to his monthly communion services at Llangeitho. He drove a highly emotional and imaginative people to frenzy by his descriptions of hell. John Gambold, who had now become a Moravian, describes how they 'would leap and jump for joy, and clap their hands crying Halleluia, Gogoniant.' 'This,' he adds, 'would continue for hours after the preacher would be over, and some fell to the ground exhausted.' Similar scenes were witnessed at Howell Davies's meetings. They won for the methodists the name of 'Jumpers' and brought them into disrepute with some of their warmest friends. William Williams was found to have a peculiar genius for writing hymns. He began to print his hymns in 1744, and in all he wrote over a thousand. They were emotional and sensuous, like the hymns of the Moravians, and were conducive to religious revival. Their excellence caused them to be adopted by other denominations, and through them the spirit of methodism permeated the dissenting bodies and greatly increased the popularity of their services. These hymns have become part of the most precious heritage of the Welsh nation. Peter Williams wrote voluminously on doctrinal matters, and on his missionary tour in 1747 was the first methodist minister to penetrate into Anglesey.

Moderate opinion was scandalised by the excesses of the methodists. Their exhorters were molested and their meetings were broken up, often at the instigation of the squire and the parson. This happened frequently in north Wales, for there their unpopularity was aggravated by the fact that all the exhorters were detested southerners. Peter Williams was imprisoned by Sir Watkin Williams Wynn of Wynnstay in his dog kennels. Often the exhorters were arrested as vagabonds, and there were frequent attempts to press them into the navy. As they were anglicans they could not avail themselves of the privileges granted to dissenters under the Toleration Act, and they were frequently fined and imprisoned for illegal preaching. This brought to a head their relations with the church of England and with the dissenters. Howell Harris had defined this relationship as early as 1741. He was resolved to adhere to the church of England, and would hold no meetings of his own during the hours of divine service. He believed in the episcopal form of church government and held that ordination was necessary for administering the sacraments though not for preaching and expounding the scriptures. On the other hand he sympathised with those who scrupled to take the sacrament at the hands of those whom they considered to be unworthy priests. When the exhorters implored that they should be allowed to avail themselves of the protection of the Toleration Act by registering themselves as dissenters, Howell Harris refused. They would remain within the church, he said, 'until the Lord should open a plain door for leaving the communion.'

His attitude, and in particular his condemnation of a society which joined the dissenters in 1742, led to the estrangement of many of his nonconformist friends. The methodists in their early days had received much help from dissenting ministers, like Edmund Jones of Pontypool and Lewis Rees of Llanbrynmair. They were united by the bond of Calvinism, and could co-operate as long as the movement sought only a religious revival irrespective of sect. It is certainly true that early methodism flourished most where dissent was strongest. But Howell Harris's uncompromising attitude led to a break. Besides, the temper of the methodists differed from that of the dissenters. The latter were absorbed in interminable theological disputes, and had a tendency towards rationalism and unitarianism. Howell Harris condemned their lukewarmness and orderliness, and their concern with morality rather than with the salvation of souls. They, for their part, had a marked distaste for the excesses of the methodists, and several dissenting ministers wrote pamphlets against them.

It may well be that the methodists were led to remain within the church, despite their disabilities, by the hope that their leader, Whitefield, might be made a bishop. For it was supposed that Frederick, Prince of Wales, favoured his claim, since like all the Hanoverian heirs to the throne, he was at variance with his father. Had this come about, Whitefield could have ordained Howell Harris and the other lay-preachers, and many problems would have been solved. But, in 1751, Frederick died, and such hopes as Whitefield may have had were frustrated. In the same year, too, occurred the rupture between Howell Harris and Daniel Rowland. Both were imperious men who found it difficult to work together. Besides Howell Harris had adopted the unorthodox Moravian doctrine that God himself had died in the death of the Cross, and Daniel Rowland had published a pamphlet against his heretical views as early as 1745. Moreover, Howell Harris fell completely under the influence of Madam Sidney Griffith, the wife of the squire of Cefnamwlch in Lleyn. She was a formidable woman, given to visions, and Howell Harris had great faith in her oracular utterances on such occasions. He took her around the country with him, with the result that her husband disowned her and Howell Harris and his wife became estranged. It may well be fortunate that she died in 1752, but by this time the rupture between Harris and the 'Rowlandists' was complete.

As early as 1736, Harris had expressed a wish to form a religious community, living together under strict discipline. This was three years before he had met the Moravians, though he may have heard of them previously. He now put his plan into operation at Trevecka, with the aid of a gift of £900 from Madam Griffith. His settlement there bore an obvious resemblance to that of Herrnhut, and that of Fulneck in Yorkshire. He acquired 765 acres of land, and his agent, an Aberdare tailor named Evan Moses, attended fairs and other gatherings to urge people to join. These began to arrive in December 1752, and soon there were over 120 members. They forfeited all their worldly goods, and shared all the profits. Three times a day they held religious services, and four times on Sundays. They practised all the rural trades and even had a printing press. Harris was receptive of new ideas. He was an early member of the Brecknockshire Agricultural Society which was founded in 1755, and he introduced to Trevecka many of the new devices of the industrial revolution. When war broke out against the hated Roman catholic power of France, he equipped five men who served in Canada, and in 1759 he persuaded twenty-four men to join the Breconshire militia. When the militia left for garrison duty at Yarmouth in the following year he accompanied them, first as ensign and then as lieutenant. In time he became reconciled with the leaders of the Welsh methodists, and in 1768 Lady Huntingdon founded a college at Trevecka so that the students should have the benefit of his inspiring presence. But he himself never returned to the methodist movement, and he died in 1773. Possibly he was the greatest Welshman of his age. He certainly had creative genius, and he left an ineffaceable mark on the life of Wales. Such faults as he had were due to impetuosity. A contemporary Moravian writer describes him as 'naturally of an open choleric disposition, undisguised in his words and actions, impetuous in his proceedings, would flatter no man nor give up a particle of what he was persuaded to be truth to please his dearest and nearest friend.'

The position of the methodists within the church became more and more anomalous. Their societies had met unobtrusively in private houses to begin with, but in 1742 they had acquired their first separate building at Groeswen, near Caerphilly. Daniel Rowland's case illustrates the difficult position into which they had fallen. He remained a curate to his brother, John, until the latter died in 1760, the year in which a meeting house was built for Daniel Rowland near the parish church. The living was in the gift of the freeholders of the parish, and they might have been expected to nominate Daniel Rowland as successor to his brother. Instead they gave the living to Daniel Rowland's son, John, who spent his life in Shrewsbury, while his father remained as curate at Llangeitho. It is probable that this arrangement was made because no bishop would accept Daniel Rowland himself without pledges that he would not preach in unconsecrated places or intrude into other parishes without invitation, pledges which he would not give. But the arrangement broke down three years later, when Daniel Rowland was deprived of his curacy by the bishop. Yet, during all the years from 1760 to 1811, the sacrament of holy communion was not once administered in the parish church at Llangeitho; the parishioners, though faithful members of the church of England, communicated in the meeting house nearby. A similar anomaly arose with regard to David Jones, a leader of the second generation of methodists. He obtained the living of Llangan in the Vale of Glamorgan in

1767, and retained it till his death, in 1810, although for the last sixteen years of his life he lived in Pembrokeshire. Yet in 1775 he built a meeting house three miles away from his parish church, and it was there that he ministered, making it a centre of methodism second only to Llangeitho.

The older methodist leaders passed away with the deaths of Howell Davies in 1770, Howell Harris in 1773, Daniel Rowland in 1790, William Williams in 1791 and Peter Williams in 1796, the last having been expelled from the connexion five years previously on account of his heretical beliefs on the nature of the Trinity. Their work had been that of evangelising, and they had done it with marked success. What was now necessary was to consolidate their gains, and for this the methodists found an organiser of genius in Thomas Charles. He was born a few miles from Llanddowror some six years before Griffith Jones's death. After graduating at Oxford he held several curacies, but on his marriage in 1783 he settled in Bala and soon devoted his whole time to itinerant preaching. Hitherto methodism had flourished only in south Wales; it was Thomas Charles who was responsible for its success in north Wales, and Bala proved a convenient geographical centre for his activities. In 1785 he revived the idea of circulating schools, which had lapsed with Madam Bevan's death six years previously. But the work progressed very slowly, partly because of lack of teachers and of support, and partly, also, because the inaccessibility of so many villages in north Wales made it difficult for the people to attend. Thomas Charles, like Griffith Jones, then had recourse to night classes, and eventually to classes on Sundays. He did so reluctantly, for he was a strict Sabbatarian and feared that even teaching to read meant breaking the Sabbath. He was reassured when he found that no 'evil effects' followed the experiments of others in this field. For Robert Raikes at Gloucester in 1782 had organised the work of other men into a system of Sunday schools, and such men as Morgan John Rhys and Edward Williams of Oswestry had forestalled Thomas Charles in Wales itself. It was about 1789 that Thomas Charles organised his Sunday schools, and they became so successful that they displaced the circulating day-schools. These Sunday schools helped to create a reading public in Wales, and the demand for Bibles led Thomas Charles, in 1804, to join with others in founding the British and Foreign Bible Society.

The Sunday schools in Wales took on a Welsh character. They were never intended solely for children. In addition to classes of the very young, being taught to sing or to read the story of the Creation, there can always be found in them classes of old men pondering over the Book of Revelation. For a century the Sunday schools alone taught their pupils in Welsh. Never had they the social purpose of reconciling the poor to their station in life. Peasantry and middle class have mixed in them with complete equality, and prominence in them has depended solely on merit, while their teachers have always been unpaid. By their very nature they have therefore provided a useful training in democracy, and have raised the intellectual standard of the people by accustoming them to the discussion of abstract ideas. Their contribution to the cultural development of Wales has been inestimable.

Thomas Charles provided Wales with a mass of religious literature and a periodical, *Y Drysorfa*, largely to counteract the heresies of Peter Williams. But he was also called upon to make, with great reluctance, the vital decision by which the methodists became a separate denomination. The Moravians had already broken away after the death of Zinzendorf in 1760, and John Gambold had become their bishop. Of their churches, that of Haverfordwest was closed only recently. The methodists still clung to the established church. But with the outbreak of the French Revolution there was a renewal of persecution, for, incredible though it seems, they were suspected of Jacobinism. In one year they had to pay nearly £100 in fines. They therefore took the revolutionary step of licensing their meeting houses. A still more revolutionary step was to follow. Ordination, they believed, was necessary for the administration of the sacrament, but the older generation of ordained methodists was passing, and methodists now were reluctant to take the sacrament from clergymen who did not sympathise with them. As early as 1788 John Wesley had ordained ministers. Both David Jones and Thomas Charles were opposed to this, but after the death of the former, Charles gave way to the pressure of his exhorters, and in 1811 the reluctant step was taken. Eight ministers were ordained at Bala in June and thirteen at

Llandeilo in August. Among them were Thomas Charles's brother, David Charles, Thomas Jones of Denbigh and John Elias of Anglesey, the leaders of methodism in the early nineteenth century. The methodists had thus become a separate denomination. In 1823 the new church drew up its Confession of Faith, and three years later it became incorporated by a constitutional deed. The decisive step, reluctantly though it was taken, led to a great release of energy, which accounts for the remarkable spread of methodism in these years.

Many reasons can be found for the success of the methodist movement. The revival had the appeal of novelty, and the early preachers were men of outstanding power, whose evangelical sermons attracted people who were tired of the formalism of the established church and of the arid theological disputes of the dissenters. Moreover the anglican church was hampered by its poverty, by the apathy of many of its clergy, and by the growth of centres of population in newly developed industrial areas inadequately served by the parish churches. But this initial success of the methodist movement would scarcely have proved lasting had it not been for the great organising ability of Thomas Charles. He was the architect of his denomination, and when he died in 1814 the structure was secure.

It would be difficult to analyse fully the influence of methodism on the development of the Welsh nation. Not only did it contribute to the growth of nonconformity by the establishment of a new denomination; it led also to the expansion of the other dissenting bodies. In this the hymns of William Williams played an important part. The older dissent became suffused with the emotionalism of the methodists. This both increased its popularity and counteracted its tendency towards rationalism. In time dissent became the religious pattern for the greater part of the nation. As the gentry remained within the anglican church this added a further element to the division between them and their tenantry. Methodism also counteracted the anglicising tendencies prevalent since the Tudor period. It gave an impetus to the study of the Welsh language and produced a considerable literature in Welsh. It may be said to have changed the tone of the nation both for the better and for the worse. The moral fibre of the people was stiffened, and they became more law-abiding. But they lost that carefree joyousness which had found expression in the 'interlude' and the 'noson lawen.' They became obsessed with thoughts of death and of the fires of hell. The movement coincided moreover with great industrial changes, and the people's concern with the world to come, while it may have saved the country from social disturbance and anarchy, rendered them apathetic to the need for reform. Yet the methodist insistence on uncompromising integrity of character, on honesty, temperance, industry and thrift, together with their belief in the sanctity of the individual and the equality of all men before God, led in time to the rousing of the social conscience and the sweeping away of many abuses.

CHAPTER XI

WELSH POLITICS: 1714–1832

THE position of the Hanoverian dynasty on the throne remained insecure for some years after the accession of George I, and many wavered in their loyalty to it. Naturally the dissenters strongly supported the new dynasty, but they were a small minority in England, and an even smaller one in Wales. Anglicans were divided by their adherence on the one hand to the high church policy of the later years of Anne's reign, and by their detestation of the Roman catholicism of the exiled Stuarts on the other. Some of the gentry were notoriously Jacobite in sympathy. Lewis Pryse of Gogerddan, near Aberystwyth, was returned as member for Cardiganshire to George I's first parliament, but, no doubt with foreknowledge of impending events, he did not appear when the house assembled in August, 1715, and went into hiding when a messenger was sent by the commons to arrest him. In the next month the Jacobite rising took place in Scotland under the earl of Mar. Its success was short lived, while the attempt of the English Jacobites was even more abortive. Their leaders were soon arrested and condemned to death. One of them was the earl of Nithsdale, the husband of Lady Winifred Herbert, daughter of the marquis of Powis who had gone into exile with James II, but she and her two Welsh maids, Mistress Evans and Mistress Morgan, had access to her husband in the Tower on the night before his execution and contrived his escape. In Wales, Jacobite mobs in Wrexham, aided by the miners of Rhosllannerchrugog, wrecked the two meeting houses in the town and smashed the windows of the dissenters. After the rising there were desultory prosecutions here and there in Wales of men who had drunk seditious healths, but that was all.

Jacobite intrigue, in fact, did much to strengthen a reaction in favour of the Hanoverians. Welsh people in London, who were to exercise a progressively important influence on Welsh affairs throughout the century, formed, in 1715, the first of their societies, that of the Ancient Britons, with the express purpose of protecting the dynasty. Its loyalty was not destined to be put to the test, but the society served a most useful purpose, for it founded, in 1718, a charity school for educating and apprenticing poor boys of London-Welsh parentage, and this, in time, has become the well-known girls' school, now at Ashford in Middlesex. The charity schools in Pembrokeshire were, meanwhile, praying daily for King George and the royal family, and Iaco ab Dewi translated into Welsh a sermon preached in London in thanksgiving for the defeat of the Jacobite rising.

Lewis Pryse of Gogerddan was expelled from the house of commons for contumacy, and in April 1717 the earl of Mar wrote to him from Innsbruck to inform him that another attempt at invasion would be made in the autumn, this time through Milford Haven. Like several other Jacobite schemes, nothing came of it, yet it helped to keep Jacobite sentiment alive. This was also the main function of various Jacobite clubs throughout the country. There was a vogue for secret societies (it was the time of the spread of freemasonry), and the Jacobites took to arranging clandestine meetings for the purpose of drinking the health of 'the king over the water' in specially designed glasses, and for other such puerilities. Two of these societies were in Wales, one of them being perhaps the most famous of all Jacobite clubs. This was called the Cycle of the White Rose, for it had been formed in 1710, on White Rose Day (June 10, the birthday of the Old Pretender). It drew its members from north-east Wales and the border, and of them by far the most important was Watkin Williams Wynn of Wynnstay near Ruabon, the greatest landowner in his area. He was the son of Sir William Williams of Llanforda, near Oswestry; it was through his mother that he inherited, in 1719, the estates of Sir John Wynn of Wynnstay, grandson of Sir John Wynn of Gwydir and the last of his line. He did not succeed to his title until 1740, but he owned vast estates, and his income was said to be £18,000 a year. He had already become member of parliament for Denbighshire in 1716, and he continued to represent this constituency until his death. Of all the Jacobites in parliament he was possibly the most active in debate and in his opposition to the house of Hanover. When the Cycle of the White Rose was revived in 1723, he was thirty-one years of age, and he soon became its leader. It used to meet periodically in the country houses of its members or at the hostelry of Daniel Porter, Junior, in Wrexham (which later became the Wynnstay Arms). The other Jacobite club was the Society of the Sea Sergeants, which was founded about 1725 and met annually at Tenby and other seaport towns in west Wales. This society, also, had its special drinking glasses, emblazoned with its badge, a dolphin. Its secretary and most prominent member was John Philipps of Picton Castle, younger son of the patron of Griffith Jones. Horace Walpole, who was his cousin, described him as 'a notorious Jacobite,' but very little is known of the club's political activities.

There is no doubt that Jacobite opinion was strong in Wales, especially along the border. The marquis of Powis, son of James II's companion in exile, had recovered his great estates, but retained his Jacobitism. His nephew, the young duke of Beaufort, owned vast lands in Herefordshire, Gloucestershire and Monmouthshire, and his family, too, supported the Jacobite cause. In Shropshire one of the greatest landowners was the Jacobite, Sir Richard Corbett. Denbighshire, Montgomeryshire and Merioneth were under the influence of Watkin Williams Wynn. Lord Bulkeley, the Anglesey landowner, was known to favour the cause, and there were many other Jacobite families in south and west Wales. But their acknowledged leader was James Barry, earl of Barrymore, a landowner in Cheshire, who held the rank of lieutenant-general in the British army. It was reported to Louis XV in 1743 that 'the twelve counties of the principality are entirely at the orders of the dukes of Beaufort and Powis, Lord Bulkeley, Sir Watkin Williams (Wynn) and those who think with them, and they have all undertaken to hold themselves in readiness to take the saddle as soon as the first signal is given by Lord Barrymore.'

But, as the crisis approached, the government took action. Barrymore was arrested and placed in the Tower. Instructions were issued to meet a possible invasion through Wales, and customs officers were ordered to keep strict watch and report the activities of suspected persons. This drew forth protestations of loyalty from various quarters. Haverfordwest, true to its tradition in the Civil War, presented a loyal address. The methodist, Howell Davies, drew up a list of 1,500 Pembroke-shire men who were willing to serve King George while the revolt lasted, and Daniel Rowland compiled a similar list of 500 Cardiganshire men, for the methodists were as violent in their detestation of Roman catholicism as were the dissenters.

Prince Charles Edward sailed on July 2, 1745, from Nantes with seven companions on the *Du Teillay*. He was escorted by the *Elizabeth*, on which was Henry Lloyd, a native of Cwm-bychan in Merioneth, at that time an officer in the French army. Seven days out the *Elizabeth* was engaged by a British ship, the *Lyon*, and both were so battered that they had to withdraw from the fight, so that the prince landed at Moidart with only his seven men. Henry Lloyd was wounded in this fighting, but as soon as his ship reached Scotland, he was sent on mission to north Wales and to reconnoitre the coasts of Wales and the west of England. The prince advanced into England, taking the Carlisle route, so that he could collect his adherents in Lancashire, Cheshire and Wales. At Preston he was joined by Richard and William Vaughan of Courtfield, members of an old Monmouthshire Roman catholic family, and by David Morgan, whose home was at Pencraig Taf, near Merthyr, and whose family was related to the leading Glamorgan gentry. He was a barrister in London, a high churchman and a leading member of a London Jacobite club. His repute was probably known to the prince, for he was given posts of responsibility and was called 'the prince's counsellor.' Meanwhile Cumberland had assembled his forces at Lichfield, thus placing himself between the prince and his Welsh supporters. The Jacobites were therefore forced to move away from north Wales, and reached Derby on December 4. There the prince realised that vastly superior forces were assembled against him and he was forced to begin his disastrous retreat.

Immediately on reaching Preston the prince had written to Sir Watkin Williams Wynn. 'The particular character I have heard of you,' he said, 'makes me hope to see you among the first. I am persuaded that you will not break my expectations, and you need not doubt but I shall always remember to your advantage the example you shall thus have put to your neigh-bours and consequently to all England.' But this letter appar-ently did not reach Wynnstay. Was this perhaps the cause of the strange inactivity of the Welsh Jacobites? For the Cycle of the White Rose played no part in the rising. The prince's own explanation, in a letter which he wrote to his father from Avignon, ten months after Culloden, was that Lord Barrymore's son reached Derby two days after the retreat had begun. He had been sent by Sir Watkin Williams Wynn and others to assure the prince that 'they were ready to join me in what manner I pleased either in the capital or everyone to rise in his own country,' but it was too late. Had the Welsh Jacobites reached Derby the prince might well have overruled his advisers and continued his advance on London. The history of the rebellion would, in that case, have been very different, but the ultimate result would no doubt have been the same.

The fortunes of the Welsh Jacobites varied considerably. David Morgan decided not to withdraw to Scotland with the prince; he is reported to have said that he would rather hang than starve. It was not long before he was captured, and after six months in prison awaiting trial he died the gruesome death of a traitor. William and Richard Vaughan fought at Culloden. They escaped to Spain and entered the Spanish army, where William rose to the rank of general. In time, Richard's son was allowed to succeed to the estate of Courtfield, and among his descendants was Cardinal Vaughan, archbishop of Westminster. Henry Lloyd was arrested on suspicion after he had examined the coast as far as Dover, but as there was no definite evidence against him, he was released and allowed to go to France. He served in the Seven Years War first on the Austrian side and then on the Prussian side, and eventually became a general in the armies of Catherine II of Russia, fighting against both the Swedes and the Turks. He was one of the most celebrated of eighteenth century writers on military science, and his books were studied in every military academy in Europe. Strange to say, Sir Watkin Williams Wynn escaped a charge of treason, although he was carefully watched by the authorities. As late as 1749 he wrote to the Old Pretender that the Welsh Jacobites were without a leader since the death of Lord Barrymore, but were still ready to rise if troops were landed. Later in the same year he died through a fall from his horse.

Any hope of Jacobite success had now gone beyond recall. The nation had become reconciled to the Hanoverian succession and did not wish to see the return of a Roman catholic king. The fear of Roman catholicism was, no doubt, exaggerated in Wales as in England, although at this very time there was a renewal of persecution in France and hundreds of French protestants were being sent annually to the galleys. The spread of methodism helped to remove the final traces of Jacobitism from among the people of Wales.

The eclipse of Jacobitism had a profound influence on the development of the party system. The two parties had arisen through disagreement on religious matters in the later years of Charles II. The Whigs drew their support from London and the towns, where dissent was strongest, but, nevertheless, they ranged themselves around a few great aristocratic magnates. The Tories were the Roman catholic and high church party, and from among them the Jacobites were drawn. A difference of attitude towards religious toleration always persisted to some degree, but otherwise the line dividing the Whigs from the Tories was becoming increasingly blurred even in the reigns of George I and George II, and, when Jacobitism ceased to be a vital issue, this dividing line virtually disappeared. It is scarcely accurate to speak of party politics in the reign of George III. There was at that time little difference in principle between the two parties, and no party discipline. Men belonged to groups formed through personal allegiance to a political leader, and the composition of these groups was constantly changing.

Political contests, therefore, were not fought over matters of national policy, but were struggles between the great land-owning families and their satellites. The magnates in Wales were the duke of Beaufort in Monmouthshire, the earl of Pembroke in Glamorgan and the marquis of Powis in mid Wales. Around them were grouped the gentry who had consolidated their estates in the previous two centuries and who were united by a whole net-work of inter-marriages, and yet divided by old enmities and rivalries. A seat in parliament had become, for them, a mark of social distinction in the centres of fashion. It also gave the member's family priority in his own district, a matter of great concern to country gentlemen, and allowed him to have a say in the nomination of the lord lieutenant of the county and its *custos rotulorum*. Besides it gave him control of a considerable amount of patronage, for he could dispose of church livings and of offices in the army and navy and the public service. The direct pecuniary corruption of members was surprisingly rare, despite all that has been written on this theme since the eighteenth century, but considerable per-quisites were placed at their disposal. In particular the amount of royal patronage available in the boroughs was very large; it was less in the shires, so that county members were, on the whole, more independent of the control of the government. Seats had come to be regarded almost as the property of parti-cular families. Sometimes it was even arranged that families should hold a seat in turn. Usually there were contests only when new-comers, who had made fortunes in eastern trade or otherwise, sought to acquire a seat for reasons of social distinc-tion. But this was an expensive matter, for the electors suppor-ted the local families with almost feudal loyalty.

The franchise in the shires was still restricted to the forty-shilling freeholders, but they were a reasonably numerous class, as the value of money had declined considerably. In the boroughs the position was not so clear. There was a variety of franchises, but the Welsh boroughs were nearly all of the 'free-man' type, that is, the franchise was vested in those who had been admitted as burgesses either through birth, through apprentice-ship, through marriage with a burgess' daughter or through the gift of the corporation. Beaumaris, however, was a closed borough; there the member of parliament was elected by the corporation, a body of twenty-five who themselves filled any vacancy which arose in their own ranks. On this account Beaumaris had fallen completely under the control of the family of Lord Bulkeley, which nominated every member of parliament from the Restoration to the Reform Act. In Brecon, also, the number of electors had been reduced to seventeen by neglecting to create new burgesses. Nor was it necessary in the majority of Welsh boroughs that the freemen should reside locally, though the house of commons decided in 1680 with regard to the Monmouth boroughs, and in 1744 with regard to those of Denbigh, that the franchise should be restricted to resident burgesses. Elsewhere, when a contest was anticipated, it was possible to create honorary freemen to swamp the poll, and this practice continued throughout the eighteenth century. Frequently, also, there were disputes between the shire towns and their contributory boroughs. Thus in 1709, the house of commons rejected the claim of Newborough to share the representation of Beaumaris, and in 1728 a similar decision asserted the exclusive rights of the burgesses of the tiny borough of Montgomery to elect a member, as against the claims of the growing towns of Llanidloes, Llanfyllin and Welshpool.

Such contests as there were in Glamorgan were between the satellites of Cardiff castle and its opponents. Here the unreality of politics was shown in 1789 when the son of the previous member for the shire, a nominee of the earl of Bute (whose family had succeeded to the estates of the Herberts, earls of Pembroke) was asked to stand down in order that one of the Bute family might obtain a seat. He refused to do so, and then held the seat for a quarter of a century in opposition to the Bute interests. The member for the Glamorgan boroughs was more amenable, when the earl's heir came of age in 1790 and wanted a seat. In Monmouthshire political interest was shared between the duke of Beaufort's family and that of the Morgans of Tredegar, for there were two seats. From the time when the shire had first obtained representation in parliament a member of each of these families, or one of their nominees, had represented Monmouthshire. Valentine Morris of Piercefield, who had made his fortune in the West Indies, decided in 1771 to contest a Monmouthshire seat, but he was unsuccessful and ruined himself by doing so. The Beaufort interest was predominant in the town of Monmouth, so that the seat for the Monmouth boroughs invariably went to this family. On the other hand, Brecon, with its restricted electorate, was a pocket borough of the Morgans, and, for the eighty years before the Reform Act, a Morgan represented Brecon almost without a break. The same was true of Breconshire, but here, in 1806, a nabob appeared in the person of Thomas Wood of Gwernyfed, and the Morgan nominee withdrew. Great efforts were made to unseat Wood in 1818, but he retained the seat until 1847. In Cardiganshire, the Vaughans of Trawsgoed, who obtained an Irish peerage as earls of Lisburne for their support of the Whig revolution of 1688, were opposed by the Pryses of Gogerddan and the Powells of Nanteos, yet in 1761 their common interests in lead mines led the Powells to support the Vaughans. Contests in Carmarthenshire were fought with great bitterness, and here, again, a nabob appeared in the person of Sir William Paxton. His unsuccessful attempt to secure a seat in 1802 has become famous, for his expenses are said to have amounted to £15,690, 4s. 2d., a sum which covered 11,070 breakfasts, 36,901 dinners, 684 suppers, 25,275 gallons of ale, 11,068 bottles of spirits, 8,879 bottles of porter, 460 bottles of sherry, 509 bottles of cider, eighteen guineas for milk punch, £786 for ribbons and 4,521 separate charges for horse hire. He succeeded in being returned unopposed for the boroughs in the next year, and in transferring himself to the shire in 1806, but in 1807 he was again defeated. The contest for Flint in 1734 is said to have cost the two candidates £70,000, and the successful candidate, after three such elections, died in a debtors' prison. In the boroughs and shire of Denbigh the Middletons of Chirk maintained the Whig traditions which the family had acquired in the seventeenth century, until there arose the great house of Wynnstay, the ruling dynasty of north-east Wales.

Apart from the intrusion of an occasional interloper, the political domination of the Welsh gentry seemed likely to continue as undisturbed as it was undistinguished. (In the two centuries after the Restoration, with the exception of some five years, a Morgan sat continuously in Westminster, yet in all this time the family did not produce one political leader of any distinction whatsoever.) But two factors now emerged which were to produce a change. One was the spread of nonconformity and the other was the growth of industrialism.

The dissenters of Wales remained few in the first half of the eighteenth century, and they were mainly concentrated in the south. (Anglesey may well have been the only shire in England and Wales with no dissenting congregation.) But in the next fifty years the number of congregations more than doubled, largely through the influence of the methodist revival, and after that their growth was rapid. Besides, the social status of the dissenters was fairly high, for they were mostly substantial farmers. They were therefore in a position of some independence, and they showed a marked tendency towards radicalism in their political views. Memories of the Civil War and of opposition to the government still persisted among them, and counteracted the countryman's inclination to passive obedience and loyalty to the landowning families. Church and state were then inextricably interwined, and as the dissenters were, by nature, opposed to the established church, they were predisposed, also, to opposition to the state. Nor had they any sentimental reverence for the established order. They had divested religion of all its outward trappings, its traditional ceremonial and usages, and they set no value on the continuity of the church or its apostolic succession. A disparagement of tradition is part of the make-up of all radicals, and this critical attitude of mind the dissenters transferred to the realm of politics.

This tendency was strengthened by the growing rationalism of the age. Unlike the methodists, the dissenters did not feel themselves to be humble suppliants for grace, dependent for their salvation on the mercy of God. Their religion was more intellectual, and their religious beliefs had to be proved by argument. They were engaged in interminable theological disputes. Newtonian science had provided the eighteenth century with an almost complete explanation of the universe, so that divine revelation became almost superfluous. Their disputes, therefore, turned largely on the divinity of Christ, and the very term 'presbyterianism' ceased to have any bearing on the form of church government and became synonymous with liberalism in theology. The centre of these ideas in Wales was the Presbyterian Academy at Carmarthen, especially in the early years of the century when Thomas Perrot was its tutor. His chief pupil was Jenkin Jones, who, in 1726, founded at Llwynrhydowen in south Cardiganshire the first Arminian church in Wales. Under Jenkin Jones's ministry and that of his successors, David Lloyd and David Davis, Castell Hywel, the church moved towards Arianism, that is, a partial denial of the divinity of Christ, and the foundations of these beliefs were firmly laid in this locality. Less than twenty miles away at Llangeitho, Daniel Rowland threw vast crowds into paroxysms of fear and exaltation by expounding the redemptive powers of Christ, but on this solid core of Arianism his passionate eloquence had no effect whatsoever.

It must be remembered also that the dissenters were a minority subject to disabilities for their religious beliefs. The Toleration Act had only removed the penalties for non-attendance at church; it had not granted religious equality. The dissenters still had to be married with anglican ceremony; they were still excluded from the universities, and the Test and Corporation Acts still debarred them from public office. The Corporation of London had in fact passed a by-law inflicting heavy penalties on those who refused to serve in public office when called upon by the lord mayor, who then proceeded to nominate dissenters in expectation of the fines which would accrue. The Corporation obtained £15,000 in this disgraceful way, until the practice was stopped in 1767 by the decision of the house of lords in the case of Allan Evans, the decision which, through the judgement given by Lord Mansfield, established that nonconformity was no longer a crime. Naturally the dissenters clamoured for religious liberty. Influenced by the radical political theory of the day, they claimed that this liberty was one of the inherent natural rights of man. It was but a short step from this to advocating political liberty, that is, the right of each individual to participate in the government of his country. Much of the political theory of radicalism emanated from the dissenting academies, and the unitarians were in the forefront of the struggle, but the dissenters never formed a political party. They differed among themselves on questions of theology too widely for this, but they all shared a common desire for political freedom.

The exclusion of John Wilkes from parliament, despite his election on three occasions for the county of Middlesex, had some repercussions in Wales, for in 1771 the shires of Pembrokeshire, Carmarthenshire and Cardiganshire presented addresses of support to him through Watkin Lewes, a Pembrokeshire man who was treasurer of the Society of Ancient Britons and who became lord mayor of London in 1780. London Welshmen were also active in the movement started in 1771 by a number of men of unitarian sympathy for the abolition of the subscription to the Thirty-Nine Articles which was compulsory for students and others. Their petition to parliament was strongly opposed by Edmund Burke and was rejected. But these incidents were of very minor importance compared with the outbreak of the American War of Independence, for the Americans were themselves descended from the puritans of the seventeenth century, and shared common traditions with the dissenters of England and Wales. It was the American War which developed a political awareness in Wales, and it is significant that the first publication in Welsh of a purely political nature appeared in 1776, and was a translation by David Jones of Trefriw of a pamphlet on the nature of the dispute in America. The war, also, in addition to arousing political consciousness in Wales, crystallised the attitude of the dissenters towards politics.

This attitude is thrown into high relief by the writings of Dr. Richard Price. He was fifty-two years of age when fighting began, and he had long been a leader among the dissenters. His own mental development, in fact, clearly illustrates the changes which came over nonconformity in this century. His father was a Calvinist, but Price reacted against this stern creed. After the death of Perrot the Presbyterian Academy had been moved from Carmarthen to Llwynllwyd in Breconshire, in an attempt to stamp out its heterodoxy, and Price was educated there, and subsequently in London at Coward's Academy. In these institutions he became progressively an Arminian and then an Arian, and he spent his life as minister of a presbyterian congregation at Stoke Newington, at that time a village outside London. Early in 1776 there appeared his pamphlet on the American war, entitled *Observations on the Nature of Civil Liberty*. Hitherto the dispute with the colonists had been about taxation; it was Price who taught the Americans to appeal not to English usages and constitutional practices but to the inherent natural rights of man. The struggle thereby ceased to be an altercation about facts and precedents, and became an argument on the principles of government. Price argued that sovereignty rested in the people; the power of the government, he said, was merely delegated to it by the people in order that it might accomplish certain ends; the king and his ministers were the servants of the people and not their masters. This was revolutionary doctrine in the eighteenth century, so that his pamphlet caused a stir and sixty thousand copies of it were sold in the first year.

Even more radical were the opinions of another Welsh dissenter, David Williams. He was fifteen years younger than Price, and when he proceeded to the Academy it had returned to Carmarthen, but had once again become so heterodox that the congregationalists refused any longer to support it. Williams served as minister to presbyterian churches at Frome and Exeter, and finally at Highgate on the outskirts of London, where a frequent member of his congregation was Alderman Wilkes, the father of the tribune. But Williams developed into a deist, and with the help of Benjamin Franklin, then representing the American colonies in London, he tried to establish a cult of nature. The liturgy which he composed for this cult won the commendation of both Voltaire and Rousseau. He was less restrained in his language than Price, and in his *Letters on Political Liberty*, which he wrote in 1782 to defend the Americans, he advocated manhood suffrage, the ballot, the payment of members, small constituencies, annual parliaments, the publication of parliamentary debates and the freedom of the press. He thus put forward a complete radical programme. His pamphlet was translated into French, and embellished with notes which were more radical even than the text, and which landed the translator in the Bastille.

Another friend of Franklin was Jonathan Shipley, the absentee bishop of St. Asaph. His son-in-law, Sir William Jones, the son of an Anglesey father, was the greatest orientalist that this country has produced. Inspired by his detestation of the American war, Jones wrote in 1782 a pamphlet entitled *The Principles of Government in a Dialogue between a scholar and a peasant*. This was reprinted in Wrexham in his absence by his brother-in-law, William Davies Shipley, dean of St. Asaph, who was both a radical and one of the worst pluralists in Wales. The dean was thereupon prosecuted for seditious libel at the instigation of the sheriff of Flintshire, and there ensued a trial which became celebrated, for in it Erskine, who defended Shipley, vindicated the rights of juries in trials for libel. The case dragged on for nearly two years, and did much to disseminate the ideas put forward by William Jones, and the dean's acquittal was received with rejoicings and bonfires as he returned through Wrexham and Ruabon to his home in St. Asaph.

To these radicals the French Revolution was but a continuation of the revolutions of 1688 and 1776. This view was expressed by Richard Price in the anniversary sermon which he preached on November 4, 1789 to the Whig 'Society for the Commemoration of the Revolution of 1688,' and which was published with the title *On the Love of Country*. The light which the Whig revolution had 'struck out,' he said 'after setting America free, is reflected in France, and there kindled into a blaze that lays despotism in ashes, and warms and illuminates Europe.' He was now an old man, but he rejoiced to have lived to see this glorious day, and when he died some eighteen months later the French Assembly went into mourning for him. His sermon had, however, provoked Edmund Burke to write his *Reflections on the Revolution in France*, one of the great classics of English conservatism. Unlike the Welsh dissenter, the Irish writer glorified the English constitution on just those grounds of tradition and continuity which the radicals disparaged. A disposition to preserve, he claimed, was as important as an ability to improve.

David Williams, in his *Letters to a Young Prince* published in 1790, considered the English constitution a 'fraudulent deception.' But he was equally critical of the first French constitution which was to some extent modelled on it. Therefore, when the middle-class regime which had started the revolution was itself overthrown in August 1792, Williams was made an honorary citizen of the French Republic, and invited to Paris to help in the forming of yet another constitution. He arrived there in December when power was already slipping out of the hands of his friends, the Girondists, and stayed in Paris during the trial and execution of King Louis XVI. When France declared war he returned home, bearing, however, remarkable overtures for peace from the French foreign minister.

The leading London-Welsh society of the day was that of the Gwyneddigion. It was founded, in 1771, for convivial reasons, but its interests were historical and literary. It was the Gwyneddigion who, in 1789, revived the eisteddfod in its modern form, and for the meeting to be held at St. Asaph in the following year they announced the now popular subject of 'liberty' as the theme of both the prize poem and prize essay. Among the members of the society was Edward Williams (Iolo Morganwg), a literary stonemason of Glamorgan. He was, without doubt, the most erudite man of his day in Welsh history and antiquities, but the romantic atmosphere of the time, and his own perversity, led him to fabricate a wealth of ancient Welsh texts, to the confusion of Welsh scholarship. He produced a considerable body of verse in both Welsh and English, much of it of pronounced radical, and even republican, tendencies. The Gwyneddigion also sponsored *Y Cylch-grawn Cymraeg*, the first periodical in Welsh to discuss social and political matters. This was edited by Morgan John Rhys, a young baptist minister. He had given up his church in Pontypool in the late summer of 1791 and crossed to Paris to distribute Bibles, actuated by his hatred of the Roman catholic church and by his belief that the Revolution had ensured its overthrow in France. He returned to Wales early in 1792 to collect more funds. He then availed himself of the printing press at Trevecka to set up his periodical, to the distress of Evan Moses and other methodists, who did not share his opinions, and who were glad to see him leave after the second number had appeared in April 1793. In all he published five numbers before he had to abandon his project through lack of support. His sympathy for the Revolution was evident in all his writings, but he was more particularly concerned with religious freedom, with the Christian missions and the abolition of slavery. He is said to have been in close contact with the radical societies in London, of which there were many, and, in the late summer of 1794, he left for America, just at the beginning of the trials for treason of members of these societies.

The attempt to establish a periodical was then taken up by Thomas Evans, of Glyn Cothi, who published *Y Drysorfa Gymmysgedig* in 1795, but only three numbers appeared. He was even more radical than Morgan John Rhys, both in theology and in politics, for under the influence of Priestley he had become a unitarian, and it was he who founded the first unitarian church, properly so-called, in Wales.

The Gwyneddigion fell into disrepute through the writings of John Jones of Glan y Gors, one of the society's most prominent members. He had fled to London to escape service in the militia and became, in time, the innkeeper of the Canterbury Arms in Southwark. He was a satirist of considerable ability, and held extreme views on church and state. In 1795 he published a pamphlet entitled *Seren Tan Gwmmwl* which contained bitter attacks on royalty, on aristocracy and on the bishops. He was not a thinker of any originality, and his ideas were derived entirely from Tom Paine's *Rights of Man*. His second pamphlet, *Toriad y Dydd*, which appeared in 1797, was little more than a translation of some of the more virulent passages in Paine's works.

It is difficult to estimate the influence of these pamphleteers on the Welsh people. Echoes of their teaching appear in the popular ballads of the time. There was, in addition, much opposition to recruitment for military service and to the press gang, and considerable rioting occurred. Yet the effigy of Tom Paine was burnt in the streets of Cardiff in the winter of 1792, even before war had broken out, and several writers attacked Glan y Gors, notably in *Y Geirgrawn*, another short-lived periodical which appeared in 1796. Besides, such sympathy as the French Revolution had gained in Wales was quickly dispelled by the attempt to land in Pembrokeshire in February, 1797.

This attempt arose out of an attack on Ireland. The French general, Hoche, had suppressed a royalist rising in La Vendée, which had been helped by the British and had led to much destruction. He determined to carry the war into Britain itself. Ireland was seething with disaffection, and Hoche was led by Wolfe Tone and other Irish leaders to believe that the Irish would rise as soon as the French landed. He therefore prepared to attack Ireland. To distract the attention of the English authorities, Hoche decided to send a force to maraud in England. In view of its purpose, it was not necessary that it should consist of trained soldiers, and the majority of the 1,300 men who composed it were drawn from the prisons and the galleys. Detailed instructions for the raid were drawn up by Hoche. Bristol was to be attacked and burnt to the ground, and the force was then to advance on Liverpool. The soldiers were to live on the country and might loot at will, but while 'making war on the castle' they were to 'spare the cottage' and if possible rouse the countryside. Command of this force was given to an American adventurer named Tate, who was entirely incompetent both through his lack of experience and his advanced age.

The attack on Bantry Bay in December 1796 proved a fiasco, and Hoche had returned to France before Tate had set out. Nevertheless it was decided to proceed with the venture, and the force sailed in three corvettes and a lugger. Contrary winds prevented them from going up the Bristol Channel beyond Porlock, and drove them back around St. David's Head. On Wednesday, February 22, 1797, they reached Carreg Gwastad near Fishguard. Here the French decided to land, and the ships sailed away, as had been arranged, leaving the marauders to fend for themselves. They were soon looting the country, and were quickly drunk and demoralised. The local fencibles were under the command of Colonel Thomas Knox, but he decided to withdraw his few troops before what he supposed to be the superior forces of the enemy, an action which led to much recrimination later on. Word was soon sent to the lord lieutenant, Lord Milford, son of Sir John Philipps, the 'notorious Jacobite,' but he entrusted command to Lord Cawdor, captain of the Castlemartin Yeomanry, who immediately advanced on Fishguard. There had, in the meantime, been skirmishing between the country folk and bands of the invaders, twelve of whom were said to have been taken prisoner single-handed by a woman cobbler, Jemima Nicholas, armed with only a pitchfork, an exploit for which she received a pension from an appreciative government. Tate soon realised that his situation was hopeless, for his troops were drunk and mutinous, and superior forces were approaching. Therefore, on Thursday night he offered to capitulate, and on the following afternoon the French laid down their arms on Goodwick sands.

This episode, insignificant in itself, had profound effect in Wales. Terrified people had fled inland, driving their cattle before them, and their panic was kept alive by rumours of further landings. The shock cured the Welsh people of their vague radicalism. The reaction fell heavily on the dissenters. Six men were detained for alleged complicity in the affair, among them the ministers of the neighbouring baptist churches of Felinganol and Llangloffan. All were released except two yeomen farmers, Thomas John and Samuel Griffiths, the former a baptist and the latter an independent. The authorities went to great lengths to obtain evidence of treasonable conspiracy, and French prisoners were induced to make statements incriminating them. The two men were kept in prison for six months, but when they were brought to trial at Haverfordwest in September, the French witnesses withdrew their perjured depositions and the case for the prosecution collapsed. The methodists, in particular, were now strengthened in their opposition to radicalism. They had been unjustly accused of fomenting the riots against conscription in 1795 in Denbigh and elsewhere, whereas, in fact, they were extreme conservatives in politics. Their belief in predestination paralysed any inclination they had towards reform, and their conviction that this world was but a place of trial in preparation for the after life led them to teach that everyone should be satisfied with his lot. These ideas were embodied by their leader, Thomas Jones of Denbigh, in a pamphlet which appeared in both languages in 1798, namely *Gair yn ei Amser* (*A word in Season*), which stigmatised the French Republic as anti-Christ, and maintained that there was no need for reform. Soon the struggle against Napoleon roused patriotic fervour. Even Glan y Gors sang in praise of Nelson, and Iolo Morganwg in honour of the Glamorgan volunteers. A few extremists alone persisted in their radicalism, among them Thomas Evans of Glyn Cothi, who was sentenced in 1803 to two years' imprisonment, and to two appearances in the pillory, for singing seditious songs.

At the end of the war agitation for parliamentary reform began again. It now found a powerful advocate in the baptist minister, Joseph Harris. He had issued on January 1, 1814, the first number of a weekly paper, *Seren Gomer*, but in August 1815 it was discontinued, because the tax of fourpence on each copy and the difficulties of distribution involved its promoter in heavy financial loss. Nevertheless it reappeared in 1818 as a fortnightly, subsequently changed in 1820 to a monthly, and it continues to appear at the present day. Joseph Harris was a moderate reformer; he was opposed to violence and bloodshed. But he pointed out the anomalies in the political life of his day, especially as they affected Wales. Cornwall, he showed, had forty-four members to Wales's twenty-seven; Swansea, the second largest town, was but a contributory borough of Cardiff, while Haverfordwest had its own member. The expense of elections, he claimed, made it impossible for independent men to come forward as candidates. He clamoured for a redistribution of seats, an extension of the franchise and electoral reform. Above all he sought in every way to break down the apathy of the Welsh people in political matters, and he may be said to have done as much as anyone to create a political consciousness among them.

The effects of industrialisation, also, were now being felt. A class of wealthy capitalists had arisen whose interests differed from those of the landed proprietors and who were rich enough to oppose them. The first to enter the field was Benjamin Hall, proprietor of the Rhymney iron works (and son-in-law of

Richard Crawshay, the 'iron king' of Cyfarthfa), who was returned for Glamorganshire in 1814. In view of Hall's enormous wealth, the Bute nominee withdrew before the contest. In 1818 Lewis Weston Dillwyn, the Swansea industrialist, came out for the Glamorgan boroughs, in the first contest held there since 1734. There were riots in Cardiff, but Dillwyn thought wise to withdraw. The younger Benjamin Hall, son of the Rhymney iron master, even ousted the Marquis of Worcester from the Monmouth boroughs in 1831. In addition to the appearance of great industrial magnates, there came the growth of a considerable middle class in these years, for whom a number of English weekly newspapers began to appear, starting with the Swansea *Cambrian* in 1804. Finally the industrial population generally, and even the peasant farmers, came to nurse exaggerated hopes that a reduction in taxation would follow parliamentary reform.

Reform meetings were therefore held throughout the country, and when the reform bill was rejected in 1831 there was rioting in Carmarthen and meetings of protest elsewhere. In the ensuing elections there were only six contests in Wales, but the greatest efforts were made to secure the return of members favourable to reform. The Reform Act of 1832, when it was passed, gave an additional member to the shires of Glamorgan, Carmarthen, and Denbigh, and a separate member to Merthyr Tydfil, while the Glamorgan boroughs were now divided into two constituencies, centering around Cardiff and Swansea. Wales thus obtained thirty-two members, In the shires of Wales the new provisions made little difference, for there were hardly any copyholders and few large farms let to tenant farmers, but in the boroughs there was considerable extension of the franchise. Even so, the results of the great act were meagre in so far as Wales was concerned. In the boroughs, it is true, landowners were replaced by employers of labour, but in the shires their influence remained undiminished. Such is the power of ancient loyalties that the Morgans and the Wynns continued to represent their constituencies as before, so that the victory of the middle-class reformers in 1832 was more apparent than real.

CHAPTER XII

A PERIOD OF CHANGE

THE social life of Wales in the sixteenth and seventeenth centuries was marked by the emergence of a class of gentry and by the consolidation of their estates. The changes which took place in those years were, therefore, changes in the structure of society, rather than changes in the occupations of the people or in methods of production within these occupations. Welsh life remained predominantly rural. The country was still sparsely populated, for at the beginning of the eighteenth century the number of its inhabitants can hardly have been much greater than 400,000. These were evenly distributed over the countryside, the relatively higher density of some areas being due solely to the greater productivity of the soil. The majority of the people were engaged in stock-breeding and agriculture, and in the crafts dependent upon them.

Owing to the isolation of Wales, which was due both to its geographical position and to its bad roads, and owing to its lack of great financial centres, the transition to industrialism which characterised contemporary England was retarded in Wales. Such industries as there were scarcely affected the general landscape of the countryside. They were financed by the local gentry, and required little capital or machinery. The numbers engaged in them were small, and, as their workers generally cultivated some land as well, the industrial and rural populations shaded imperceptibly into one another. But the growth of great industries in England in time had its effect on industry in Wales. Besides, the increasing demand for greater food supplies for the new industrial population accelerated changes in agriculture, which, again, were introduced into Wales from England. The needs of the new industry and of the new agriculture made it imperative that improvements should be made in the means of communication and transport, and these in turn, facilitated the introduction of further changes. At the same time both the rural and the industrial populations of

Wales were increasing at an unprecedented rate. All these developments were further complicated by warfare, waged continuously for nearly a quarter of a century. So closely did these factors interact on one another that it is impossible, as far as Wales is concerned, to separate the changes in agriculture from those in industry, in transport or in population, in the period before the end of the Napoleonic wars.

As the eighteenth century proceeded, wheat and barley were grown more extensively in Wales, but the chief crop was still oats, and methods of cultivation and farm implements still remained primitive. The cattle trade became increasingly important with the growth of London, and of towns in the Midlands and on the border. Droves of black cattle were assembled at convenient places and shod before their long journey to be fattened in the home counties, or to be sold in the great fairs of Barnet and Smithfield. Whenever possible, they were driven across country along open trackways in order to avoid the English villages, and frequently they forded streams and swam across the larger rivers. Thousands of beasts crossed the border each year, and this constant selling of the best stock had a bad effect on the Welsh herds. The trade was financed by the drovers themselves, who became important members of the community, for they executed commissions for their fellow countrymen in London, conveyed rents to absentee Welsh landowners in the metropolis, and paid local taxes into the exchequer. They were the unofficial bankers of the people, and, in addition, one drover, David Jones of Caeo, even became celebrated as a Welsh hymn-writer.

Store sheep, also, were driven to be fattened in Kent and Essex, but sheep were reared more particularly for their wool. In many parts of Wales almost every farmer spun his own thread and wove it into cloth on looms which were sometimes centuries old. All kinds of wool were used, so that the cloth was very coarse. Nevertheless it was made up into clothes for the farmers' own families, and was also sold for use in the army, as well as for export to European countries, to Africa, the West Indies and the American colonies. This export trade showed a steady and very remarkable expansion throughout the eighteenth century, particularly the trade with the West Indies and the southern American colonies, for Welsh cloth was used extensively on the slave plantations. The trade was entirely in the hands of English merchants, especially those of London, Liverpool and Bristol. Some parts of Wales, notably Merioneth, were also celebrated for their stockings. Men, women and children were to be seen knitting along the road sides, and they would frequently gather together in each others' houses in winter or on the village green in summer for their *cymorth gwau* (knitting meeting). Stockings to the value of several hundred pounds were sold in the weekly market at Bala on Saturday mornings, and the trade remained of considerable importance until the demand for long hose decreased as knee-breeches went out of fashion. By the middle of the century, woollen manufacture at Llanidloes had already reached the factory stage, as it did at a slightly later date at Newtown and Welshpool, but the textile industry in Wales was too small to produce any 'industrial revolution.'

Of the industries unrelated to agriculture, the most important in Wales was lead mining. This had been revived in Cardiganshire at the end of the seventeenth century when a rich vein was discovered at Esgair Hir on the lands of Sir Carbery Pryse of Gogerddan, and especially when an act of 1693, abolishing the monopoly of the Society of Mines Royal, opened the way to private enterprise. Sir Carbery died in the following year, and a controlling interest in the mines was purchased by Sir Humphrey Mackworth. The new owner had developed coal mining on his wife's estate at Neath, and had restarted copper smelting there. He now founded a joint stock company, the Mine Adventurers of England, to exploit the Cardiganshire lead mines. Much of the ore he transported to Neath to be smelted, and lead entirely displaced copper in importance there. He also opened a furnace at Garreg on the Dovey estuary, using the coal brought back in his ships from Neath. But, despite his philanthropic interest in the S.P.C.K., his company was not financially sound, and a committee of enquiry set up by the house of commons found him guilty of fraudulent practices. He was saved by the fall of the Whig government in 1710, but because of these financial difficulties the lead industry fell into a period of depression. It revived with the discovery of yet another rich vein of solid lead ore in 1751 at Esgair y Mwyn near Strata Florida. This was on crown land, and the superintendent of crown mines in Cardiganshire at the time was Lewis Morris, one of three Anglesey brothers who were prominent in the literary life of Wales. But Lewis Morris's endeavour to exploit the newly discovered vein met with bitter opposition from the local landowners, who claimed that the land was freehold, and Powell of Nanteos and Lord Lisburne of Trawsgoed sank their political differences in their opposition to the crown. Powell, as a magistrate, succeeded in having Morris arrested and kept in Cardigan gaol for six weeks awaiting trial. Rioting, instigated by the landowners, occurred at the mines, and protracted lawsuits followed. Eventually a settlement was reached, but once more the industry suffered a period of depression.

Another centre of small industry was Pontypool, where iron works had been in the possession of the Hanbury family since Elizabethan days. Early in the eighteenth century, John Hanbury elaborated a method of rolling iron plates. There is considerable doubt as to the origin and the date of this invention, but the commercial prosperity of the industry began in 1728. By using mechanical rollers thin sheets of iron of good quality could be produced at considerable speed, and these were coated with tin to form tin-plate. Some of this was decorated, and because it resembled Japanese lacquered wood it was called Japan ware. It was used to make a variety of boxes and containers, but in time it was displaced in public taste by less clumsy materials, and the very secret of japanning died out with the last craftsman in the following century.

The difficulty of feeding the growing industrial population in England led, in the mid-eighteenth century, to an agricultural revolution. Its occurrence in Wales was delayed for a number of reasons, the chief of which were the isolation of the country, its distance from large markets, and the deplorable condition of its roads which hindered the sale of its agricultural products. The great landowners, who were the prime movers elsewhere, were generally non-resident as far as Wales was concerned, and took little interest in their estates apart from the collection of their rents. The smaller gentry lacked the necessary capital, and the holdings of individual farmers were too small to allow the introduction of improvements. The increasing number of English books on the subject were unfamiliar to most Welsh farmers, who were unaccustomed to reading in English, although Jethro Tull's classic work *The Horse Hoing Husbandry*,

CYFARTHFA IRON WORKS

[The National Library of Wales]

CYFARTHFA CASTLE

Built in 1825 by William Crawshay

which appeared in 1733, was carefully read by Lewis Morris and, no doubt, by other enlightened Welshmen. Towards the end of the century a number of county agricultural societies were formed, and these sponsored new methods of farming. The first in Wales (and one of the first in the British Isles) was that of Breconshire, founded, in 1755, mainly on the initiative of Charles Powell, the squire of Castell Madoc. It was followed by that of Glamorgan in 1772, and by the Cardiganshire society in 1784, until, by 1815, there were local or county societies in all parts of Wales. These encouraged the introduction of turnips, potatoes and clover, and offered premiums for the best crops. They gave awards for the planting of trees, for the best bulls and herds of cattle, for superior craftsmanship in spinning and knitting and in other rural trades, for care of the roads, and for the good behaviour and service of farm servants. These county societies were the channels through which the agricultural revolution came to Wales.

As the revolution was primarily due to the need for more food it was natural that attention should first be paid to animal husbandry, and many 'spirited proprietors,' such as Corbett of Ynysmaengwyn, near Towyn, tried to improve their herds. But the improvement of stock was largely dependent upon the provision of adequate winter fodder. Hitherto there had been a general slaughter of cattle at the *Calan gaeaf* (November 1), because of the lack of fodder, and the country folk had lived throughout the winter months on salted meat. Animal husbandry therefore led inevitably to a consideration of crop husbandry. To maintain the productivity of the land at all, it was necessary to alternate between tilling it and allowing it to lie fallow. The simplest form of rotation was to exhaust the soil by growing corn for several years in succession, and then attempt to restore it by allowing it to remain fallow and by fertilising it with the natural manure of the cattle turned on it to graze. Arthur Young, the eighteenth-century traveller and writer on agriculture, noted with astonishment that this primitive system still prevailed in many parts of Wales. It had been adequate while the population was small, and while the standard of life was very low, but there was now real danger that it would break down. The chief difficulty lay in the inadequate supply of grass, for if there was insufficient grass the stock of cattle would have to be kept low and there would then not be enough manure to restore the soil. In an attempt to remedy this there was a great extension in the use of lime in Wales in the latter half of the eighteenth century, for lime not only supplied an essential plant food but counteracted the acidity of the soil in the upland pastures and produced the conditions necessary for grass to grow. Through the use of lime, also, it was possible to cultivate clover and other artificial grasses. But even more important than this was the extensive growing of turnips as a field crop. Turnips had been cultivated for some time on a small scale, but it was only now that they were used to any great extent to feed cattle, and even then only by the more progressive gentry. Arthur Young noted carefully the rotation which he found on the estates of the landed gentry of Wales, as did the reports published by the Board of Agriculture in 1794 and 1796. It varied from place to place, but frequently it consisted of growing turnips one year, followed by barley, then clover and finally wheat. In this way it was unnecessary to allow the land to lie fallow, so that the area under cultivation was increased, and, moreover, since turnips provided adequate winter feed, it was also unnecessary to slaughter the stock in the autumn months.

One way of meeting the increased demand for food was, therefore, by more intensive farming; another was by utilising the waste lands. The enclosure movement of the sixteenth century had continued with varying intensity in the succeeding years, and the great enclosures of the late eighteenth century differed from earlier ones only in extent. Throughout the intervening period the gentry had encroached upon the hill-pastures and open moorlands, and the hostility which this had roused is reflected in Ellis Wynne's *Gweledigaetheu y Bardd Cwsc*. It had led to much litigation, generally when enraged villagers had taken the law into their own hands and destroyed the squire's fences. But the crofters also had continued to encroach upon the waste. The old practice of transferring flocks and herds to the upland pastures in summer was gradually dying out, and the *hafod*, or summer residence, had usually become a separate farm kept by a branch of the family. It was therefore a temptation to encroach on land beyond the former limits of the *hafodydd*. Squatters, too, carved out small holdings for themselves in isolated spots far away from any other enclosed land. Actions were frequently brought against them by the stewards of the crown, which claimed possession of all the waste.

From the beginning of the eighteenth century it was possible to effect enclosures only by obtaining a private act of parliament, except where there was complete agreement. The first act relating to Wales dates from 1733, and concerns some 3,000 acres of land in the Dee estuary. But there were relatively few acts until the outbreak of war with France in 1793, and it was the war period from 1793 to 1815 which saw the great enclosures of Wales. They were primarily in the highlands, and were due to the great rise in the price of corn, which led to attempts at cultivation at a higher altitude than ever before, and, indeed, than at any subsequent time until the Second World War. The act already passed in 1788 to enclose some 3,000 acres of the marsh at Malltraeth in Anglesey was now put into effect. In the years 1796 and 1797 35,000 acres were enclosed in the Kerry hills of Montgomeryshire, followed by the enclosure of 40,000 acres in Breconshire in 1808. In 1813, some 10,000 acres were enclosed in north Cardiganshire, including Cors Fochno, and two years later there was another enclosure of 11,500 acres in Montgomeryshire. By the end of the war by far the greater part of the uplands of Wales had undergone enclosure.

There was opposition to this from the start, but it was of little avail, for the movement was in the interests of the landowners, and parliament was composed of members of this class. To petition against an act involved much expense, and, even though, after 1774, it was necessary to give information of a proposal to enclose, by public meeting or by fixing a notice on the church door, it was still difficult for the villagers to organise resistance. Moreover the hedging and ditching which followed enclosure were expensive, and many peasants preferred to abandon their claims to the open moorlands. The case of the squatters was more difficult, and in 1809 there were riots at Llanddeiniolen, caused by 'misguided people,' as they were described by the *North Wales Gazette*, 'who occupied some cottages from which they foolishly conceived they could not legally be removed.' But while the war produced an artificial prosperity for the farmers there was comparatively little opposition; this came later when the period of depression which followed the war threw the grievances of the peasantry into high relief. For enclosures were undoubtedly in the interests of agriculture as a whole. The draining of the marshes of Malltraeth and Cors Fochno and at Portmadoc was beneficial to everyone. The enclosure of the hill slopes, again, led to an improvement in the herds of cattle, for scientific breeding was impossible while these could roam unhindered, and the characteristic Welsh breeds, the Castlemartin blacks and Glamorgan reds, emerged only at this time. Moreover enclosures and road improvement generally went together; indeed, improved communications were sometimes their primary purpose. Tracks over the waste had frequently been impossible to follow in winter, but with enclosures roads were properly laid out and drained. And, even though the social consequences of enclosures may have been deplorable, it is certain that worse social evils would have followed the continuation of the old system.

These enclosures cannot be said to have caused depopulation, but this was undoubtedly the result of the tendency in these years to consolidate farms. Generally Welsh farms were too small to be economically profitable, and landowners began a practice of reducing three or four, or even more, tenements into one. This meant that the smaller farmers must either become labourers or drift to the new industrial towns. At the same time there occurred a further change in land tenure. Hitherto tenant farmers had generally held their land on lease, either for a period of years, or, more often, for a number of lives. Thus a lease might be for 'three lives,' that is, until the death, possibly, of the farmer and his wife and his son. Now, such leases, when they fell in, were not renewed, and the land was instead let on a year to year tenancy. This happened to nearly all tenants on the Vaenol estate in Caernarvonshire about 1800. Before the end of the war there was little leasehold left in north Wales, though leases were rather more common in the south. Under the old system a tenant had reasonable security of tenure, and could hope to benefit by any improvements which he might carry out. The new system, on the other hand, favoured the landowner, who could take advantage of the great rise in prices to increase the rent of his tenants at short notice, and this, again, led to bitter grievances in the period of general depression which followed the war, as rents, once raised, were seldom reduced.

The remoteness of Wales also accounted for the slow development of the iron industry there. Iron manufacture in England had, in fact, suffered a decline in the late seventeenth century because of the exhaustion of timber supplies. So, while the iron-masters had usually continued to keep their forges in old-established places, they had scattered their furnaces in remote areas where timber was available, as, for example, in the Severn valley in mid-Shropshire, a district which was destined to become the matrix of the Welsh iron industry. Moreover, the lack of fuel made it necessary to develop new technological processes, and, early in the eighteenth century at Coalbrook-dale in this part of Shropshire, Abraham Darby succeeded in smelting iron with coke by increasing the strength of the blast in his furnace. This epoch-making discovery was introduced at Bersham, near Wrexham, when the furnace there passed, in 1753, into the hands of Isaac Wilkinson (later of Broseley, near Coalbrookdale). The outbreak of the Seven Years' War soon afterwards created a demand for munitions, and Bersham was reconstructed for the manufacture of armaments. Under Isaac's son, John Wilkinson, the Bersham works became famous throughout Europe.

It was the Seven Years' War, also, with the increased demand for iron and the interruption of supplies of ore from abroad, which turned attention to south Wales. The estates of the Herberts in Glamorgan had passed, through his mother, to Lord Windsor (whose own daughter and heiress was, in turn, to marry the earl of Bute). A lease of the mineral rights on land belonging to Lord Windsor on the Dowlais brook, near the hamlet of Merthyr, was taken over in 1759 by a local magnate, Thomas Lewis of Llanishen, together with eight partners, one of whom was Isaac Wilkinson. As the yearly rent eventually decided upon (in 1763) was only £31, with no provision for the payment of royalties, it is not likely that any great development was expected in this area. Nor were the partners drawn there by the presence of coal. The great attraction lay in plentiful iron ore, in addition to the timber from the thickly-wooded slopes and the water supply from rapid mountain streams. In the early years, workmen spent much of their time in wood-cutting and charcoal-burning, and the nodules of ironstone were obtained partly by 'scouring,' that is by damming the brooks and then loosening the ore by suddenly releasing the water. But as early as 1760 the partners engaged John Guest of Broseley as their manager, and it is probable that he began immediately to experiment with the use of coal. Moreover Guest was interested in ventures of his own, for in 1763 he and Isaac Wilkinson leased land, at a rental of £60 a year, on the neighbouring estate of the earl of Plymouth, who, also, had succeeded to his Welsh property through his mother, the heiress of Thomas Lewis of Van, near Caerphilly. Two years later, Anthony Bacon, a Cumberland ironmaster, leased a vast domain of 4,000 acres in the Merthyr district from Lord Talbot of Hensol, yet another English nobleman who had inherited Welsh estates through his mother, the heiress of Charles Mathew of Castell Mynach. Soon Anthony Bacon had set up both a furnace and a forge here at Cyfarthfa, and at the same time he took over the Plymouth concession from Guest and Wilkinson.

Progress, however, remained slow for a number of years, and it was not until the eighties that any great development took place. Once more the impetus came from renewed war in America. In 1780 Anthony Bacon took over the lease of Hirwaun, on Lord Windsor's property, at the western end of the iron field. Two years later John Guest was taken into partner-ship at Dowlais by Thomas Lewis. Guest died within three years, but in time his descendants acquired a controlling in-terest in the works. In the same year as this development at Dowlais, Francis Homfray of Broseley leased some land from Bacon for the erection of a forge at Cyfarthfa. He surrendered this lease within two years, but then, in conjunction with his two sons, Jeremiah and Samuel, he acquired from a freeholder the lease of a tract of land at Penydarren for ninety-nine years, on payment of a shilling royalty on every ton of ore raised. Here he set up a furnace, and as Penydarren had possibly the richest iron deposits in this neighbourhood, these works expanded rapidly under the management of Samuel Homfray. Meanwhile, in 1786, Anthony Bacon died, and left his 'mineral kingdom' in trust for his illegitimate sons. Their executors leased Cyfarthfa to Richard Crawshay, a Yorkshireman who had sought his fortune in London, and, under his charge, Cyfarthfa became so prosperous that within eight years Crawshay was able to buy

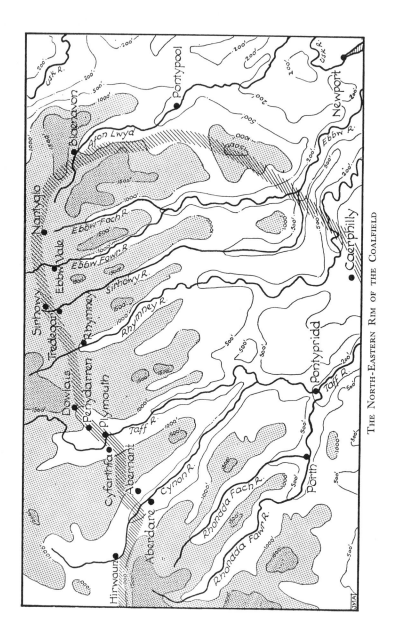

The North-Eastern Rim of the Coalfield

the works outright. The Plymouth works were leased in 1788 to Bacon's brother-in-law, Richard Hill.

Thus had the great industrial enterprises of Hirwaun, Cyfarthfa, Plymouth, Penydarren and Dowlais come into existence in close proximity to one another. Their expansion was helped within this decade by two technological developments of the first importance. One of these was Watt's perfection of the steam engine, which both provided a new motive power and increased the demand for iron, although the penetration of industry by the steam engine was, it is true, surprisingly slow. Of more immediate importance was the invention of puddling. Hitherto the iron produced in the furnaces, which was too brittle for various purposes, had been worked into 'wrought' iron by being beaten by tilt hammers. This was a slow process and it took twelve hours to make a ton of iron bars. But in 1783 and 1784, Henry Cort, at his works at Fontley in Hampshire, devised a method of stirring the molten iron so that its carbon impurities were removed, and then passing it through rollers at a welding heat. This enabled fifteen tons of bars to be made in the twelve hours, and the quality of the iron also was greatly improved. It would appear that Peter Onions had struck upon much the same process at the same time at Cyfarthfa and there was acrimonious controversy and litigation over the patent, but so general did puddling become in south Wales that it was known as 'the Welsh method.'

From Merthyr and Dowlais the iron industry spread along the north-eastern rim of the coalfield. To the west of Merthyr lay the valley of the Cynon, a tributary of the Taff. At the far end of this valley was the Hirwaun works, and to the south of it Jeremiah Homfray acquired (1801) and developed the great works at Abernant. To the east of the Taff, and parallel to it, ran the Rhymney, and, in its upper reaches the 'iron King,' Richard Crawshay, acquired for £100,000 the Rhymney works (1803), which, on his death in 1810, became the sole property of his partner and son-in-law, Benjamin Hall. Further east came the Sirhowy valley, at the far end of which lay the Sirhowy works, which passed in 1794 to Richard Fothergill of Clapham, who thereby entered the industrial life of Monmouthshire. But more important was the establishment lower down the valley of the Tredegar iron works, on land leased by Sir

Charles Gould Morgan (who, again, had acquired a Welsh estate through marriage with an heiress, and had adopted the family name) to Richard Fothergill and Samuel Homfray who had now become the baronet's son-in-law. The Tredegar works, named after the family seat, became the most important in Monmouthshire. East of the Sirhowy ran the river Ebbw, and the great works there, at Ebbw Vale, which had been acquired by Jeremiah Homfray in 1789, passed in 1796 to James Harford. On a tributary to this river, the Ebbw Fach, Harford acquired an interest in furnaces at Nantyglo, but work was suspended there until these were bought in 1810 by Joseph and Crawshay Bailey, nephews of Richard Crawshay who had followed him from Yorkshire, and who became legatees under his will in that year. Lastly, on the eastern rim of the coalfield, came Blaenavon, in the upper reaches of the Afon Lwyd, and there a Thomas Hill of Staffordshire and two partners started in 1789 the great Blaenavon works.

The iron works of south Wales had thus sprung to importance within a very few years. They were all concentrated in a narrow stretch of land, some eighteen miles long and scarcely more than a mile wide, from Hirwaun to Blaenavon. Despite their proximity, however, they were located in narrow valleys separated from each other by high ranges of hills, and difficult of access from the coast. Their prosperity was due to the presence in the same neighbourhood of ample coal, which was near the surface and could easily be worked, of rich iron beds, of limestone for use in smelting and of stone to line the furnaces. Owing to the absence of an industrial tradition in Wales, the iron works were developed by capitalists from across the border, for Thomas Lewis of Llanishen was the only Welsh industrialist among them. These immigrant iron masters brought with them their technical skill. Yet for their capital they were, at first, largely dependent on the banks. But they established great industrial dynasties, and control of the huge concerns was consolidated in a few dominant families. These were able to take the fullest advantage of the enormous demand for iron produced by a quarter of a century of warfare against France.

The growth of the iron industry had naturally led to an increase in coal mining in this area, but an independent coal trade was hampered by the difficulty of transport. As late as

1782 a customs official at Cardiff wrote: 'We have no coal exported from this port, nor ever shall, as it would be too expensive to bring it down here from the internal part of the country.' Nevertheless the coal trade of Wales in the eighteenth century experienced a gradual and continuous, though unspectacular, expansion. Naturally the chief mines were located on the south-western rim of the coalfield where it touched the sea, first at Neath and then at Swansea. In the mid-eighteenth century Chauncey Townshend, an alderman of London, opened collieries at Llansamlet near Swansea, and in 1752 he acquired coal lands on the Stepney estate at Llanelly. Charles Raby, also, opened collieries at Llanelly and began developing the anthracite coal of the Gwendraeth valley. Much of this coal was carried coastwise to Bristol and Bridgwater, and some of it was exported to Ireland and to France.

Coal had always been used to smelt the non-ferrous metals, and, as these were imported, the furnaces for this purpose were located on this maritime rim of the coalfield. It was cheaper to transport ore to the coalfield than to take coal to the copper mines, especially as coal could then be carried in the returning ships as ballast, whereas if coal were taken to the mines, and the smelting done there the ships would have to return empty. Moreover, in smelting copper it was found more economical to use ores of different quality together, so that it was less profitable for each copper mine to do its own smelting. Therefore Cornish copper had been brought to Neath as early as 1584, and a tradition was started which kept the industry in this area. It was revived by Sir Humphrey Mackworth a century later, but in the early eighteenth century Swansea gradually replaced Neath because of its better port. Chauncey Townshend built new copper works at Swansea in 1755. Some years later the position was entirely revolutionised. This was because of spectacular developments in Anglesey, where, after many unsuccessful attempts, a rich vein of copper ore was struck in 1768 on the Parys mountain, on land belonging to Sir Nicholas Bailey, followed within a few months by another discovery on the neighbouring land of the Reverend Edward Hughes. The veins were enormously productive; moreover the ore was near the surface and could easily be worked, so that the Welsh copper industry began a period of great prosperity.

Both landowners had recourse to the services of Thomas Williams of Llanidan, a local solicitor, who soon became a partner in their firms, and proved to be a commercial genius of the first order. There was no coal in Anglesey, so he built a new copper smelting works at Swansea, and then opened others at Amlwch, using the coal brought back in his returning ships. Hitherto the smelters had controlled the copper trade at the expense of the mining companies, and they did their best to ruin Williams, but by undercutting their prices he destroyed their power. There then ensued a struggle between him and the Cornish mine-owners, but by 1787 Williams had become the selling agent for the ore raised in Cornwall as well as for his own. For some years he dominated the copper trade of the whole world. His companies had a capital of £800,000. He employed 1,200 miners in Anglesey and owned his own fleet of ships. In addition to the works at Swansea and Amlwch he had rolling mills and manufacturing works at Great Marlow. His peculiar genius lay in finding new uses for copper and new markets. In particular he was a pioneer in supplying copper sheathing and bolts for ships, and soon his products were used in the dockyards of Great Britain, Holland, France and Spain. The outbreak of war upset the balance of his civilian trade, but led to a greater demand for copper for armaments. But when he died in 1802 the ore of Anglesey was already becoming exhausted, and Cornish ore had to be brought to his copper works at Swansea. Charles Nevill, a Worcestershire industrialist, had meanwhile begun smelting at Swansea, and in 1805 his son, R. J. Nevill, opened copper works at Llanelly. John Vivian, of Truro in Cornwall, had also become interested in this area. With his sons he opened the great Hafod copper works at Swansea in 1810, and established the ruling metallurgical dynasty of that town.

The slate industry of north Wales sprang to importance in the same years. As in the case of coal, slate quarrying had first of all been carried out by individuals working on their own account. When Richard Pennant succeeded to his estates in 1765 there were about eighty such undertakings on his land, each paying a rental of one or two pounds a year. He decided not to renew their leases, and from 1782 onwards began to develop the industry on a large scale. Within twenty years the productive capacity of his great quarry at Bethesda had been multiplied over ten times. His example was copied later by Assheton Smith in the Dinorwic quarry at Llanberis. The quarries in the Ffestiniog area, however, did not undergo the same progress of consolidation, but early in the nineteenth century they were taken over by a group of Lancashire speculators.

Both the agricultural and the industrial developments of the eighteenth century made it imperative that the roads of Wales should be improved. Three great roads had emerged in the course of late mediaeval and early modern times. One ran through Chester, Denbigh, Conway and Caernarvon to Holyhead, and it became increasingly important with the growth of traffic with Ireland. The second ran from Hereford and Hay to Brecon, then up the Usk valley and across to the vale of Towy, passing through Llandovery and Carmarthen, and continuing to Haverfordwest and St. David's. The third was the coastal road of south Wales. Difficulties in traversing the Forest of Dean and in crossing the south Wales rivers near their mouths had long delayed the importance of this route, but by the end of the seventeenth century it had gained priority over the Brecon road. But these roads were for through traffic, primarily with Ireland; they neither integrated the country nor even served the needs of the small market towns. The by-roads were unbelievably bad, and came in for scathing criticism from Arthur Young and other writers. Valentine Morris of Piercefield informed a committee of the house of commons that Monmouthshire had no roads, the people having to travel in ditches. Responsibility for the roads still rested with the parishes under the act of 1555, but the surveyors nominated under this act were untrained and unpaid, and could gain no experience as they were changed annually. Parishes were frequently 'presented' at quarter sessions for neglecting their roads, and were sometimes fined, but the local magistrates did little to see that improvements were carried out. For such improvements were primarily in the interests of the commercial classes of the towns and not of the country magistrates or of the parishioners. Without doubt the roads of Wales were worse than those of England, for there were fewer large towns and great country seats, and there was no military motive for building roads as in the highlands of Scotland.

The old system remained tolerable as long as wheeled traffic was infrequent and people not only travelled mostly on horseback but conveyed their marketable commodities, such as cloth or stockings, by means of pack-horses. The coming of the wagon and the private coach changed all this, and the compulsory annual labour on the roads, the 'corvée,' now proved quite inadequate. Besides, the cost of repair, which was due mainly to through traffic, fell heavily on country villages, and a new principle of making travellers pay for use of the roads was introduced. Toll gates, or turnpikes, were therefore erected, but, in 1750, they still remained very few in number.

It was the demands of agriculture which led to the building by William Edwards in 1755 of the celebrated bridge at Pontypridd, on the road leading to Llantrisant and the Vale of Glamorgan. Edwards was an entirely self-taught man, a farmer and independent minister, then aged thirty-five, but, after three unsuccessful attempts, he built a single span bridge which was not only the largest arch in the world in its day but which still remains a thing of beauty. In the succeeding years he and his sons built a number of other bridges in south Wales. The new county agricultural societies all offered premiums for well kept roads, and, in some cases offered to bear part of the cost of repairs. But voluntary efforts proved insufficient. Therefore, in the decades after 1750 numerous road trusts were established. These were composed of persons, generally local landowners, who obtained authority through a private act of parliament to take over a specified length of road and repair it, being authorised to borrow money to do so on the security of the tolls which they would then levy. The first charge on the tolls should go to repay the cost of obtaining the act, which was usually high, then for the payment of interest on the loan, and finally to repay the loan itself. It was thought that this repayment could be completed within a few years, and the trusts were established for a limited period, generally twenty-one years, but, if the loan were not repaid within that time, the trust could be renewed.

Trusts first appeared in the border counties and were then extended into Wales. By 1759 the whole of the north Wales route had been covered by trusts, and by 1772 this was true of the two south Wales roads. Industrialists as well as landowners were interested in the trusts, for their works were usually in inaccessible moorland areas, and there are traditions associated with the early days of most furnaces that iron was carried to the coast on packhorses. Anthony Bacon, in 1767, seems to have been the prime mover in repairing a road from Merthyr to Cardiff, apparently through Caerphilly, but it was soon superseded by a trust road along the Taff valley, through the Tongwynlais gap. Later a branch of this road penetrated the Cynon valley. Soon, also, Merthyr was joined by a trust road to Abergavenny in the east, and by another to Neath and Swansea in the west, thereby again linking the industrial strip with the sea. A south Wales Association for the Improvement of Roads was formed in 1789 and published a valuable report three years later, but its interest was largely confined to the coastal route. With the union of England and Ireland in 1800 the Welsh trunk roads gained added importance. The great road engineer, Thomas Telford, was commissioned by the government in 1811 to survey the north Wales route, and in 1815 the house of commons authorised a grant of £20,000 for its improvement. It was at that time administered by six small trusts, which were amalgamated in 1819. Telford's supreme achievement was the building of the Menai Bridge, which was opened in 1826. In that year he also reported on the south Wales roads, and, with a view to expediting the Irish mail, suggested many improvements, few of which were carried out. John Macadam had, in the meantime, been consulted by several Welsh trusts concerning the surfacing of their roads.

There has always been much misunderstanding of the functions of the road trusts. It must be borne in mind that they were never intended to replace the parish system; at no time did the trusts control more than one-fifth of the roads of Wales. Nor did they in any way eliminate the corvée, for the parishes still remained responsible for the repair not only of their own roads but of those of the trusts. Misunderstanding on these two points gained the trusts undeserved odium, for it is certain that in their early period, before 1815, they rendered Wales an inestimable service, and provided the country with a network of roads such as it had never had before.

The transport of coal and iron by horse drawn vehicles, even on these improved roads, was still difficult and slow. The great Bridgewater Canal begun in 1759, had already provided an alternative method, and it was copied in minor enterprises in Wales, as for example, at Kidwelly. But the 'canal age' in Wales came later, following the enormous expansion of the iron trade in the eighties; for all the great Welsh canals were constructed in one decade, from 1790 to 1800. In the east the Monmouthshire canal ran from Newport to Pontypool along the Afon Lwyd, and then across to the Usk valley at Abergavenny, being eventually extended to Brecon. Above Newport it was joined by a branch which ran along the Ebbw river as far as Crumlin Bridge. The Glamorgan canal joined Cardiff to Merthyr, with a branch along the river Cynon to Aberdare. The Neath canal ascended the river Neath to within five miles of the iron works at Hirwaun, while the Swansea canal, along the river Tawe, linked the iron works of the upper Swansea valley with the port. In north Wales the services of Telford were secured for an ambitious scheme to link the Severn and the Dee with the Mersey. The project to join the coalfield at Bersham with Chester, which was part of this scheme, proved a fiasco, but Llangollen was linked to the English system by the Ellesmere canal, which Telford took over the Dee and Ceiriog rivers by the magnificent aqueducts of Pontcysyllte and Chirk. In time the Montgomeryshire canal was built to join the Ellesmere, and ascended the Severn through Welshpool as far as Newtown, thus linking the woollen towns with Manchester and the Midlands.

But Wales, with it steep gradients, was a difficult country in which to build canals, and the more inaccessible areas were served by a supplementary system of tram roads. Along these lines heavy loads could be conveyed down hill, for the iron works were all at a high altitude, and the empty trams could be drawn up with comparatively little difficulty. Blaenavon was linked in this way to the Monmouthshire canal at Pontypool, and Nantyglo to its branch at Crumlin. As there was no canal in the Sirhowy valley a tramroad was built by Samuel Homfray from Sirhowy and Tredegar to Newport. The controlling interest in the Glamorgan canal lay with Crawshay, and because of the intense rivalry between them, Samuel Homfray threatened to build a tram-road from Merthyr to Cardiff which would compete with the canal. He failed to put his scheme into operation, but because Penydarren was inconveniently placed at a distance from the canal head, he did build nine miles of tramroad to link his works with the canal lower down the valley at Quakers' Yard. It was along this line that Richard Trevithick, on February 21, 1804, successfully ran his steam-driven locomotive, drawing a load of ten tons and seventy persons. This was a foretaste of the new development which was soon to render the canals obsolete, but nevertheless their usefulness continued well into the railway age for they provided direct access from the iron works and coal mines to the ships at sea.

Throughout this period the population of Wales kept increasing. It had reached about 480,000 by 1750, but when the first census was taken in 1801 it stood at 587,000 and by 1811 it had even reached 673,000. This remarkable increase was due primarily to natural causes and not to immigration, and it is particularly noteworthy that each succeeding census until 1841 showed an increase in the population of all the shires of Wales, despite migration from the rural to the industrial areas. It is evident, therefore, that natural increase was sufficient to off-set the loss through migration even from the most rural parts of Wales. Migration into the industrial areas came, in fact, from the neighbouring districts in the first place, from within circles of ever-lengthening radius. And with industrial development came the growth of towns. Merthyr, a small hamlet in 1760, had by 1801 become a town with a population of 7,705. The next town to it in size was Swansea, which had a population of 6,831, and whose development had been more gradual since some of its industries were old-established. Cardiff, with its 1,870 people, was still merely a small market town, scarcely larger than Aberystwyth which had a population of 1,758, while Newport, with 1,087, was even smaller. The towns of Wales, built, as so many of them were, around a castle, had, throughout the centuries, been islands of English speech within a Welsh countryside, but the incursion of persons from their immediate hinterlands now made them predominantly Welsh for the first time in their history. Yet the coalfields of Wales, both in the north and in the south, were situated near the English border, so that, in addition to skilled English workmen brought in by the ironmasters, the Welsh industries had drawn on English areas for their workers almost from the start, and in time the English element swamped the Welsh population of the towns. But the outstanding fact which emerges from a consideration of the first two censuses is that the population of Wales was still evenly distributed over the whole country at the end of the Napoleonic wars, and that three out of every four people were still concerned with agriculture. The transition to industrialism, remarkable though it was, had thus not proceeded very far. The new division of Wales into two nations, the one rural in its occupations and Welsh in speech, the other English and industrial, two nations between whom there were few cultural ties, was essentially the work of the following century.

The Chartist Attack on Newport 1839

THE REBECCA RIOTERS

CHAPTER XIII

AGRARIAN DISCONTENT

THE long war against France brought prosperity to the land-owners of Wales, and to the farmers of the rich lowland valleys and coastal plains. Its effect on the fortunes of the upland farmers was more varied. They profited by the rise in the prices of dairy products, but they grew very little wheat, and therefore suffered acutely from the scarcity of corn, especially in 1800, when it reached the highest price until that date in England and Wales. A series of wet and unproductive harvests from 1789 to 1802 brought great distress, which is reflected in many of the popular ballads of the day. But with the end of the war came a period of depression affecting the whole rural population, upland and lowland alike, and lasting, with minor fluctuations, until about 1850. For the coming of peace brought with it a sudden cessation of the employments directly dependent on the war. There was, in consequence, much unemployment in the industrial areas, whence workers tended to return to their homes in the country, begging as they went. At the same time the introduction of machinery was increasing the number of these displaced persons, while the countryside was being flooded by immigrants from Ireland. This industrial unemployment seriously affected the local market for farm produce. Moreover, war had left its usual heritage in an enormous national debt and heavy taxation, while a sense of insecurity was generated by the high cost of living and by the unsound financial expedients adopted by the government.

The immediate consequence of the return of peace was a sharp decline in prices. An act of 1815, which fixed the lowest price for imported wheat at 80/- a quarter, for barley at 33/- and for oats at 22/-, gave some protection to corn growers, but, nevertheless, the price of corn fluctuated violently in the succeeding years. Farmers, even in the Vale of Glamorgan, found that they were farming at a loss. They dismissed their workmen to reduce their labour bill, and neglected both to hedge and ditch their land and to give it sufficient lime, since the carting of lime over long distances was expensive. In this way, by less intensive farming, they lowered their immediate costs, although ultimately the land suffered. It became uneconomical to plough in the uplands, where the land had been cropped year after year without adequate manuring, and had become exhausted. Within twenty years there was a loss of 2,000 acres of arable land in Glamorgan alone and in many cases it was allowed to return to waste. Even substantial farmers became insolvent in these years. Yet so great was the demand for corn that it had to be imported from Ireland, to the intense chagrin of the local corn growers. By 1835 the amount of corn imported into Cardiff had risen from very little to about 160,000 bushels a year.

The stock breeders and dairy farmers showed more resilience than the corn growers, but for a time their distress was even more intense. This was due to a number of unexampled bad harvests in the years immediately after the war. The winter of 1814 had proved to be one of the coldest on record, while 1816 has been called 'the year without a summer,' on account of its constant rain and low temperature. As a result the hay harvest failed, and in the following year rural Wales was faced with famine. Again in 1818, tremendous gales and floods in the vale of Towy and elsewhere reduced the people to destitution. Farmers sold their beasts to buy the necessaries of life, and obtained only a fraction of their normal price because of the bad market. For many years the land was therefore under-stocked, to the prolonged injury of Welsh agriculture. Even so, farmers' goods were distrained upon for rent in many cases; the sheriff's officers, remarked one observer, were the only persons fully employed in these years in Wales.

Scarcity of food led to sporadic rioting. A crowd, assembled on the quay at Carmarthen, prevented the shipment of a cargo of cheese on September 25, 1818, and three days later, when another attempt was made to load the cheese, the infuriated mob ransacked the vessel. The lord lieutenant had to call out the yeomanry and militia, and order was restored only when some merchants agreed to dispose of their cheese locally. In the following July, the Montgomeryshire yeomanry suppressed a riot at Abermule. Even in Monmouthshire a government investigator spoke of 'the great, unexampled and increasing distress.'

This distress, too, brought to the surface the opposition to the economic changes of the previous period, particularly to enclosures. In 1820 there was rioting at Maenclochog in Pembrokeshire, where the house of a farmer who had enclosed much of the mountain side was destroyed. Two years later the mansion built by a person who had bought 850 acres of enclosed land on Mynydd Bach in Cardiganshire was burnt, and a second house was similarly destroyed in 1826. The ring-leader of the incendiaries was caught, and because of popular feeling his trial was removed to a neighbouring English shire. In one instance an enclosure bill was successfully opposed. This related to land in the parishes of Llandwrog and Llanwnda in Caernarvonshire. The son of a local crofter who had prospered in London organised opposition to it, and when the bill was introduced for its second reading in 1827 it had to be withdrawn. The indignation of the peasantry fell particularly on those of their number who rented more than one farm. The transfer from leasehold to yearly tenancy was almost complete, and thereby the owners had greater opportunity to consolidate their estates into larger and economically more profitable units, but this reduced the number of farms available. The peasants had, however, no other means of livelihood, and the reckless bidding for farms to which they were driven kept the rents high. Some landowners reduced their rents in face of the prevailing distress, but the majority took full advantage of the demand for farms. Moreover they were often non-resident, and employed English or Scottish land agents for the precise reason that these were alien to their tenants and therefore unlikely to be favourably disposed towards them. The 'agent' remained the most detested character in the popular literature of Wales throughout the best part of the nineteenth century.

The depression in industry and agriculture also produced a banking crisis which, in turn, intensified this depression. To meet local needs a number of country banks had sprung up towards the end of the eighteenth century. Such a bank was opened at Merthyr about 1770; another was opened at Brecon in 1778, and soon there were banks in all the larger market towns. Frequently the bankers were the new industrialists, but sometimes they were prosperous drovers, as is indicated by such names as Banc y Ddafad Ddu (the Black Sheep Bank of Aberystwyth and Tregaron) or Banc yr Eidon Du (the Black Ox Bank of Llandovery). They issued their own notes in considerable quantities during the war years. Some crashed immediately the war was over, as, for example, the banks at Denbigh and Welshpool, and their notes became worthless. All observers were agreed on the bad effects of insufficient currency on the economy of the countryside at this time. The position was eased in the following years, but in 1825 and 1826 there occurred a banking crisis during which more than seventy houses failed in England and Wales. Every bank in Pembrokeshire was wiped out, as were many others elsewhere, while those banks which survived did so only with difficulty. This ruined innumerable people, and the shortage of ready money which ensued crippled the farmers and retarded recovery.

Poverty was therefore the keynote to this period in Wales, and it was natural that attention should be fixed on the administration of the poor laws. For the war, while it had enriched the landowner and affected the tenant farmer in a variety of ways, had pauperised the labourer. His wages had risen some forty per cent in the war years, but this bore no relation to the rise in the cost of living, and it was only in areas such as Monmouthshire, where the proximity of iron works tended to send up wages, that a farm labourer, supplying his own food, would get two shillings a day in 1815. Farm servants who lived in received from £6 to £12 a year. Since the Restoration and the Settlement Act of 1662, responsibility for the relief of the poor had fallen entirely on the parish. There was little central control, so that administration varied considerably according to the public spirit and the efficiency of the local magistrates. While the problem of pauperism remained relatively unimportant, the system worked well enough. The sums distributed were very small, and were often given for a specific purpose, such as to buy a pair of shoes, and parish relief was often supplemented by gifts from the local gentry. But from about 1770 to 1815 the poor rate for the whole country increased by over four hundred per cent, and the law came to be ever more harshly applied. This fell heavily on the impotent poor. The lot of poor children, apprenticed by the parish, became very hard, and they were often brutally treated. The sick and the old also suffered, for any goods of value they might possess were immediately seized, and a pauper's possessions were all sold in aid of parish funds when he died. Iolo Morganwg was highly indignant in 1796 when the cottage, built by Ben Simon, the bard of Abergwili, who had transcribed manuscripts at Jesus College and elsewhere, was taken from his daughter since her father had been forced to seek parish relief in the last two or three years of his life. The poet-preacher, Ap Vychan, remembered with horror all his life the day in the year of famine, 1817, when the overseer removed a feather-bed from beneath his father, who was in delirium through fever and semi-starvation, as it was the only chattel of any value which he possessed. The vestry of Dolgelley in 1822 decided that no relief should be given if there were 'a clock or any useless furniture in the house.' In Dolgelley, also, the aged poor were let out in a sort of Dutch auction at the annual vestry to those who would take them for the least amount. In addition, some parishes, for example Cowbridge in 1770, decreed that all relieved persons should carry a badge to indicate that they were paupers.

The harshness of the old poor laws was most evident in the provisions for the removal of those likely to become chargeable to the parish. Expectant mothers of illegitimate children were obviously in this position, and it was doubly important that they should be removed, for the 'settlement' of a child would be determined by the place of its birth. As the poor creatures concealed the fact as long as possible, their removal was often carried out in circumstances of gross indignity and brutality, and in 1814, a woman, removed from Bedwellty to Haverfordwest, gave birth to a child on the way. Removal often caused litigation because of doubt as to a pauper's 'settlement,' and this, while it proved a remunerative source of revenue to lawyers, added considerably to the poor rate. Where there was doubt, the parishes concerned would generally negotiate, and, if they could not agree, would bring the cases before the quarter sessions. Most frequently these disputes arose between neighbouring parishes, but sometimes paupers were removed long distances at great expense. Appeals to quarter sessions were very rare in the early eighteenth century, but after 1815 they amounted for the whole of Wales to several hundreds a year. Besides, removal could apply also to the able bodied, and, in places, it restricted the movement of labour. Although the slate quarries of Ffestiniog required additional labour, the parish vestry in 1817 ruled that anyone letting a dwelling house to a stranger would be liable for the cost of removal should he fall on the rates, and since an act of 1691 allowed anyone hired for a year to obtain settlement, the Maentwrog vestry decided in 1827 that persons who hired labourers for more than six months at a time should be fined.

Despite the harshness with which the law treated the impotent poor there were numerous abuses. In particular, relatives were able to shift their responsibility on to the parish. Aged poor in Dolgelley were sometimes let to their own children, and youths apprenticed at the parish expense to their fathers. Parents were paid sums from the rates for looking after their children at Maentwrog and elsewhere, and there were instances where people refused to accept their relatives on the terms offered them by the parish.

But the problem of the impotent poor was simple when compared with that of the able-bodied, especially of those who were willing to work. For those who preferred vagrancy there were houses of correction at Bala, Cowbridge, Dolgelley and elsewhere, though the commissioners of 1834 spoke of the 'almost incredible ineptitude' with which the vagrancy laws were applied in Wales. But the war had produced conditions in which the landless labourer even when in work could not live without aid from the parish in addition to his wages. As early in the war as 1796 an investigator employed by the Board of Agriculture had urged, even with regard to the relatively prosperous shire of Glamorgan, that where wages were too low to buy the necessaries of life the parishes must relieve their parishioners according to their wants. This set a problem entirely beyond the competence of the poor law officials. Many of the parishes of Wales had neglected to appoint overseers, and those who were appointed served only under compulsion; (in 1723, a warrant had been issued to compel a person to act as overseer in Llandebie). Even when overseers came to be paid they were equally incompetent. The sole overseer for Dolgelley for twenty years, from 1795 to 1815, was totally illiterate, and this was true also of his wife, a midwife by profession, who succeeded him till she was dismissed in 1822, but their illiteracy had not prevented both from embezzling the funds of the parish.

Such supervision as the magistrates exercised was very per-
functory. Various expedients were tried now to provide work for
such able-bodied poor as were unemployed. Houses of industry
were set up in many places, especially in market towns, and the
inmates were employed in spinning wool or beating hemp and
picking oakum. There were attempts to run these houses at a
profit, and in some places, Carmarthen, for instance, the poor-
house was farmed out to an individual, the parish contributing
some 2/- a week per head, and the 'farmer' obtaining in addition the fruits of the labour of the inmates. But all attempts to
employ the poor proved unsuccessful. The parish was too small
a unit to do this, and even when parishes combined, as they
were allowed to do by law, the result in most cases was financial
failure. The officials therefore fell back on the payment of small
doles to individuals in immediate relief of their distress.

The Berkshire magistrates had in 1795 decided upon a
scale of relief to supplement wages varying with the price of
corn, and according to whether a labourer were single or married and to the number of his children. These Speenhamland
tables were widely adopted, and had disastrous effects in
pauperising the working class. They were never applied in
Wales in this particular, systematic form, and it has therefore
been argued that the evils of the old poor law were non-existent
in Wales. Yet the poor law commissioners reported that 'if they
were called upon to produce from parochial account books
proofs of the maladministration of the law, the parishes of Wales
were those which they would offer.' For the system of allowances
was not new in 1795, but was inherent in the working of the poor
law, and although no single able-bodied man in regular employment ever obtained parochial relief in Wales, this was almost
universal for labourers with more than three children. It stands
to reason that some scale was adopted, and the difference in
Wales was that the scales were haphazard and less scientific
than those of Speenhamland. The result was the same. In 1817
the farmers of the Cardiff district were urged to employ the
poor on the understanding that their wages would be made up
out of the rates, with the result that they immediately dismissed
their independent labourers. It was the general practice for the
parish to pay the rent of married labourers. Of the £2,000 a
year spent on the poor in Llanidloes in 1834, £800 was paid in

rent. Paupers were indeed very desirable tenants, for the land-lord was sure of his rent, and could generally get more from the parish than from other occupiers. The roundsman system, by which the unemployed poor were sent around to those who would hire them, was not common in Wales, but it did exist, and the Llanpumsaint vestry decided in 1817 that the workers should be allocated to the farmers by drawing lots, the employ-ers paying eightpence a day to each pauper, who however, was required to supply his own food.

The problem of the able-bodied poor reached such propor-tions as to create a panic, and the new government, elected by a middle-class vote after the reform act of 1832, resolved to find a solution. It approached its task in a logical and efficient manner but with an almost complete disregard of human con-siderations, and with no enquiry into the causes of poverty. By the act of 1834 outdoor relief to the able-bodied was to cease forthwith; parishes were grouped into unions with boards of guardians who were to build workhouses, and the condition of those who sought relief in these institutions was to be made less desirable than that of the poorest paid labourer outside. Immediately the poor rate for the whole country was reduced by a half. By 1837 the allocation of parishes to unions was complete in Wales, but the building of workhouses took longer. In the meantime there came a cry of protest from all parts of Wales. The act was said to outrage natural feelings by separating hus-bands from wives, and parents from children, and so dreaded were the new 'Bastilles' that aged people went to the most piti-ful extremes to avoid being taken into them. The clause which made mothers solely responsible for their illegitimate children, and denied them relief except in the workhouse, was univer-sally deplored. The nonconformist press was unanimous in its condemnation of the new system. Ten thousand people in Merthyr are said to have signed a petition to the house of com-mons for its repeal. The magistrates and clergy of Cowbridge declared it to be contrary to divine will, and to be cruel, unjust and impolitic. The guardians at Dolgelley petitioned for a return to the old system, 'the new poor law not having been found to work beneficially in this parish.' Prominent Chartists, such as John Frost in Newport and Hugh Williams in Carmarthen, sought to mitigate its effects, and even to render it inoperative.

Soon less responsible persons were to take the law into their own hands and resort to violence.

The same passion for standardisation led the Whig government in 1836 to enforce a compulsory commutation of the tithes, despite the prevailing depression. In no part of the kingdom had so large a proportion of the tithes passed into lay hands as in Wales, and their payment, always unpopular, was now made more so both by the economic distress of the time and by the growth of nonconformity. The better farmers particularly objected to tithes as they were a charge which increased with good farming. In some places they had already been commuted, but as long as the farmer had the option of paying in kind he could always bargain, because of the difficulty which the tithe owner would encounter in collecting if they could not agree. The act of 1836 prescribed that the tithe owners and payers should meet to decide the value of the tithes, and that the annual payments thereafter were to be calculated on the average prices of wheat, barley and oats over seven years. This change took several years to administer. It would, in any circumstances, have been accompanied by disagreement and dissatisfaction; it was particularly unfortunate that it should take place in a period when there was economic distress and when a lack of ready money made cash payments more difficult. Moreover, the government commissioners of 1844 were forced to agree that, taking Wales as a whole, the change had meant an increase of seven per cent in the value of the tithes paid.

Local magistrates were invariably drawn from the gentry and the clergy, and the spread of nonconformity, which was responsible for the growing objection to tithes, also sapped the confidence of the people in the magistrates and produced an unhealthy condition in the countryside. There was much agitation in Bala at Easter, 1838, when the local landowner and his clerical colleagues on the bench refused to serve because a Calvinistic methodist grocer had been placed on the commission of the peace. A government investigator defended their action as 'the dictate of pure patriotism, the spirit of aristocracy in a county magistracy being the salt which alone preserves the whole mass from inevitable corruption.'. The education and early associations of dissenters, he felt, did not generally qualify them to mingle with gentlemen, and if such persons acquired wealth they should rest content with the thought that their grandsons might aspire to the bench. Because of this lack of confidence the peasantry clamoured for a paid magistracy. They complained also that the excessive fees demanded by magistrates' clerks, even in respect of trivial cases where the fines themselves were very light, constituted an intolerable grievance.

This smouldering discontent blazed out in an attack on the toll gates of west Wales. For there were defects inherent in the turnpike system from the start. The existence, side by side, of parish roads and trust roads led to endless confusion, as the trusts were often content with repairing old roads and did not trouble to build new ones, so that the country people were uncertain as to who was responsible for a particular road. Both trusts and parishes sought to evade this responsibility by throwing it on each other, and, because of the extension of the trusts, the parish roads came to be even more neglected than formerly. Much dissatisfaction arose from the erroneous belief that the payment of tolls did away with the corvée. The road system was, in fact, both wasteful and inefficient, and with the enormous growth of traffic the problem became acute. The legislation with regard to roads had also become chaotic, so the Whig government, with its delight in tidiness, proceeded to set it in order in a general Highways Act in 1835. This definitely abolished the corvée, and it was at least the intention of the act that the tolls should be made sufficient to pay for repairs on the trust roads. But the confusion between trust and parish roads remained, and the road authority was still the parish, which could levy a rate for the maintenance of the roads. The Reform Parliament thus missed an opportunity of reorganising the road system completely on a national basis, and making it subject to the control of the central government.

There is little doubt that the road trusts of Wales were exceptionally inefficient. This was mainly because they were too numerous, and because their districts were too small. In consequence their outlook was parochial. There was much rivalry between them, and they sometimes built uneconomical roads rather than use those of each other. They could ill afford to pay trained surveyors, so that repair work was inefficiently done. On the financial side there was gross mismanagement and occasional dishonesty, and the majority were heavily burdened with debt. Sometimes this was due to grandiose schemes of improvement beyond their means. The trust covering the Pembrokeshire part of the Brecon to Milford Haven road was ruined by carrying out the improvements suggested by Telford. Yet all tourists were agreed that the roads of west Wales were intolerably bad. 'Nothing but love of glory,' wrote one traveller, 'should tempt a man to pass along them.'

Bad roads were nothing new; it was the frequent toll gates which now made them oppressive. These were so arranged that persons, leaving the side roads, had to pay however short might be the distance they travelled on a trust road. When they had paid they were given chits which 'cleared' the gates for a certain distance. But the chits of one trust did not 'clear' the gates of another, and as the trusts were small and their roads interlocked there were frequent 'plague spots' where travellers might have to pay twice or even three times within a short distance. This often happened near a town; both Swansea and Carmarthen were like besieged cities, so surrounded were they by toll gates. Country people taking their produce to these towns were seriously handicapped in this way, and it is noteworthy that in Breconshire, where all turnpike roads belonged to one trust, there were few riots. The farmers found the toll on lime particularly oppressive, for many had to cart their lime over long distances. The farmers of the north Pembrokeshire uplands, for example, had to go to the lime-kilns of the south, and since it was possible to pass both ways through a gate in one day for a single payment, they would assemble with their carts at the first gate at midnight in the hope of doing their long journey and returning within twenty-four hours. It is significant that the first gates to be destroyed were in this upland area, across the Carmarthenshire border, and that this took place as the lime burning season was beginning. The tolls levied were not generally high, although they were often increased when the act establishing a trust had to be renewed. Nor was there much evidence of deliberate overcharging. The gates of a trust were generally let by auction to the highest bidder, and the toll keeper was usually a local person, possibly disabled, who might connive at minor evasions of payment. But in the late thirties one Thomas Bullin, who had farmed the tolls of several trusts in England, extended his interests into south Wales. The collection of tolls then became much more stringent, and as he paid his toll keepers on a commission basis, it was to their profit to exact all they could. He also had side-bars and chains erected to stop any traffic which managed to avoid the gates. His actions were no doubt legal, but once more the argument arose as to whether certain roads on which these bars were placed were parish roads or trust roads, for the trusts had spent no money at all in improving some of them.

The wet summer and autumn of 1838 and of the succeeding year reduced the farmers to despair and the countryside became unsettled. The magistrates of Llandovery asked the home secretary in August 1838 to send down an officer of the metropolitan police who was acquainted with the Welsh language. In October an angry crowd at Llangoedmor burnt a farmer in effigy in his own farm yard, to the great danger of his haggard, to frighten him from taking on another farm as well as his own. The hatred of the poor law was shown by the burning, on January 16, 1839, of the new workhouse at Narberth. The guardians offered a reward of £50 for information, and the government an additional £100 with a free pardon for any accomplice who turned informer, but with no result. A few weeks later a Chartist missionary visited the area, and added to the ferment of discontent. Then, on the night of May 13, a newly erected gate at Efailwen in Carmarthenshire, a mile or so from the Pembrokeshire border, was destroyed. This belonged to the Whitland Trust, which was notorious for neglecting roads, and whose tolls were now farmed by Thomas Bullin for £800 a year. The gate was re-erected, whereupon placards immediately appeared announcing a meeting for June 6, 'to consider the necessity of a toll gate at Efailwen.' The magistrates hastily swore in special constables. Nevertheless at 10.30 on that night a crowd of some three to four hundred assembled, many of them with blackened faces and dressed in women's clothes. They drove away the special constables and again destroyed the gate. The Rebecca Riots had begun. It is said that the leader on this occasion was Thomas Rees of Carnabwth, nearby, and that the riots took their name from the scriptural assurance that the seed of Rebecca should possess the gates of her enemies. A few nights later another gate was destroyed a few miles away at

Llanboidy. Then the tumult subsided, and within a month the magistrates of the neighbouring county of Pembroke, anxious not to place an additional burden on the local rates, passed a resolution that they did not consider it necessary to establish a rural police as the population was 'well conducted and peaceable.'

The lull continued for no less than three and a half years. But in the winter of 1842, disturbances broke out again in the same area, the hilly country to the north-west of St. Clears, and, once more, it was the gates of the Whitland Trust which were destroyed. Its roads crossed the Carmarthenshire border into Pembrokeshire, and soon not one of its gates was left in either shire. This time the rioting spread rapidly and affected other trusts in Pembrokeshire and Carmarthenshire, and even in south Cardiganshire. Troops were drafted into the area, but met with little success. In the daytime the countryside was quiet, but at night bands of disguised countrymen would assemble on their heavy horses, proceed to a gate and destroy it. Each band had its Rebecca, its leader for the occasion, and the work of destruction was sometimes preceded by a pantomime in which Rebecca and her daughters decided upon the 'necessity' of the particular gate. For this jacquerie had its frolic side, and many a farm lad was glad to substitute the excitement it afforded on moonlit nights for the high delight of poaching. The rioters showed remarkable ingenuity in preserving secrecy and in spreading false rumours of their movements, so that they were able to elude both the military and the London police who were sent down to cope with them. By the end of the summer the country was reasonably clear of gates.

But with success Rebecca became bolder and proceeded to administer rough justice and remedy particular grievances. Threatening letters were sent to clergymen who were grasping in the matter of tithes, and the plantations and hay ricks of unpopular magistrates were burnt. Then, on June 19, some three to four hundred fantastically disguised horsemen, led by Mike Bowen of Trelech, entered the town of Carmarthen in broad daylight. They carried placards bearing the inscription Cyfiawnder (Justice), and it may well be that they intended only to demonstrate. But they were joined by rabble from the town, and when they appeared before the workhouse they proceeded to ransack it. This destruction was interrupted by the arrival of a troop of dragoons, and immediately the rioters scattered, many of the horsemen having to leave their 'steeds' behind in the congested streets in order to make good their escape.

This incident drew the attention of the nation, and so the London *Times* sent an investigator to west Wales. He described the situation in a series of lengthy and most remarkable letters, which were so sympathetic to the farmers that he entirely won their confidence. He was invited to attend mass meetings, at which they discussed their grievances and at which they drew up petitions of redress for submission to the queen. At these meetings their spokesman very frequently was Hugh Williams, the Chartist. He was a native of Machynlleth, and his sister later married Richard Cobden. On his own marriage Hugh Williams had settled in St. Clears, and it was he who had introduced Chartism into Carmarthen and had defended the Llanidloes rioters. He was opposed to the violence of Rebecca, but he drafted her petitions and helped to defend those of her followers who were captured.

In the late summer the movement spread to east Carmarthenshire and west Glamorgan, and in this semi-industrial area a sordid and even sinister aspect of the rioting appeared. Early in September there was an attack on a gate at Pontardulais, but the authorities, who now had spies among the rioters, had been forewarned. They surprised the attackers, and shots were fired for the first time, three rioters, including the leader, being captured. A few nights later, in an attack on the Hendy gate nearby, a stray shot fired by some irresponsible person killed the old woman toll keeper. This alienated the sympathy of moderate people, yet the coroner's jury had the effrontery to return a verdict of death from the effusion of blood, the cause of which was to them unknown. There now appeared in this area the two most redoubtable of Rebecca's leaders, John Jones (Shoni Sguborfawr) and David Davies (Dai'r Cantwr). Both were Glamorgan men, the former being a pugilist who had drifted into west Wales in search of work, while the latter was a ballad singer and hedge-poet. In the last days of September both were captured. Nevertheless rioting spread north-eastwards in October, into the Rhayader district of Radnorshire, but by this time its fury seemed to be burnt out.

The authorites had used stern measures to put down the disturbances. They employed large detachments of troops and of London policemen, and in addition to the use of spies they offered enormous awards of £100 for information leading to the conviction of any rioter, together with free pardon for the informer. At a special assize in Cardiff in October the three Pontardulais rioters were sentenced to transportation for a period of years. Shoni Sguborfawr was sentenced to transportation for life at the winter assizes in Carmarthen, and Dai'r Cantwr for twenty years. Both men signed a full confession, and the Cantwr composed in gaol a threnody on his own fate which is not without literary merit. Others received lesser sentences at the spring assizes at Carmarthen in March 1844.

Fortunately the government was not content with mere repression. Largely because of the publicity given to the riots by *The Times*, three special commissioners were appointed in October 1843. They held numerous meetings and heard much evidence, and their report, together with this evidence, was published in March 1844. The commissioners analysed the general causes underlying the riots, and, in particular, exposed the abuses of the turnpike system. Nor was this all, for a turnpike bill was immediately introduced into parliament and became law in July 1844. This embodied the main proposal of the commissioners, the consolidation of the trusts, for county road boards were set up in Wales to take over all the trusts in each shire. Arrangements were made by which these boards could liquidate the debts of the old road trusts. The tolls were simplified and made uniform, and a toll once paid would now 'clear' seven miles of road within a shire or two miles in the neighbouring one. The toll on lime, the peculiar grievance of the upland farmers, was reduced by a half. Rebecca had won a substantial victory.

Other measures helped to ease the situation in rural Wales. The general enclosure act of 1845 decreed that a local enquiry by enclosure commissioners must precede the introduction of a private enclosure bill into parliament. Thereby the poor could at least make known their grievances beforehand. In 1846 came the repeal of the Corn Law. The Anti-Corn Law League had conducted extensive agitation in Wales through an organiser, Walter Griffiths. It naturally won the support of the industrial areas of north and south Wales. But since rural Wales was not a corn growing area, the peasantry too, were led to believe that only by repeal could the price of bread be reduced. Moreover the nonconformist press strongly supported repeal. The repeal agitation was, in fact, of great importance in the political development of the nation, for, through it, Welsh nonconformity became politically articulate for the first time. Besides, the farmers were shown that their economic interests did not coincide with those of the great Tory landowners who opposed repeal, and the peasantry were weaned thereby from their traditional political allegiance to the ruling families. Finally, in 1847, a Poor Law Board was established and the working of the poor law was made more humane. It was never afterwards the object of violent and widespread agitation. But possibly of more importance than any single measure was the general improvement in economic conditions which converted the hungry forties into reasonably prosperous fifties. In particular, the railways not only ushered in a new period of development, but also brought prosperity to rural Wales. It could then be seen that Wales had emerged from half a century of depression as a country of small farms, whose occupants were still poor but were no longer desperate. There was not in Wales that great disparity of wealth which was evident in the English countryside. The number of magnates was small, and the tenant farmers who in England were often allied to the squires, did not, in Wales, differ much in social status from their labourers, who, in many cases, could hope to hold farms of their own. This social equality did much to mitigate the evil effects of economic poverty, and to engender peace and contentment.

CHAPTER XIV

THE INDUSTRIALISATION OF WALES

THE close of the Napoleonic war brought a fall in the price of industrial commodities as of farm produce. Iron fell immediately from £20 to £8 a ton. The iron industry of south Wales, which produced about a third of the total for the United Kingdom, was seriously affected. Yet its regression proved to be only temporary, and, with minor fluctuations, it experienced afterwards a quarter of a century of constantly increasing prosperity. By 1840 there were over twice as many furnaces in blast as there were in 1815, and the amount of iron produced in them was, in proportion, considerably higher, since their efficiency was greatly increased as well as their number.

The prosperity of the iron industry in these years was primarily due to technological improvements of great importance. One of these was the use of steam engines. These had only been very slowly adopted in industry, for there were probably only eight steam engines in the whole of Wales in 1800, but they now became general. Through its use to pump water out of the iron mines, the steam engine made it possible to work the deeper seams. It could also be employed to crush the ore before smelting, and, above all, by its use the blast could be enormously strengthened, so that the heat in the furnaces was greatly increased. A further innovation was the use of the hot blast in the manufacture of iron. Strangely enough, some ironmasters had hitherto believed that the quality of the iron was improved if the air driven into the furnace was cold, and they had even sought means to refrigerate it. However, James Neilson, in 1828, proved this theory to be completely wrong, and showed that, by first passing the air through a heated chamber, the heat within the furnace could be made still more intense. One enormous advantage of the new method was that raw coal could be used instead of coke, with a great saving in expenditure. The hot blast was soon adopted by all the Welsh ironmasters, and by its use and that of the steam engine the average output per furnace was more than doubled.

As a direct consequence of the use of the hot blast came another discovery of great importance to Wales. This was a process by which anthracite coal could be used in smelting iron ore. West of the River Neath the northern part of the coalfield is all anthracite. The coal produced there had hitherto been of little value because it could not be converted into coke, so that the furnaces in the area were small and unimportant. As in the case of most of the discoveries of the time, the new process was later to be the subject of much litigation between inventors, but there is no doubt it was first successfully applied at the Ynyscedwyn iron works near Ystalyfera, and that credit for it should be shared between George Crane, the proprietor of the works, and David Thomas, his superintendent. There is some doubt about their respective roles, but it is significant that success came in February 1837, after a visit by David Thomas to James Neilson in Scotland. The discovery led to the industrialisation of west Wales, especially of the Aman and Gwendraeth valleys, although, by this time, the great iron works to the east were well established, and the new centres could not hope to compete with them. Scarcely of less importance was the development of the trade in anthracite coal, for it now came to be used for other purposes as well, and west Wales has always produced ninety per cent of all the anthracite in the United Kingdom. The new smelting process at once attracted world-wide attention, so that an American company immediately entered into agreement with Crane and Thomas to construct furnaces on the great anthracite bed in Pennsylvania. In 1839 David Thomas was induced to settle in Pennsylvania, and so vital was his role in its development that he has been called 'the father of the American anthracite iron industry.' So many, also, were the Welsh iron workers and miners who followed him in the course of the next half-century that the names of the two chief towns on this coalfield, Scranton and Wilkesbarre, became household words in the mining valleys of Wales.

Scarcely less important than these new processes in accounting for the growth of the iron trade was the increased demand for iron for various purposes. For example, the cables of the suspension bridge across the Menai Straits were made at Penydarren. But all these purposes were dwarfed by the great expansion in the building of tramroads and railways, especially after

the introduction of steam locomotion in 1825. The rails for
the Stockton to Darlington railway were made at Ebbw Vale,
and those for the Manchester to Liverpool railway at Penydarren. Nantyglo, under Crawshay Bailey, developed a world
reputation for iron rails, and for many years the iron works of
south Wales were almost exclusively employed in this trade.

The prosperity of the iron industry was dependent upon an
abundant supply of cheap coal, and the ironmasters continued
to open new levels and pits. The deep, parallel gorges which
rivers had cut through the coal bed made it possible to reach the
lower series of coal layers, but the coal was still generally worked
in levels, and the undertakings were small, each employing only
a few men. It was very slowly that the steam engine was introduced, but with its use for pumping water and hauling coal it
became possible to sink deeper pits, and the safety lamp, first
used in Wales in 1816, lessened the danger of working in them.
In time the mining of coal for sale began to acquire importance. The trade was concentrated at first almost entirely on
Newport, for acts of parliament passed in connection with the
Monmouthshire canal had exempted coal brought along this
canal, and then carried to ports east of the Holmes, from the
heavy duty on exported coal. A thriving trade grew up with
Bridgwater and Bristol, and, to a lesser extent, with Gloucester
and Chepstow, for the coal was carried from these ports inland
along the rivers and canals. There were repeated protests from
Cardiff and Swansea against this unfair advantage, but it was
retained by Newport until the repeal, in 1834, of all export
duties on coal carried in British ships. Above all else this
privilege had established the prosperity of Newport, which,
for a few years, completely outstripped Cardiff in size and
importance.

The 'sale coal' trade was not in the hands of the ironmasters
but of small local capitalists, notably Thomas Prothero, a
Newport attorney, and Thomas Powell, a timber merchant.
These two men entered into an association to control prices at
Newport, thereby founding the first 'coal ring' in south Wales.
The Glamorgan coal vendors, also, were independent of the
ironmasters. Walter Coffin, the son of a Bridgend tanner,
opened levels early in the century at Dinas, near the confluence
of the two Rhonddas, and in 1832 sank a shaft there and struck

a rich seam of coal. He was the pioneer in the development of the Rhondda valleys, but he little appreciated the untold mineral wealth which they contained. Of far greater immediate importance was the striking of the famous 'four foot seam' in the Waunwyllt level at Abercanaid, near Merthyr, by Robert Thomas, some four years previously. This was smokeless coal of the highest quality, and his widow, Lucy Thomas, who carried on the business after his death and opened two more levels, conceived the idea of selling the coal further afield. She therefore entered into agreement with an agent at Cardiff, George Insole, and he, on November 12, 1830, sent four hundred tons by ship to London. This was the beginning of the coal export trade from Cardiff. Within a few years the superiority of Welsh coal over the smoky coal of Newcastle became widely recognised, and other speculators hastened to share in its success. The centre of this new development was the adjoining valley of Aberdare. Here Thomas Wayne was fortunate enough to strike the same 'four foot seam' in 1837. Thomas Powell of Newport had equal good fortune five years later, and in 1844 he sank two pits at Duffryn, thereby originating the name, Powell Duffryn, which was to become familiar in many parts of the world. Meanwhile, John Nixon had started as a coal factor, and had taken a hundred tons of Welsh coal to Nantes. Thus he began the coal trade of Cardiff with France. Soon he had sunk pits on his own account in the Aberdare valley. George Insole, the other coal factor, in 1844 sank a pit at Cymer, the junction of the two Rhonddas, and produced steam coal which was excellent for coking and industrial purposes. But the coal exported from Cardiff still came almost entirely from the Merthyr and Aberdare valleys; the upper reaches of both Rhondda valleys were to remain for some years a pastoral area of sheep walks and small farms.

Both the coal and the iron for export were brought along the Glamorgan canal, and loaded on to small ships at the canal mouth. It soon became clear that these facilities were rapidly becoming inadequate, for the ships were too small for the trade, and, even so, there was insufficient room for them at the quayside. The second marquis of Bute, a man of great business ability, decided therefore to build a dock at Cardiff and this was completed in 1839. Its construction cost him some £350,000, and he risked his whole fortune in the enterprise. It was, possibly, the first venture on so large a scale to be undertaken anywhere in the world by one man at his own expense, but his foresight was to be amply rewarded. The new dock made the canal appear still more inadequate to cope with the growing traffic. The canals of Wales had, in fact, never met with complete success. It had been necessary to build them along narrow valleys, almost parallel to one another, so that it had not been possible to link them into a canal system, as in the lowlands of England. Steep gradients had made frequent locks inevitable, and these had slowed down the traffic along the canals and made it impossible to use steam tugs. Besides, the locks added greatly to the cost of upkeep, while ice in winter and drought in summer made the canals undependable. Despite the enormous expenditure on them, the canals were beginning to become obsolete when the railways came to replace them. Significantly, the first railway in Wales ran from Merthyr Tydfil to Cardiff, and the canal company strongly resisted the passing of the act of parliament authorising its construction, and succeeded in obtaining a sum of money in compensation for loss of trade. The new railway was opened in 1841. It followed the trust road and the canal through the narrow Tongwynlais gap, and had an extension along the Aberdare valley, as well as to the coal pits at Cymer and Dinas. Its construction was entrusted to Brunel, one of the greatest engineers of his day, and it was regarded as a considerable feat of engineering.

The coming of the railways marks the turning point in the industrialisation of Wales. Yet, although the first of the railways of Wales had been built for industrial reasons, their early development was as part of the English railway system and was directed primarily to ensure rapid communication with Ireland. The great railways of Wales, therefore, like the trunk roads, ran from east to west, with important consequences later on. Attention was first of all directed to the north Wales route, and George Stephenson and his son Robert were consulted as to whether the railway should run from Shrewsbury through Capel Curig or from Chester along the coast. They decided in favour of the coastal route, and the act was obtained in 1844. There were great engineering difficulties to be faced, and, after much consideration, Robert Stephenson devised tubular bridges to cross the Conway and the Menai Straits. The Menai Bridge was opened to traffic on March 5, 1850, and the Irish mails were carried by rail all the way to Holyhead. The south Wales railway was the work of Brunel. He built the line from Chepstow to Swansea in 1850, and, by constructing the Chepstow bridge in 1852, linked the line with the Great Western Railway. Later in that year the railway reached Carmarthen, and in 1854 was extended to Haverfordwest. It was then taken on to Neyland, a sparsely inhabited spot on the shore of Milford Haven which Brunel had chosen to serve as a port for a steamer service to Ireland. Brunel was an advocate of a wide gauge for railway lines. This became the chief subject of controversy in railway engineering, and, in the long run, the decision went against Brunel, so that the gauge of the south Wales railway had to be changed at great expense.

In the two decades from 1850 to 1870 the majority of the railways of Wales were built. Some of these linked the growing industrial centres of south Wales with the ports of Newport, Cardiff, Swansea and Llanelly, and joined Wrexham with Chester. Others were built to carry the slate of Bethesda, Llanberis, Blaenau Ffestiniog, Abergynolwyn and Corris to the nearest point on the coast. The direction of the railways in rural Wales was not so easy to determine. We have become so accustomed to their present location that it is difficult to bear in mind that this was frequently chosen for inadequate reasons. Many ambitious schemes proved abortive; others turned out to be false starts and financial failures. A grand scheme was elaborated to tap the great industries of the Midlands by means of a railway through Worcester and Radnor to a port which would be developed on Cardigan Bay. Another plan aimed at joining Manchester with Milford by a railway through mid Wales, in the hope that Milford might rival Liverpool and Southampton. A Manchester and Milford railway did come into existence, but, despite the grandiloquent title which it retained, it ran only from Pencader to Tregaron, until the original scheme was abandoned and the railway was diverted to Aberystwyth. The Welsh railways were built by small companies in competition with one another, and the contractors were local men. Of these, one towered above the others in importance. He was David Davies, the son of a crofter of Llandinam in Montgomeryshire, who had begun by building roads and bridges near his home, had then turned to railways, and was soon to dominate the coal trade of south Wales.

The haphazard way in which the Welsh railways were built had important social and economic consequences. The railways did no more to integrate the life of the nation than the trunk roads had done, for the main lines were built to converge on London and not to unite the various parts of Wales. The absence of a well-planned railway system was, also, one factor in the decline of the smaller industries, especially those of north Wales. In the early stages of industrialisation, north Wales seemed as likely to be developed as south Wales; by 1850 the region had returned to agriculture. This was partly due to the difficult nature of the land and to the exhaustion of its mineral wealth, but partly it was due to the absence of capital, and to the consequent late development of its railways. The woollen industry of Montgomeryshire, for example, was outstripped by other areas, partly because it was far from a coalfield and partly because it was very badly served in the early railway age. When the railway did come, the countryside was flooded with Welsh flannel made in Rochdale and sold at a price with which the local mills could not now compete. The lead mines of Cardiganshire had a temporary boom between 1850 and 1870, when the important mine at Frongoch, on the earl of Lisburne's land, was being worked, but here again exhaustion and isolation made it impossible to continue the industry, although, in areas which were better served with railways, an industry, once established, was able to continue when local supplies had run out. Even the slate industry suffered through transport difficulties, although its prosperity was longer lived, for it reached its peak in 1898, when half a million tons of slates were produced and sold. By the time of the outbreak of the Great War, sixteen years later, this figure had been halved.

The continued building of railways in the United Kingdom led to an ever increasing demand for iron, with the result that, in the fifties, there were no less than a hundred and sixty-five furnaces in blast in Wales, producing almost a million tons of pig iron out of a total of 3,600,000 tons for the whole country. This enormous demand led to a search for new sources of supply. The great Cleveland iron field in north Yorkshire was now exploited, and the little market town of Middlesbrough on the Durham border sprang, within a few years, into an industrial centre of great activity. In its development Welsh industrialists played an important part, and its great works were served by a succession of highly skilled Welsh managers and technicians. So many were the iron workers who migrated there from south Wales that Welsh communities, worshipping in their own tongue, came into being by the waters of the Tees. Welsh industrialists sought other supplies abroad, and began importing, from northern Spain, iron ore which had an unusually high metallic content. Dowlais and Ebbw Vale were the pioneers in this activity, which was destined to have such vital consequences for both places. Imported ore accounted for one-quarter of the amount used in south Wales even before the revolutionary changes which transformed the iron industry.

For the demand for iron had led also to a search for new processes, and these rapidly led to the replacement of iron by steel. Of these processes the earliest was discovered by Bessemer in 1856. Briefly, it involved the pouring of molten pig iron into a pear shaped 'converter' into which hot air was blown at enormous pressure through pipes. In this way the carbon and manganese impurities were burnt out and the purified metal could be poured into ingot moulds. This took only some ten to fifteen minutes. Puddling was thereby rendered out of date, for the new process did not depend on the manual dexterity of the workman. For the first time steel, which was greatly superior to puddled or 'wrought' iron, could be produced cheaply on a large scale. It took some years to make the process a commercial success, and the cost of transforming the iron works was enormous. But this was soon done at Dowlais and Ebbw Vale, where Bessemer steel was used almost exclusively for the manufacture of steel rails. A little later there were Bessemer converters at Rhymney and Blaenavon too. Yet, within a few years, William Siemens, in his experiments at Landore, discovered still another process, and in 1868 he founded a company to establish a works there. By the Siemens-Martin method, pig iron was melted in an 'open hearth,' a shallow basin, which, despite its name, was wholly enclosed apart from the doors at each end through which the material was charged. Heat was directed at the surface of the iron, which was then tapped into a ladle, while the slag overflowed into another receptacle. This method was much more expensive than Bessemer's and took a much longer time (some eight to ten hours), but the steel produced was of superior quality.

These discoveries coincided with a crisis in the iron industry. For by the end of the sixties most of the railways of the kingdom had been built, and the demand for iron rails had greatly diminished. Besides, many of the old leases, granted in the mid eighteenth century for ninety-nine years, now fell in. The Dowlais lease, granted by Lord Windsor for £31 a year, was renewed by his great-grandson, the marquis of Bute, for £30,000 a year. Many iron works could not pay the sums demanded. At the same time cheap steel entirely displaced iron for several purposes, but the cost of erecting the new plant necessary to produce it was prohibitive. Therefore one old iron works after another closed down. That the crisis did not affect the steel industry was due to the enormous development of foreign railways, in north and south America, in India and in Russia, which produced an insatiable demand for Welsh steel rails. In some instances the steel industry was developed inside these new countries with the aid of Welsh technical skill and Welsh labour. Thus John Hughes became the pioneer of the industrial development of the Donets valley in southern Russia. He founded there the Novorossuskoe Obshchestvo (New Russia Company) in 1869, and the town which sprang up was named Hughesovka after him, but is now known as Donetsk. A large number of his workmen came from south Wales and from the Welsh community in Middlesbrough.

The local supply of iron ore was entirely inadequate to meet the demand for Welsh steel rails. Besides, the local ore contained phosphorus, and neither the Bessemer nor the Open Hearth process succeeded in eliminating this impurity. To produce steel it was necessary to import non-phosphoric ore, which came mostly from Spain. The Dowlais Iron Company and others therefore formed the Orconera Company at Bilbao in 1872. By 1879 the amount of imported ore was four times that of the local ore used. But in that year a young Welsh scientist, Sidney Gilchrist Thomas, aided by his cousin, Percy Gilchrist, a chemist at the Blaenavon ironworks, devised a process by which the phosphorus could be removed through lining the converter with a basic material such as limestone. His discovery was tried out on a large scale in Bessemer converters by Windsor Richards, the Welsh manager of a Middlesbrough firm, and proved to be a commercial success. It could be equally well adapted to the Siemens-Martin process, and the first basic open-hearth furnace was built at Brymbo, near Wrexham, in 1884. It was a development of world-wide significance, for the great phosphoric iron beds of America and of Lorraine could now be exploited. From this discovery sprang the stupendous industrial expansion of Germany, which had acquired Lorraine in the Franco-German war, and the consequent dislocation in the balance of international power. Local Welsh ore could once again be used to make steel, but increasing demand made the Welsh steel works more and more dependent upon imported supplies. By the end of the century over 800,000 tons of ore were imported annually into Cardiff, in addition to 340,000 tons into Newport and 170,000 tons into Swansea, as compared with over a million tons into Middlesbrough.

The import of ore led to a remarkable change in the location of the steel industry. For historical reasons the iron industry had been located on the north-eastern rim of the coalfield, and an industrial tradition had retained it there. But the cost of conveying each year a million tons of ore by rail for some twenty-five or thirty miles inland was enormous, and made it difficult for the steel companies to compete with others which were more conveniently placed. Cyfarthfa, which had been closed for some time, was restarted in 1883 as a Bessemer steel works, but its career until the Great War was uncertain and it was eventually closed. In 1890 the whole plant at Rhymney, including Bessemer converters, was dismantled, and the company restricted its activities to coal production. But more spectacular was the decision of the Dowlais Company to seek a better location on the coast, and to build in 1891 the great 'Dowlais Works' on the East Moors at Cardiff. This was the only British Bessemer firm to change its location, and even then, it did so only partially, because of the concern of Lord Wimborne (great-grandson of John Guest) for the dependent community at Dowlais, so that the whole of the firm's rail rolling continued on the old site. It is probable that other firms, such as that of Ebbw Vale, would have moved had they had sufficient funds. New iron-using industries which migrated from the Midlands to south Wales in these years naturally sought a location on the coast, at Newport and elsewhere. Besides, Bessemer steel, which was used with unqualified success only in making rails, was now being ousted by Siemens steel. In 1885, 433,000 tons of Bessemer steel were manufactured in Wales, and 138,000 tons of Siemens steel; by 1912 the production of Bessemer steel had dropped to 328,000 tons but that of Siemens steel had risen to 1,358,000 tons. This change reflects the enormous growth of industry on the south-western, maritime rim of the coalfield where the Bessemer process was not much used.

The growth of the industry in this area was due to the expansion of tin-plate manufacture. The tin-plate industry had always been located in west Wales because of the historical association of Welsh iron and Cornish tin. In the second half of the nineteenth century the Malay States entirely displaced Cornwall as a source of supply. Since all the tin which was used had to be imported, it continued to be convenient to have the tin-plate works near the coast, especially as a large proportion of the tin-plate was produced for export. Distance from the great iron works was therefore less of a disadvantage than might otherwise have been the case, and there was further compensation in the existence of a plentiful supply of clean water, which is particularly important in this industry. By 1875 tin-plate manufacture had become almost a Welsh monopoly. Very little tin-plate was made outside Great Britain, and, in that year, of the seventy-seven factories in Great Britain fifty-seven were located in south Wales. This was the year in which Siemens began to use steel for making tin-plate at Landore, and in the next fifteen years the expansion of the industry was phenomenal, largely owing to the development of food canning in the United States and elsewhere. The new Prince of Wales Dock was opened in Swansea in 1882 to cope with the increased traffic. In 1889, of the 430,000 tons of tin-plate exported, 330,000 tons went to the United States. But at this time tin was discovered in the Dakotas, and the United States government decided to foster a tin-plate industry at home. They therefore passed in 1890 the McKinley Act which imposed a duty amounting to 9s. 10d. per box of tin-plate of the value of 13s. 3d. This duty was to come into operation on July 1, 1891. In the early months of that year, therefore, export from Wales reached its peak, but afterwards there came disaster. Within four years, of the 514 mills in the ninety-three tin-plate factories of Wales 221 were idle, and ten thousand workmen were unemployed. Since the industry is more dependent than most on skilled labour, thousands of these tin-plate workers were induced to emigrate to America in the succeeding years. But new uses were found for tin-plate, and in the first decade of this century the petroleum industry outstripped the canning of foodstuffs in tin-plate consumption. With new uses came new markets, in Russia and elsewhere, and by 1914 the output of the Welsh tin-plate mills was fifty per cent higher than in 1890.

With the growth of heavy industry there emerged a number of colossal firms whose activities were closely integrated within themselves. Thus the Ebbw Vale Steel, Iron and Coal Company made its own plant, controlled sources of ore supply in Spain and Norway, transported the ore to this country, owned its own supplies of limestone and produced coke from its own coal, in addition to manufacturing steel. The Dowlais enterprises were in 1901 acquired by a company, called Guest, Keen and Company, in which Lord Wimborne still retained an interest. This company owned supplies of raw materials, iron ore, coal and limestone, as well as its manufacturing plant, and in the next year it combined with Nettlefolds, who were world-famous as screw makers. Guest, Keen and Nettlefolds then added enormously to their resources by absorbing Crawshay's of Cyfarthfa. Baldwins Ltd. were formed in 1902 through the combination of several firms, and constituted a self-contained unit for the manufacture of galvanised sheets, tin-plate and steel products. This tendency became, in fact, particularly noticeable in the twentieth century in the tin-plate industry, for this is dependent upon steel production for its own raw material. Steel firms, such as Baldwins Ltd., therefore established tin-plate works to use their own steel, but even more significant was the setting up in 1907 of the Llanelly Steel Works partly by a number of tin-plate makers who agreed to take all their steel from it. In addition to this 'vertical' integration, there was also the growth of 'horizontal' combination, that is, absorption or association of a number of firms of a similar nature. The tin-plate industry had at first been highly individualistic; it was carried on by a large number of small firms. But now great amalgamations took place. Many of these are associated with the name of Richard Thomas. He was a clerk in a tin-plate factory at Neath when, in 1867, he founded Richard Thomas and Company, which remained a private concern until it was registered as Richard Thomas Ltd. in 1889. The crisis caused soon afterwards by the McKinley tariff led to much reorganisation, and, while many tin-plate works were permanently closed, others were absorbed into this firm. Competition was eliminated through these amalgamations, and new firms were now unable to enter the field because of the enormous initial difficulties which they would have to overcome.

The growth of industry in the Swansea area was due also to developments in the copper trade. Once again, historical reasons accounted for the persistence of copper smelting in this area. The mines of Anglesey had now become exhausted, and Swansea had to return to Cornwall as its chief source of supply. This source continued until the middle of the century, although in 1828 the first cargoes of overseas ores had been brought into Swansea. In later years, cargoes came from Cuba, Australia and South Africa, but mainly from Chile, and ships carrying them sometimes took six months to make the long journey around Cape Horn. As in the case of tin-plate, copper smelting was almost a Welsh monopoly; of the eighteen copper works in Britain in 1860, seventeen were in the Swansea area. In the next three decades copper smelting was at its height, and several new works were opened along the strip of coast from Burry Port to Port Talbot. The Swansea Metal Exchange became the centre of the copper trade of the whole world. But then decline set in. Great sources of supply were found south of Lake Superior, and American firms entered the market. Moreover, copper smelting was started at the mines in Chile and in Australia, so that the ore was no longer brought to south Wales. One by one the copper works were closed, and the chemical industries which were subsidiary to copper smelting also declined. But a metallurgical tradition remained strong in the Swansea district, and in 1902 nickel refining was started at Clydach, on the outskirts of Swansea, at the Mond Nickel Works, the largest of its kind in the world. The Swansea area has, in this way, always retained a far greater variety of industries than any other part of Wales, and has therefore been less subject to fluctuations in employment.

The heavy industry of south Wales consumed an ever increasing quantity of coal, and, as we have seen, some of the old iron firms went over entirely to coal production. But local consumption of coal was soon dwarfed by the demand from abroad, so that Thomas Powell, the owner of sixteen collieries when he died in 1863, was the largest single coal exporter in the world. His property was mainly in the Aberdare and Rhymney valleys, and in the year after his death it was acquired for £365,000 by the Powell Duffryn Steam Coal Company, formed by Sir George Elliot, who had, himself, started life as a door boy in a Durham pit. The P.D. Company in time acquired most of the Aberdare valley. Still more spectacular was the development of the two Rhonddas. These remained a secluded pastoral area until the sixties, but were then invaded by prospectors and speculators. Among these was David Davies, who was, at this time, building the railways of mid Wales. In 1865 he sank two shafts of unprecedented depth at Cwmparc and Ton in the Rhondda Fawr valley. One reason why the Rhondda had hitherto been undeveloped was because the coal seam was here at its deepest, and David Davies's outlay was enormous on this account. He formed a company in 1867, and twenty years later this was registered as the Ocean Coal Company Ltd., with a capital of £800,000, half its shares being held by David Davies and his son.

The export of coal from Cardiff was aided by the fact that the journey from the mines to the coast was all down hill, so that the cost of transport was reduced. Besides, Cardiff coal boats returned from abroad laden with mineral ore, so that freights, also, could be lowered. Then came the revolution in shipping with the change from sail to steam. Welsh coal was particularly suitable for ships, and the advantage of having 'bunkers' in various parts of the world, that is, large reserves of coal at depots convenient for shipping, was soon realised. This idea was seized upon by John Cory, a ship's chandler at Cardiff. He opened his first colliery at Pentre in the Rhondda Fawr valley in 1868, and later acquired large interests elsewhere, especially in the Neath and Ogmore valleys. He at once established a bunkering depot at Suez when the canal was opened in

1869, and before his death in 1910 he owned about eighty such depots all over the world. Meanwhile the Admiralty had changed over to steam and had become one of the best customers for south Wales coal.

This immense development taxed to the utmost the resources of the Taff Vale Railway, and especially of the Cardiff docks. New docks had been built at Cardiff in 1855, in 1864 and again in 1874, but still proved insufficient. The marquis of Bute, through his masterful agent, William Thomas Lewis (who became Lord Merthyr in 1911), exercised a stranglehold on the commerce of the port, and independent traders complained not only of congestion and delay through the holding up of coal waggons but also of extortionate charges. Led by David Davies and John Cory they elaborated a scheme for building a dock at Barry, and a railway to connect it directly with the Rhondda valleys without passing through the narrow gorge at Tongwynlais. They sought to obtain a private act of parliament for this purpose, but met with intense opposition from the marquis of Bute. Despite this, the act was passed in 1884, and five years later Barry Dock was opened. The building of Barry Dock and railway was David Davies's last venture, and also his finest achievement. Soon another dock was called for at Barry, as well as two others at Cardiff. The opening of the Severn Tunnel had, meanwhile, shortened the journey to London by one hour, and helped in the expansion of the trade of south Wales. It was appropriate that the tunnel should be first used, on January 9, 1886, by a coal train.

During this period of great prosperity the coal magnates competed relentlessly with one another. The advantages of co-operation came to be realised, and William Thomas Lewis (himself a coal owner through marriage with Lucy Thomas's grand-daughter) succeeded, in 1871, in persuading both the proprietors of sale coal and those ironmasters who produced coal to unite in forming the Monmouthshire and South Wales Coal Owners' Association. Competition nevertheless continued, despite the repeated efforts of Lewis's chief rival, David Alfred Thomas (the future Lord Rhondda), to form a closer union. The nucleus of D. A. Thomas's own interests was the Cambrian Collieries Ltd., but he succeeded in associating with it nine other coal producing firms, including the Ebbw Vale Steel,

Iron and Coal Company and the Rhymney Iron and Coal Company, together with four coal exporting firms, to form, in 1913, the Consolidated Cambrian Ltd., with a capital of £2,000,000 and an annual output of 7,350,000 tons. That year saw the record production of 56,830,000 tons of coal in south Wales. Seventy per cent of this coal was exported, forty-five per cent of it from Cardiff alone. Cardiff had thereby become the largest coal exporting port in the whole world, and in south Wales coal undoubtedly was King.

CHAPTER XV

THE SOCIAL CONSEQUENCES
OF INDUSTRIALISATION

THE industrialisation of Wales was, as we have seen, a consequence of the transition to industrialism in England. Attention was turned to the mineral and other resources of Wales only when those of England were becoming exhausted or were proving inadequate to meet increasing demands. It follows therefore that the process began later in Wales than in England, so that it came when technological developments were already far advanced. Thus, whereas industrialism in England was a slow growth extending over centuries, the changes in Wales were more rapid and more revolutionary, and were introduced into a country almost entirely lacking in an industrial tradition. The social consequences which everywhere followed industrialism were, on this account, greatly intensified in Wales.

As might be expected, the great expansion in population which accompanied these changes began later in Wales than in Lancashire and Yorkshire, for example. But between the first census in 1801 and the fifth in 1841 the population of Monmouthshire had increased by 117 per cent, the highest percentage for any shire in the British Isles, while Glamorgan, with 77 per cent, stood third on the list. This inrush brought with it a large non-Welsh element, particularly from the south-west of England, which the indigenous population was never able to assimilate. There thus grew up a racial division within the industrial areas, giving rise to social problems which did not exist in similar regions in England. This division was further complicated by an influx of Irish workers, driven out by recurrent famines, in 1817 and 1818 and again in 1822, culminating in the great famine of 1846. The south Wales coalfield was conveniently near to Ireland, and Irish families, in extreme stages of destitution, were brought over as ballast by returning coal boats and landed clandestinely on the Glamorgan coast, whence they would beg their way to the towns. This caused great annoyance to the country folk. There were constant complaints, and rewards were offered for information which would lead to the conviction of the captains of vessels who illegally landed persons at places other than the recognised seaports. The standards of life of these immigrant Irish were incredibly low and they were prepared to accept lower wages than the native workmen. There was constant strife between them and the Welsh. The heterogeneous nature of the industrial population was further accentuated by the fact that, in the early days, it was almost entirely unskilled. Agricultural labourers were attracted to the coalfield by higher wages. They brought with them no industrial traditions, and the constant flow of new recruits prevented such traditions from growing. The absence of any sense of cohesion made it difficult for a working class movement to emerge.

It was a grave misfortune for Wales that industrialisation took place in sparsely inhabited tracts of bleak, open moorland, and in steep, narrow valleys. The workmen lived in clusters of houses hastily thrown up around an iron works or a coal mine. These houses belonged to the employers, who were able to use the threat of eviction to bring pressure to bear on their workmen in the industrial disputes which arose later in the century. Apart from Swansea there were no well-established towns to act as centres around which a healthy communal life could grow. Besides, the geographical nature of the mining valleys made it impossible to create such centres, for houses had to be built in long narrow ribbons, extending for miles. Moreover the narrowness of the valleys prevented the growth of a variety of industries on the coalfield itself, as was the case in the Midlands. This, together with the fact that south Wales formed a natural coal-exporting area, since the loaded trains could so easily be brought downhill to the coast, led to concentration on the basic industries of iron and coal, and this, again, accentuated the distress which was caused by fluctuations in these industries, since there was no alternative employment. Moreover the narrow valleys gave rise to insoluble problems of drainage and sanitation. The houses were built in terraces one behind the other, along steep slopes, which were dominated by overhanging coal tips and were frequently in positions where they received very little sun.

There was a great deal of overcrowding, as houses could not be built rapidly enough. Several families lived together, and since the male population greatly exceeded the female, as in all newly-developed areas, the congestion was increased by innumerable lodgers. These conditions took their toll of health and well-being, and when the dread new disease of cholera appeared in Great Britain in 1831, the south Wales mining valleys proved a fertile breeding ground. In the great cholera epidemic of 1849, no less than 1,400 died of the disease in Merthyr Tydfil alone.

Geographical isolation made it necessary for the employers not only to provide houses but to arrange for the provisioning of the new communities. Thus began the company shops, or truck shops, which were to become for a time the chief grievance of the workers. The 'long pay' system, by which workers were paid monthly, was almost universal, and the workers often received their wages in the form of vouchers which could be used only at the company shops. That the workers were constantly in debt to these shops gave their employers an additional hold over them in times of industrial dispute, while their provisions could be entirely cut off if necessary. It was inevitable that most company shops should take advantage of their virtual monopoly, and their prices were generally 25 per cent to 30 per cent above those of independent traders in the towns.

Conditions in the iron industry were bad, for hours were excessively long and the work was heavy and dangerous. Yet in the primitive coal levels and mines conditions were even worse. There was an almost total absence of safety devices; the foul atmosphere led to frequent explosions, and the individual deaths annually from accidents such as falling roofs, greatly exceeded in number those caused by major disasters. Women as well as men were used in heavy industry; in fact, while men hewed the coal the task of carrying it in baskets to the surface had always been allocated to women, and when trams were introduced these were drawn and pushed by women, often scantily clad because of the intense heat and frequently unable to stand upright because of low roofs. Children of both sexes were used to open doors underground and shut them immediately to prevent draughts, which were thought to interfere with the ventilating of the mine. Sometimes these infants were not five years of age, and had to be carried to their work.

Moreover they sometimes helped in filling trams. There is little evidence of deliberate ill-usage, for the children worked with their parents. Generally they were taken down the mines because of the system which prevailed by which a man with a 'helper' could get more trams to fill than one working alone.

The attitude of the workers towards social and political problems throughout the century was determined by their living and working conditions. They were herded together in extreme discomfort and brutalised by long hours of heavy and dangerous work. In winter the miners saw daylight only on Sundays. They received their pay in public houses, and had little recreation except drink, which was provided in innumerable beer-houses. In the early days there was little provision for religious worship. There were no resident magistrates on the coalfield and few police. A heritage of lawlessness and a tendency to unrest and extreme actions were thus generated and persisted even after conditions had improved.

The Napoleonic war, with the increased demand for iron which it produced, accelerated industrial changes even in Wales, where they were already very rapid. At one and the same time the war led to spasmodic over-production, causing alternating high wages and unemployment, and also checked any movements towards social amelioration. Working class agitation was regarded with great alarm. The combination acts of 1799 and 1800, which forbade workmen to associate for the purpose of increasing wages or reducing hours, represented no change in policy but nevertheless aggravated the relations between the men and their employers. Five Swansea rope makers were committed to gaol in 1806 for conspiracy to raise wages. Sporadically during the war years there was rioting, as for example in Merthyr in 1800, when two of the rioters were hanged, and again in 1810. The chief grievance in both instances seems to have been dissatisfaction with the truck shops.

The sudden end of the long war brought a complete dislocation of the iron industry, so that furnaces became idle and wages were immediately reduced. As a result there was rioting on a considerable scale. It began at the Tredegar iron works in October 1816, and the rioters then moved over the mountain to Dowlais, where they were fired on by special constables and one rioter was killed. Soon there was rioting in all the iron works from Merthyr to Blaenavon. As there was no adequate police, yeomanry were summoned from Cardiff, Swansea and Carmarthen. But the employers decided to withdraw their notices for the reduction of wages, and the rioting ceased. Moreover, in 1817, with a revival in the iron trade, Crawshay not only raised wages but decided to discontinue his company shop. A depression in the coal trade five years later led to rioting in Monmouthshire, when the miners tried to destroy the coal waggons of the Tredegar company as well as the Sirhowy tramroad. Once more the yeomanry had to be called upon to restore order. Few employers had followed Crawshay's example in abolishing truck, and agitation against it continued. In 1830 there was an anti-truck meeting in the parish church at Merthyr. In the same year the miners of Llansamlet and Landore marched, on separate occasions, to lay this grievance before the Swansea magistrates, and the Monmouthshire justices drew up a petition to parliament for its abolition. The Denbighshire yeomanry were called out in December to quell a riot among the miners of Rhosllannerchrugog during a strike due to the same reason. There was a slight skirmish in which the yeomanry fired on the crowd (the 'Battle of Chirk Bridge' was celebrated in a ballad) and two of the men's leaders were sentenced to imprisonment at the Ruthin assizes.

The outbreak in Merthyr six months later, in June 1831, was far more serious. Here again it was the miners who were primarily involved, and the immediate cause was a reduction in their wages by Crawshay. The town was in ferment because of the agitation for parliamentary reform, and numerous meetings were being held on the hillside. At one of these the Merthyr Court of Requests, a local court for the recovery of small debts, was violently criticised, and the crowd, before dispersing, sacked the premises of the court and burnt its records. The magistrates immediately summoned troops, and a detachment of Highlanders arrived from Brecon on Friday, 3 June. They halted in front of the Castle Inn, and a hostile crowd gathered. The mob was harangued by several ironmasters; nevertheless the men rushed the troops in an attempt to seize their arms. The Highlanders panicked; they bayoneted some of their assailants and fired on others, so that about twenty were killed and over seventy seriously injured. Twenty of the soldiers, also, were wounded. Before the evening a troop of cavalry arrived, but next morning a mob outside the town stopped the troops bringing ammunition from Brecon, so that it had to be taken back. The Swansea yeomanry were waylaid the same day, and surrendered their arms without a struggle. Large crowds arrived in Merthyr over the week-end from the neighbouring iron works and dragoons were brought from Newport, but there was no further fighting.

Over twenty ring-leaders were arrested and two were condemned to death at the Cardiff assizes. Of these, one was a haulier, Lewis Lewis (Lewsyn yr Heliwr), who was said to have been hoisted on to a lamp post and to have directed the crowd in disarming the soldiers. The other was Richard Lewis (called Dic Penderyn from the cottage in Aberavon where he was born), a young married man, aged twenty-three, who was accused of having wrested a musket and bayonet from one of the Highlanders and of having wounded him in doing so. Petitions were organised on behalf of both men, and Lewis Lewis was reprieved. But despite considerable doubt concerning the evidence, and despite the exertions of Joseph Tregelles Price, the quaker ironmaster of Neath, who obtained an interview with the implacable Melbourne, Dic Penderyn was hanged in Cardiff gaol. His body was buried in Aberavon churchyard amid scenes of great emotion, and a strangely persistent suggestion of martyrdom has always been attached to his name.

The Merthyr riots had one beneficial consequence; they led to an anti-truck act which became effective on January 16, 1832. An active supporter of this measure was the grandson of the first Richard Crawshay, Benjamin Hall, the member for the Monmouth boroughs, who was later, as Commissioner of Works, to give his name to Big Ben, and whose wife, Lady Llanover, played a prominent part in the intellectual life of Wales in the nineteenth century. The act forbade the payment of wages in goods. But it did not effectively abolish truck as was shown by the frequent prosecutions which followed. Nor did it in any way eliminate the company shop, while the 'long pay' system ensured that workmen remained constantly dependent upon credit. Besides, it was easy to circumvent the provisions of the act, for workmen could be given a hint of dismissal if they did not deal with the company shop. Yet it is significant of the diversity of opinion on this question that as late as 1838 the men of Cyfarthfa, in one of their meetings on the mountain side, decided to petition their employer to open a shop, as they considered· that they were being cheated by the tradesmen of Merthyr.

It was during the Denbighshire riots of 1830–31 that unionism made its first appearance in Wales. The Friendly Associated Coal Miners' Union was formed in Lancashire in October 1830, and soon extended into Flintshire. During the strike oaths were administered to ensure that no miner would accept lower wages than his fellows. The employers used every means to destroy the new movement, and despite the arrival in north Wales of the Union's chief organiser in June 1831, its activities ceased. It secured a firmer footing in south Wales after the Merthyr riots, and numerous 'union clubs' were formed. These provided for mutual assistance during unemployment, but their primary purpose was to resist reductions in wages. Secret oaths were taken which provided that no member would instruct anyone in his trade other than a fellow member or apprentice; that he would not work where a fellow member had been dismissed for standing out for his price, and that he would employ no one to assist him but a fellow member. Clubs formed in the mines attached to Joseph Tregelles Price's iron works at Neath, and in Walter Coffin's pit at Dinas, were dissolved by agreement with the employers, who were highly sympathetic to their workmen. But the response of the sale-coal owners and ironmasters elsewhere was resolute and relentless. Six employers in the Merthyr neighbourhood announced in September 1831 that they would employ no union men, and for two months there was an almost complete lock-out. But the clubs had no funds. Parish relief was refused to the workers, though large sums were spent in removing them to their original places of settlement. The workers therefore had to admit defeat and return to the mines.

It was difficult for unionism to take root among the miners of Wales because of the absence there of any tradition of trade regulation or co-operation. The miners' work was unskilled, and new labour could always be recruited from among immigrants into the coalfield. Besides, the influence of the nonconformist denominations was thrown in against them. These were rural in their outlook and decried working-class combinations. They regarded secret oaths as blasphemous, and disapproved of the clubs because they met in public houses. The Calvinistic methodists meeting in their association at Tredegar, on October 19, 1831, while the lock-out was on, formally passed a series of resolutions condemning unionism and prohibiting church membership to any member of a club. On the north Wales coalfield the *sasiwn* meeting at Mold in the following year, adopted the same attitude. This was in keeping with the middle-class mentality of most leaders of nonconformity at this time.

The result of suppression was violence. Bands of disguised men 'scotched' those who accepted lower wages or were obnoxious to them for some other reason. They destroyed their houses and even mutilated the workmen themselves. These bands first appeared at Nantyglo in February, 1832, and were active in the Pontypool valley in April and May. They came to be known as the Scotch Cattle and adopted a red bull's head as their symbol. Large rewards were offered for information as to their identity, and troops were called in, so that for a time the outrages ceased. The legitimate aspirations of the workers then found an outlet in Robert Owen's attempt at organising labour, culminating in his Grand National Consolidated Trades Union in February 1834. But although the combination acts had been repealed, workmen could still be prosecuted for conspiracy at common law if they combined to increase wages or administered secret oaths, and the sentences of transportation passed in March on the Tolpuddle agricultural labourers led to the collapse of Robert Owen's flimsy structure. Once more the Scotch Cattle became rampant in the Monmouthshire valleys, attacking, as before, not the employers of labour but their own fellow workmen, as well as tradesmen against whom they had grievances. In November 1834 one of their victims at Blackwood died from injuries, but the murderer was hanged and his accomplices transported, and once more the outrages ceased.

The year 1834 saw not only the trial of the Tolpuddle 'martyrs' but the passing of the Poor Law Amendment Act. This was the first-fruit of the middle-class regime established by the Reform Act of 1832. The workers had based exaggerated hopes of an improvement in their lot on the reduction in taxation which they believed would follow a reform in the administration, and the Poor Law Act completed their disillusionment. There was a storm of protest from industrial as from rural Wales, and this now replaced truck as the chief grievance of the industrial population. Agitation against the poor law merged into further demands for constitutional reform, and in 1836 the Working Men's Association was formed in London with this end in view. Soon a branch was established at Carmarthen by Hugh Williams. When the People's Charter embodying the celebrated six points was published in May 1838, Chartism had started on its course. It flourished in the summer of that year in the woollen towns of Montgomeryshire, where, owing to a financial crisis in London, many workers were unemployed. By the end of the year several W.M.A. branches came into existence in the Monmouthshire valleys, and the Chartist missionary, Henry Vincent, came down to address them in preparation for the summoning of a Chartist convention to London in February 1839. The Monmouthshire delegate to this convention was John Frost, a prosperous tradesman of Newport, who had served as the second mayor of the town after the passing of the Municipal Corporations Act, and who was, moreover, a guardian of the poor and a justice of the peace.

The first outbreak of violence came in April in Llanidloes. London policemen had been brought into the town, and this aggravated the dissatisfaction of the textile workers, who wrecked the Trewythen Arms where the police were stationed. For a week the Chartists held Llanidloes, but infantry from Brecon and the Montgomeryshire yeomanry restored order. One of the Llanidloes Chartists was transported for fifteen years and two others for seven years. In May Vincent was arrested and placed in Monmouth gaol. This produced a crisis, for Vincent was enormously popular with the Monmouthshire miners and iron workers. Great mass meetings were held, addressed by Frost and others. Nevertheless Chartism seemed to wane in the late summer, but on October 3, a secret meeting held at Nantyglo apparently favoured recourse to violence, and on Friday, November 1, a meeting of delegates at Blackwood determined upon a great demonstration at Newport to take place on the following Sunday night. The Chartists were to assemble in three contingents, one in Blackwood under the leadership of John Frost, a second on the mountain above

Ebbw Vale under Zephaniah Williams, a master miner, and a third on the racecourse below Pontypool, led by William Jones, a beer-house keeper. They were to meet at Risca in the night, and march into Newport in the early hours of Monday morning. But the night proved tempestuous, and Jones's contingent never arrived. When the bedraggled Chartists at last entered Newport the authorities were prepared for them. There was a scuffle in front of the Westgate Hotel, where, unknown to the Chartists, troops had been stationed. These fired into the mob, who fled in great disorder leaving several dead behind. The three leaders were soon arrested and were condemned to death, but through the intervention of the chief justice who had presided over their trial, Melbourne's cabinet reluctantly changed the sentence to one of transportation for life. Chartism in Wales never recovered from this fiasco. It survived for a time in Merthyr where a Chartist periodical, *Udgorn Cymru*, was published, and there was a revival in 1842 and again in 1848, but with that it suffered complete eclipse.

Chartism for a time had united within itself both the reforming zeal of the union clubs and the violence of the Scotch Cattle. Its radical programme had received the support of the nonconformist periodicals, notably *Y Diwygiwr*, and dissenting ministers incurred much odium through their association with it, though the Calvinistic methodists held strictly aloof. But there was no solidarity within the working class, and it is significant that no Irish workers took part in the march on Newport. Even with regard to this incident there was no unity of purpose, for there were innumerable gradations among the advocates of moral and of physical force. Nevertheless the Chartist movement marked the first emergence of the working class as a political force, and it provided the motive power behind much of the social legislation which followed.

The Chartists had hoped to obtain social amelioration through political changes; their failure led to a return to industrial action. In the following years there was a spread of small craft unions, mainly to restrict entrance into the crafts and thereby to keep up wages, but also to provide benefits during sickness and unemployment. The copper workers of Swansea came out on strike in 1843, when their employers announced the huge reduction of twenty-five per cent in their wages. The strike lasted five weeks, but their unions had no funds, and the men were forced to accept defeat. None of the craft unions was powerful enough to be effective in industrial disputes. These years also saw the spread of friendly societies, which competed with the unions, for they provided benefits during sickness and adversity without advocating strikes or political agitation. By their pageantry, their brass bands and processions, they introduced some colour into the bleak industrial towns. The only indigenous Welsh society was the Order of True Ivorites, which had the furtherance of the Welsh language among its objects. It was founded in Wrexham in 1836, but it soon moved its headquarters to Carmarthen, and hundreds of its lodges were set up throughout south Wales. Numerous mechanics' institutes, established in the fifties, also helped to foster local culture and alleviate the social disintegration which menaced the industrial population. Then in 1860 there was opened the first co-operative store in Wales, at Cwmbach, Aberdare. These stores counteracted the pressure which employers could bring to bear on their workmen through the company shops during industrial disputes.

The fifties and sixties were relatively free from industrial strife, partly because of the return of prosperity, though there were brief periods of over-production and unemployment. These years saw the great development of the Rhondda valleys, and work was plentiful. In consequence wages were relatively high. Throughout the century there had been competition between the iron-masters who produced coal and the independent coal owners, and the latter paid higher wages in order to attract labour to their pits. This was accentuated with the opening of the Rhonddas, for the coal owners had to persuade workmen to settle once more in an undeveloped area which offered few of the amenities of life. There was, at times, a disparity of 25 per cent between the wages paid in the Rhondda valleys and in the Merthyr mines. There occurred in consequence a 'coal rush' into these valleys which was quite unprecedented, and the immigrants came not only from rural Wales and from England but from other parts of the coalfield. The population of the valleys in 1861 stood at 3,000, but had risen to 17,000 at the next census. Working conditions, however, became still more dangerous in the deeper pits. The Mines Act of 1842 (the only 'factory act' which had much bearing on Welsh industry) had prohibited female and child labour in the mines. Providentially this had come before the development of the Rhonddas, and this abuse was unknown there. It persisted however in remote districts, and the government inspector, Tremenheere, drew particular attention to its continuance in south Wales. The added danger came from gas. On July 15, 1856, there occurred an explosion at the Cymer colliery in which 114 of the 156 miners employed were killed outright and the remainder were seriously injured. From this date until the end of the century there were seven other major catastrophes (that is, explosions involving the death of over a hundred men), including a great disaster at Abercarn, on September 11, 1878, when 268 miners were killed. In addition to these there were in this period many smaller explosions, and several thousand deaths from accidents in the pits. This continuous danger produced among the miners a restlessness and disquiet which aggravated industrial strife.

It is highly significant that, at least until 1871, not one single strike of any importance whatsoever was caused by a demand for increased wages; strikes were invariably attempts to resist a reduction in wages. This was true, for example, of the disastrous, if exceptional, strike of some four to five thousand miners in the Aberdare valley in 1857. The employers announced a reduction in wages of 15 per cent, and the workers began a strike which lasted seven weeks. Troops were called in to preserve order, and the miners were not only forced by privation to return to work but had to accept yet another 5 per cent reduction to compensate the owners for their losses during the strike.

A new militancy appeared in the early seventies. Unionism among the miners had progressed more rapidly than among other workers because of the absence of any great cleavage between skilled and unskilled workers within the industry. Several local unions had been established, and in 1869 the Amalgamated Association of Miners, formed in Lancashire, quickly spread to the Rhondda and Aberdare valleys. This coincided with a depression in the coal trade, and so there occurred the first great struggle since the thirties. In February 1871 the owners gave notice of a ten per cent reduction; the

A.A.M. countered this by a demand for a ten per cent rise in wages. It was evident that a trial of strength was impending, and eleven thousand men ceased work in the Rhondda and Aberdare areas. The owners commissioned one Paul Roper, an illiterate strike-breaker, to bring in workers from outside the area, paying him six shillings a head, but he succeeded in inducing only some 400 miners to come from Staffordshire, Cornwall and Yorkshire. After twelve weeks it was decided that the workers should return pending arbitration, and this resulted in an increase in wages and a levelling out of the differences in the rates paid in the mines of the ironmasters and of the 'sale-coal' owners. The miners had won a considerable victory. Their position was further strengthened later in the year by the passing of the Trade Union Act which recognised the complete legality of unionism. Strangely enough, the home secretary who guided this act through parliament was a liberally-minded Welsh coal owner and ironmaster, Henry Austin Bruce, who was soon to become Lord Aberdare. The success of the workers, however, caused the different types of coal owners to close their ranks, and William Thomas Lewis (the future Lord Merthyr) induced them to form the Monmouthshire and South Wales Coal-Owners' Association.

But the depression in the coal trade continued, and in 1872 the employers once more gave notice of a ten per cent reduction in wages. The workers refused to accept this, and in protest against it and against the newly introduced double-shift system, they came out on strike in January 1873. Some fifteen to seventeen thousand men were affected, but this time the unions were unable to support them and they drifted back to work. The price of coal continued to fall (it was 22/- a ton in 1872 but had fallen to 12/- in 1874), and yet again the employers announced a ten per cent reduction. The strike which began in February 1875 affected nearly all the pits in south Wales. It was the greatest strike which had yet occurred, and it was fought with great bitterness. Realising that the miners could not hold out, the owners' association increased the reduction to one of 15 per cent in April, and in May the miners accepted defeat. The A.A.M. had meanwhile become bankrupt and was now dissolved.

The terms on which the miners had returned to work were a 12½ per cent reduction in wages and the introduction of the sliding scale system. This was a device, already known in other industries, by which wages were regulated according to prices. A standard wage was calculated, and a change in the price of coal of one shilling a ton was henceforth to involve a change of 7½ per cent in wages. Wages and prices were to be adjusted every six months, and six months' notice was necessary to terminate the agreement. The first agreement was reached on December 11, 1875. The scale was to be worked by a joint committee of five employers and five representatives of the miners. For eighteen years the presidency of this committee fell to William Thomas Lewis. He was the most autocratic of the coal owners and a strong opponent of all collective bargaining. The vice-president was the miners' leader, William Abraham, better known as Mabon. In 1875 he was thirty-three years of age, and he had emerged as a leader only in the industrial conflicts of the early seventies. An incomparable orator in both Welsh and English, he exercised great influence over his followers and was equally prominent in the activities of Welsh nonconformity, as well as in the eisteddfod and in Welsh cultural life. After the Reform Act of 1884, he entered parliament, possibly the first miner to do so, and he retained a seat until 1920. He was a radical in politics, but he had little sympathy with socialism, for he believed that the interests of employers and workmen were identical and could be adjusted through argument. It was through his influence alone that the sliding scale worked with reasonable smoothness from 1875 to 1902.

The early seventies had seen the growth of craft unions in the metal industries also, notably the Independent Association of Tin-Plate Makers, formed in 1871, which was active mainly in the Swansea district. A demand for a ten per cent reduction in wages led, in May 1874, to a strike which closed nearly all the tin-plate works, but, through the weakness of their unions, the men had to return to work in the following month. This has proved to be the only general stoppage in the tin-plate industry. The dislocation caused by the McKinley tariff led to mass unemployment, and there were numerous strikes in 1891 and 1892. In the general confusion the tin-plate unions disintegrated. These years had, however, seen the growth of unions of unskilled workers, especially after the famous dock strike of 1889 led by John Burns and Tom Mann, and many tin-plate workers joined the Dockers' Union. A conciliation board, comprising representatives of employers and tin-plate workers, was established in 1899, and has proved to be the most remarkable example of collective bargaining in Welsh industry, for, despite conflicts, there has been no strike for half a century. In strange contrast to coal mining, the steel and tin-plate trades of Wales have a remarkable record of industrial peace.

It was in the early seventies, also, that the quarrymen of north Wales became organised. They formed a union in 1874. This met with persistent opposition from Lord Penrhyn, and when the workers at Bethesda submitted certain grievances to him in September 1896 he suspended their representatives from work. Three thousand quarrymen immediately came out on strike. They asked the Board of Trade to arbitrate, but Lord Penrhyn insisted on impossible conditions before he would accept the intervention of government officials, and the strike lasted till August 1897, when the quarrymen obtained the terms which they had originally submitted to him. Intense dissatisfaction continued, however, and in 1900 began a second strike which lasted for no less than three years and in which the quarrymen were beaten. This strike contributed in a marked degree to the ruin of the slate industry. The closing of the largest slate quarry in the world, and the dislocation in supplies and in prices which this produced, led to a search for substitutes, and manufactured tiles came to replace slates in the public taste. Whereas 16,000 men had been employed in the industry in 1898, by 1914 the number had fallen to 8,000.

Industrial relations in Wales, however, continued to be primarily of interest in the coal industry. The sliding scale had met with opposition from the start, particularly since the price of coal fell constantly in the first four years of its operation, so that the scale worked against the interests of the miners. It was not until 1882 that wages had returned to their standard in 1869. There began, therefore, an agitation among the miners for a living wage, that is, a minimum wage independent of prices, as well as for an eight hour day. This agitation was led by younger men, notably William Brace, who attacked not only the mine owners but also Mabon with great bitterness. It led, in April 1898 to a strike for a ten per cent increase on the basic rate for the calculation of the sliding scale. The strike lasted for six months, and half the pits in south Wales were closed, but the workers were defeated, and the sliding scale continued. Yet out of this defeat came the amalgamation of seven miners' unions (including Mabon's Cambrian Miners' Association) into the South Wales Miners' Federation. Mabon still retained sufficient ascendancy to be nominated its first president, and William Brace became vice-president. The Federation then became affiliated to the Miners' Federation of Great Britain. This body was opposed to the sliding scale, which had been abandoned in all other regions, and in 1902 notice of its termination was given by the S.W.M.F. Mabon's personal influence continued to act as a restraint on his associates, but he was now out of sympathy with the militant section of his own federation. Besides, in 1900 Keir Hardie was returned as member of parliament for Merthyr, and with this event working-class radicalism broke away from its associations with the middle class, and a new Labour Party emerged. Mabon became formally a member of the Labour Party only in the last decade of his parliamentary career, and he never advocated socialism.

The miners won a substantial victory in the Eight Hours Act which became operative in July 1909. For the first time in his history the working miner would now be able to see daylight on work days, even in the winter months. But industrial unrest continued, and a dispute in one of D. A. Thomas's pits over work in abnormal places led to a widespread strike in October 1910. There was rioting in Tonypandy in November, and throughout the winter there was upheaval in the coalfield. Large numbers of metropolitan policemen and of soldiers were brought in, and serious trouble was avoided only through the careful handling of the situation by the stipendiary magistrate, Daniel Lleufer Thomas. But the strike ended in disastrous failure for the miners. It was soon followed in 1912 by a general strike of all the miners of Great Britain, involving over a million men, and as a result of this a Minimum Wage Act was passed which, through district negotiation, led to the award to the miner of a minimum wage of about four shillings and sixpence a day.

Opinion among the miners of south Wales had, however, abandoned even the standpoint of such men as William Brace. The younger leaders advocated not only a shorter working day and better conditions but open hostility to their employers. They had completely forsaken Mabon's ideal of a unity of interest. Their ideas were incorporated in a pamphlet, *The Miners' Next Step*, which led to widespread discussion, for it not only advocated a minimum wage of eight shillings for a seven hour day, but also the adoption of methods for decreasing production while remaining at work, methods which were held to be more effective than strikes, and by which the employers would in time be ruined and eliminated. Opinion was further inflamed by a disaster on an unprecedented scale in Lord Merthyr's pit at Senghenydd in 1913 when 439 lives were lost. Thus, on the eve of the First World War, when great combines were being formed by the coal owners and the export trade had expanded so that Cardiff had become the largest coal-exporting port in the world, the coalfield was seething with industrial unrest and its future was ominous.

The century between the end of the Napoleonic wars and the beginning of the First World War had thus seen a social transformation in Wales. Its population had almost quadrupled, and, far from being evenly distributed throughout the country, five-eighths of it was now concentrated in the two shires of Glamorgan and Monmouth. Large towns had grown up, especially along the coast. Merthyr Tydfil retained its priority in the size of its population as late as the census of 1861, with Swansea in the second place, but with the opening of the Rhondda valleys, and the phenomenal growth of the coal export trade, Cardiff entirely outstripped its rivals. The population of the rural areas had, in the meantime, declined, and the balance of Welsh life had been changed. To the time-honoured differences between north and south Wales, and the class distinction between the English speaking landowners and their Welsh peasantry, there had now been added a further division between rural and industrial Wales, a division which was greatly accentuated throughout the century by the influx of a non-Welsh population.

CHAPTER XVI

NONCONFORMITY AND POLITICS

THE political life of Wales in the nineteenth century was determined to a great extent by the spread of nonconformity. In England the different religious denominations which had emerged since the seventeenth century cut across social divisions, and to some degree neutralised them. Landowner and tenant worshipped in the same parish church, while commercial expansion produced in the towns an upper middle class of considerable wealth and eminence which became the backbone of English dissent. But in Wales social distinctions coincided with and were intensified by differences not only in religion but also in language. The gap between the tenant farmer and his landlord, who had become anglicised despite his pride in his long Welsh pedigree, was increased by the spread of nonconformity. In the industrial areas the iron-masters, many of whom had their origins in English middle-class dissent, became allied, through marriage and association, with the gentry, and adopted their anglicanism. Seldom did Welsh workmen attain to high administrative posts. 'In the works,' says a government investigator in 1847, 'the Welsh workman never finds his way into the office. He never becomes either clerk or agent. He may become an overseer or contractor, but this does not take him out of the labouring and put him into the administering class.' The division therefore became as distinct in the coalfield as it was in rural Wales. The English-speaking landowner and the iron-master were anglicans; the Welsh-speaking tenant-farmer and industrial worker became increasingly nonconformist; in fact, nonconformity proved to be the most important link between rural and industrial Wales. Therefore it is seldom possible in the nineteenth century to disentangle social and economic considerations from religious motives.

At the opening of the century the great majority of the people still belonged to the established church, despite the formation of a new denomination in 1811, when the Calvinistic

methodists finally broke away. Conditions within the church
had changed very little in the course of the eighteenth century. In
the reign of George III there were no less than twenty-nine
appointments to Welsh sees, and seventeen of the bishops
obtained transfers to more lucrative places. Obviously appointment was still determined by political reasons. Not one of the
twenty-nine bishops had any association with Wales; needless
to say none had any knowledge of the Welsh language. Absenteeism and nepotism still persisted. Jonathan Shipley, a liberally-
minded prelate, who was appointed to Llandaff in 1769 and
transferred to St. Asaph in the same year, became obnoxious to
the government because of his support of the American colonies.
He was therefore forced to stay in St. Asaph for the long period
of twenty-one years, but, on an average, he visited the see only
once in four years. His son, William Davies Shipley, celebrated
because of his trial for seditious libel in 1783, held the deanery
and chancellorship of the diocese together with three livings for
over fifty years, yet lived in none of his benefices. One of his
vicarages he even let as a public house. Richard Watson,
appointed to Llandaff in 1782 during a brief liberal administration, remained there till his death in 1816. He was one of the
most learned men of his day, but his independence of mind
stood in the way of further preferment. It is noteworthy that the
only two bishops who supported a motion for the repeal of the
Test and Corporation Acts in 1787 were Shipley and Watson.
Yet Watson resided in the Lake District, contenting himself
with visiting his see (where there was, indeed, no provision for
his residence) once a year for confirmation. Despite this he
sharply criticised non-residence among his own clergy, though
he, himself, held sixteen livings. Bishop Luxmore, who was
transferred from the still poorer see of Hereford to St. Asaph in
1815, had not even the intellectual distinction of Shipley and
Watson in his favour. Yet, together with his two sons and a
nephew, Luxmore drew an annual income of £25,000 from the
sees of Hereford and St. Asaph, though the total income of the
working clergy of St. Asaph amounted to only £18,000.
Nepotism was, admittedly, no more common in Wales than in
England, but there was the added objection in Wales that each
relative of a bishop was yet another non-Welsh incumbent in a
Welsh benefice.

Of the lower clergy some belonged to the gentry and were themselves landowners, while others were known to act as land agents for their relatives. Frequently clergymen of this class were non-resident. But the great majority were of humbler origin. Their stipends were low, and, in many cases, their poverty, combined with their illiteracy and insobriety, led to a neglect of their duties. Few could afford to go to a university; many had to be content with a year's instruction at Ystradmeurig, or even at the celebrated school which the Arian divine, David Davis, kept at Castell Hywel. An attempt at reform was made by Samuel Horsley, bishop of St. David's from 1788 to 1793 and of St. Asaph from 1802 to 1806. He was the son of a dissenting minister who had conformed, but he is most celebrated for his controversy with Dr. Joseph Priestley and the unitarians. He refused any longer to ordain candidates who had been taught at Castell Hywel, but he succeeded in raising the minimum stipend of curates in his diocese from £7 to £15 a year.

This state of affairs in Wales caused grave concern to the great reformer, Thomas Burgess, who was bishop of St. David's from 1803 to 1825. He proceeded to licence four schools, at Carmarthen, Ystradmeurig, Lampeter and Brecon, and insisted on seven years' study in them before ordination. He established libraries and encouraged the work of the S.P.C.K. He required proof of proficiency in Welsh from incumbents in Welsh-speaking parishes. Above all, he set out to establish a college, allocating a tenth of his own income each year for this purpose, and encouraging his clergy to do the same. By 1820 he had collected £11,000. He then obtained grants from the king and the universities, and in 1822, the foundation stone was laid at Lampeter. Burgess was transferred to Salisbury before the college was opened in 1827, yet he continued to support it, and bequeathed it substantial legacies. The college obtained the right to grant the degree of Bachelor of Divinity in 1852 and of Bachelor of Arts thirteen years later. Burgess had founded a college to serve his diocese; it was destined to serve the church in the whole of Wales. Of all the English bishops in Wales since the Hanoverian succession, the church and the nation have most reason to be grateful to Thomas Burgess.

The most remarkable aspect of the religious life of Wales in the first half of the nineteenth century was, however, the spread of nonconformity. Separation from the church in 1811 seemed to have released latent energies within the methodist denomination, and it spread rapidly, especially in north Wales. The older dissenters had always been weak in this area, but in these years extensive 'missions' were also undertaken by their preachers from south Wales. Outstanding among these was Christmas Evans, who, for thirty years, served the baptist churches in Anglesey, and went on preaching tours throughout Wales to collect funds in order to build new meeting-houses. William Williams ('o'r Wern'), a native of Merioneth, founded many independent churches in north-east Wales. These two, together with their contemporary, John Elias, formed a triumvirate of preachers such as Wales has at no other time produced, and the spread of nonconformity was due in no small measure to their incomparable oratory and to that of other lesser men.

Even more marked numerically was the growth of dissent in the coalfield. The established church was slow to adapt itself to new conditions. Industrialisation took place in sparsely inhabited areas, where the parishes were enormously wide, and the parish churches were frequently miles away from the new centres of population. Chapels, on the other hand, were hastily built where they were required. As late as 1840 there was only one anglican church in Merthyr, in contrast to twelve nonconformist chapels, while in the industrial strip from Hirwaun to Blaenavon, with a population of 100,000, there were only thirteen anglican churches, in not one of which were the services conducted entirely in Welsh. Moreover, in the welter of conflicting opinions and beliefs which existed in the coalfield, an evangelical religion made a strong appeal to industrial workers, oppressed by the insecurity and hazards of their lives. Thus, when the census of 1851 was taken, it was seen that the anglican church had 1,180 places of worship in Wales, as compared with 2,769 belonging to the dissenters, and, although accurate figures are almost impossible to compute, it can be estimated that dissent accounted for three-quarters of the population.

The surprising vitality shown in the constant effort and financial sacrifice involved in building churches, and in the flood of books and pamphlets published by the various denominations, found expression also in social attitudes and political activity. The chapel, where farmer and labourer, shopkeeper and industrial worker, were on an equality and conducted their own affairs, proved to be a school in democratic management. The Welsh peasantry had hitherto been remarkable for its servility, but this now disappeared. Also, as the nonconformists ceased to be a minority they became less tolerant of the religious disabilities from which they suffered. The Test and Corporation Acts were repealed in 1828, but there were still other grievances, notably exclusion from the universities, the payment of church rates towards the upkeep of ecclesiastical buildings, and restrictions with regard to marriage and burial, restrictions which were the more irritating since they affected the intimate emotions of the people.

The leaders of nonconformity based great hopes on the Reform Act of 1832, but the authority of the anglican landowners (as we have seen) continued unimpaired, and, although the Municipal Corporations Act of 1835 did extend the influence of nonconformists in the towns, while Peel's Marriage Act of 1836 removed one grievance by allowing them to solemnise their own marriages, the leaders deplored the apathy of their followers in not insisting more strongly on their rights. The nonconformist periodicals set out to break down this apathy. *Seren Gomer* continued its advocacy of political reform, and in 1830 the independents started a periodical, *Yr Efangylydd*, with the same purpose in mind. It was edited by David Owen (Brutus), a very remarkable journalist. He had been a baptist pastor, but had been expelled by his denomination because, in his poverty, he had sought financial aid from an unitarian association. His periodical was, however, not sufficiently radical to please his readers, and they, in 1835, started a monthly, *Y Diwygiwr*, edited by David Rees of Llanelly. Brutus, thereupon, undertook to edit an anglican paper, *Yr Haul*, for a Llandovery publisher. This was moderate to begin with, but became increasingly hostile to the nonconformists. In it Brutus lashed his former associates mercilessly. He poured bitter satire on their way of life and their religious services, and held them responsible for all the social and political unrest. The *Diwygiwr* had, in fact, adopted for its motto O'Connell's war-cry, 'Agitate, agitate, agitate.' It eagerly supported Chartism and defended the Rebecca rioters. Indeed in its pages may be seen not only opposition to church rates and to tithes, but the growth of a movement for disestablishing the anglican church, a movement which proved that the dissatisfaction of the nonconformists went deeper than a demand for the removal of grievances.

The leadership of political nonconformity fell to the independents. The baptists were less definite in their standpoint, for Christmas Evans, a convinced Calvinist, preached obedience to those in authority. The methodists remained sternly aloof. They still retained the political quietism of their predecessors, and their periodical, *Y Drysorfa*, declared that political agitation was identical with atheism, involving a disregard for divine scripture as well as for the law of the land. This attitude was reinforced by the enormous influence of John Elias. He had secured the excommunication of those members of the Welsh Calvinistic methodist church in Jewin Crescent, London, who had joined in agitation for Roman catholic emancipation. It was under his direction that the methodists condemned trade unionism. In 1839 the *sasiwn* at Llandovery forbade any member to become a Chartist, and in the following year, at Llanidloes, expressed joy that not a single methodist had joined the rioters. Already the *sasiwn* at Bala in 1834 had unanimously adopted John Elias's proposal formally condemning the movement for disestablishment. But his extreme standpoint and his dictatorial attitude produced a reaction, and, before his death in 1841, younger leaders such as John Jones, Talysarn, were already in revolt against him.

The forties saw a tremendous increase in periodical literature. Many of these papers were short-lived, for they encountered great difficulties. The tax of 3½d. on each copy had been reduced in 1836 to one penny, but still remained a burden. Distribution also was difficult, and people had not yet become accustomed to taking a paper. Yet in 1843 there appeared two periodicals of considerable significance. One of these was a monthly, *Y Cronicl*, edited by Samuel Roberts of Llanbrynmair. Samuel Roberts (who is known in Welsh letters as S.R.) was then forty-three years of age. After a period in dissenting academies he had returned to help his father in the pastorate of ten small independent churches. For the support of the family the father also rented a farm, Y Diosg. S.R.'s politics thus arose out of his experiences as a country pastor and as the tenant of an upland farm, and his periodical, published at three half-pence and written in simple language, was intended for countryfolk such as those whom he met every day. He championed the cause of the peasants of Wales against the tyranny of the landlords and their agents, against heavy taxation, tithes and church rates. He was foremost in advocating reforms, such as the penny postage, the railway, and new methods in agriculture. Above all he was an advocate of the cause of international peace.

The other new periodical was a fortnightly, *Yr Amserau*, published at threepence by a firm of Liverpool printers, and edited for ten years by William Rees (Gwilym Hiraethog). William Rees was two years younger than S.R. He was born in a farm on the Hiraethog moorlands. His elder brother, Henry Rees, became the recognised leader of the methodists after John Elias's death, but by temperament William Rees was more akin to the older dissenters, and he became an independent minister. Nothing illustrates the contrast between Calvinistic methodism and the older dissent better than the difference between these two brothers, for whereas Henry Rees was entirely non-political in his outlook, William Rees was primarily a politician. In *Yr Amserau* he discussed all matters of domestic and foreign politics. A series of letters written by him in the Hiraethog dialect, and purporting to be the compositions of an old farmer (Llythyrau 'Rhen Ffarmwr), proved immensely popular, for in them he discussed with wit and humour all the problems which faced his readers. It is probable that he had greater influence than anyone else in the formation of Welsh public opinion in the nineteenth century.

A periodical of a very different kind was founded two years later by Lewis Edwards, principal of the methodist college at Bala. This was a quarterly, *Y Traethodydd*, modelled on the great English quarterlies of the day. Lewis Edwards was one of the best writers of Welsh prose, and the literary and philosophical essays in *Y Traethodydd* were of a very high standard. They did much to break down the prejudice amongst Calvinistic methodists against secular literature.

The problem of education stood on the border line between religion and politics, and for a time the controversies which it aroused absorbed the attention of nonconformists almost to the exclusion of everything else. The provision in Wales for both primary and secondary education was totally inadequate. There were a number of grammar schools together with some schools of the genteel sort which provided secondary education. Most of the others were 'private adventure schools' conducted by individuals for their own profit. Some of these were very remarkable men, such as James Davies, the pedlar of Devauden, but many were utterly incompetent, being not too unlike the wooden-legged reprobate, Robin the Soldier, immortalised in Daniel Owen's novel, *Rhys Lewis*. Neither the undenominational British Society nor the anglican National Society made much headway in Wales. The assistance they gave depended upon local demand. The nonconformists, however, refused to send their children to the National schools, because they were taught the catechism there and compelled to attend church on Sundays. On the other hand, the nonconformists were too poor to bear the initial burden of establishing British schools, and could hope for no support from their anglican landowners. The grant of £10,000 to each society made by the government in 1833 proved of little benefit to Wales, for the money was still distributed on a pound for pound basis in proportion to local subscriptions.

The close connection between education and religion was thrown into high relief in 1843 by a bill, introduced into parliament by Sir James Graham, which proposed to place the education of children employed in mines and factories under the control of the established church. The bill was eventually withdrawn, but it caused great outcry in Wales, not merely because it would have placed the established church in a privileged position but because a large section of nonconformity objected in principle to state grants for education. They regarded education as an essential part of religious training, and as they objected to state control of religion they objected, also, to a state system of education. David Rees strongly upheld this standpoint in *Y Diwygiwr*, and S.R., with characteristic asperity and exaggeration, denounced state grants as 'a social injustice of the most detestable type.' Others, however, appreciated that education could not be effectively provided without aid from the state. Prominent among these was Hugh Owen. He was a native of Anglesey, and at this time was clerk in the poor law commissioners' office in London. In 1843 he was only thirty-nine years of age, and for nearly forty years he was to be the leading figure in Welsh educational movements. To bring his views to the attention of his fellow-countrymen he addressed to them, on August 26, 1843, a 'Letter to the Welsh People,' and had it widely distributed. He sought to justify the acceptance of state grants towards secular education, and explained in simple terms the means by which a British school could be set up in a particular locality, gratuitously offering his own services as an intermediary with the British Society and the government. Later in the year he induced the British Society to appoint a special agent for north Wales, where there were in existence only two British schools.

The next three years were a period of considerable educational activity. Through the labours of their agent, John Phillips, the British Society established forty-two schools in north Wales. The voluntaryists, that is, the opponents of state aid, were strongest in south Wales, and there they formed the South Wales Education Committee to build their own schools, and, in 1846, established a 'normal' school at Brecon for the training of teachers. The National Society, also, devoted much attention to Wales, and, in 1845, published a report which strongly criticised the inadequate provision for education in the principality.

It was this report which led William Williams, the member of parliament for Coventry, to raise the matter in the house of commons. He was a native of Conwil, of working-class parentage, who had prospered in London, and this may account for the precise terms of reference of the commission which he induced the government to appoint: 'to enquire into the state of education in the Principality of Wales, especially into the means afforded to the labouring classes of acquiring a knowledge of the English language.' However this may be, the commission was to prove the main landmark in the nineteenth century, not only in the educational but in the social and political history of Wales.

The instructions drawn up for the guidance of the commissioners by James Kay-Shuttleworth, secretary to the committee of the privy council on education, were clear and unexceptionable. They were to ascertain the facts which would enable the government to improve the provision made for education, and were to hear evidence from all, dissenters and anglicans, rich and poor, with courtesy, sympathy and impartiality. But the commission was unfortunate even in its composition. Three young men, Lingen, Symons and Vaughan Johnson, were appointed as chief commissioners. One of them had recently become a barrister while the other two had not yet been called to the bar. They were exceptionally able, but all three were anglicans, and had no knowledge of education, of Wales, or of the working class. Ten sub-commissioners were chosen to assist them, but of these seven were anglicans, five being students at St. David's College, Lampeter, and not themselves of a very high standard in education, while of the remaining three, who were nonconformists, two thought good to resign immediately. Some three hundred witnesses were examined, but four out of every five of these were anglicans. The commissioners did their work with great thoroughness and published their findings in 1847 in three enormous volumes, but, even without any deliberate intention to be unfair, they could hardly be expected to present an impartial picture of a nation which had now become predominantly nonconformist.

The state of education in Wales was shown in these reports to be deplorable. Many parishes had no schools at all, and in very few parishes was there adequate provision. In some instances a room in a farmhouse, a part of an outbuilding, a loft over a chapel, or even a stable, was used as a school-room. In particular, many of the teachers were absurdly incompetent. Frequently they had taken up teaching late in life, because of some misfortune, such as the loss of a leg or an arm, and had had little or no training. Their knowledge of English was often very defective, although they taught only in English. By and large the judgement passed on the schools in the reports was justified, yet it is doubtful if they were quite as bad as they were made to appear. For the commissioners assumed that ignorance of the English language was, in all respects, synonymous with illiteracy, and impartial commentators, such as Dean Cotton of Bangor, deplored the use made of the methods of the bar to trap bewildered and unsuspecting children into making absurd statements, which were then reproduced in the reports, in astonishing detail, as evidence of backwardness.

Education and religion were as inseparably connected in

the minds of the commissioners as in those of the voluntaryists, and this led them to strictures on the morals of the Welsh people. On the evidence of clerical witnesses they held that Welsh country-women were 'almost universally unchaste,' and, further, that the week-night services of the dissenters were the occasion, if not even the cause, of this incontinence. The Welsh language, also, was 'a manifold barrier to the moral progress,' as to the commercial prosperity, of the people. It pandered to prevarication, if not to perjury and worse. There was, it is true, a marked absence of the greater crimes, but Symons was inclined to attribute this 'to the extreme shrewdness and caution of the people,' rather than to any virtue on their part.

The reaction to the reports was painful in the extreme. Some nonconformists were inclined, at first, to accept the dark picture as merely confirming their view of the general depravity of human nature. But this soon gave way to a wave of indignation, the intensity of which can scarcely be overestimated. On the analogy of Brad y Cyllyll Hirion (the treachery of the long knives), a mythical incident in the ancient wars between the Saxons and the Welsh, the reports were invested with the epithet, Brad y Llyfrau Gleision (the treachery of the blue books), and as such they are still known. Innumerable writers and speakers attacked them with violence, and two, in particular, should be specially noted. Dr. Lewis Edwards in *Y Traethodydd* analysed the reports with care, and pointed out the deficiencies of the commissioners, as well as their unfairness in accepting the opinions of clerical witnesses as being equal to facts, and in neglecting the merits of schools while minutely recording their faults. The other writer, Evan Jones (Ieuan Gwynedd), was a young independent minister of twenty-seven when the reports appeared, and died five years later. He had already shown much vehemence in attacking those of his fellow dissenters who were prepared to accept state grants for education, and he brought to his attack on the reports an intensity of emotion to which his sickly and febrile constitution no doubt contributed. But he was tireless in subjecting the evidence of the reports to rigorous criticism, in collecting data which enabled comparisons to be made with rural areas in England, and in proving that even on the basis of the reports themselves the sweeping conclusions of the commissioners were not justified.

THE SCHOOL OF JAMES DAVIES, A PEDLAR, AT DEVAUDEN

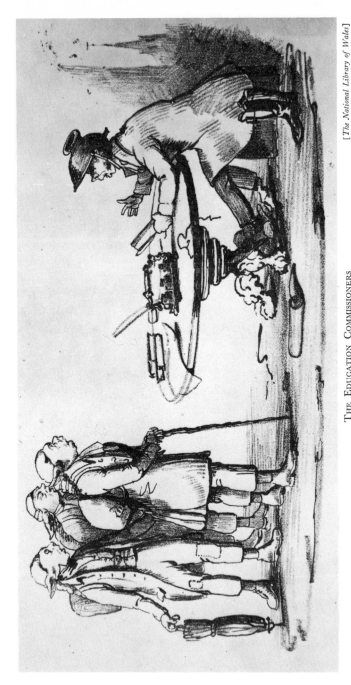

THE EDUCATION COMMISSIONERS

[*The National Library of Wales*]

Note the asses' ears beneath their barristers' wigs. The coal scuttle is a reference to Sir James Kay Shuttleworth's name.

Eminent churchmen, such as Dean Cotton of Bangor, deplored the reports, and, in fact, the best reply to them came from a devout anglican layman, Sir Thomas Phillips, the defender of Newport against the Chartists in 1839. Two years after their appearance he published a reasoned examination of the state of education in Wales in a book entitled, *Wales, the Language, Social Condition, Moral Character and Religious Opinions of the People, considered in their Relation to Education*, which still remains the standard work on the subject. But the chief result of the reports was to exacerbate the relations between the nonconformist majority of the Welsh people and the anglican minority, and the bitterness of the struggle between them later in the century was attributable, in large degree, to the ineptitude of Sir James Kay-Shuttleworth's commissioners and their disregard of his instructions.

In their effect on education the reports strengthened the hands of the voluntaryists, for they were a painful object lesson of what government interference might mean. But, by 1853, it was clear that voluntaryism had failed; even David Rees's schools in Llanelly accepted government grants in that year. In the same year also, Hugh Owen induced the British Society to appoint a special representative, William Roberts (Nefydd), in south Wales. The chief impediment to progress now came from a lack of teachers, and it was decided, again on the initiative of Hugh Owen, to establish a Training College at Bangor. Temporary premises were acquired in 1858, and the college itself opened in 1862 with John Phillips as its first principal. The National Society had already established a training school at Caernarvon in 1846 and had expanded it into a college in 1849, while in 1848 the Society opened the Carmarthen Training College to serve the needs of south Wales.

The eighteen-forties, therefore, saw not only social disturbances in both rural and industrial Wales, but bitter sectarian differences over education. They saw also a remarkable revival in efficiency within the anglican church. By the Pluralities Act of 1838 the age-long abuse of pluralism was, at last, removed. But the change in Wales was due primarily to the appointment of four reforming bishops of outstanding ability and great personal integrity. Of these the most eminent was Connop Thirlwall, appointed bishop of St. David's in 1840.

He was soon followed by Vowler Short at St. Asaph and Alfred
Ollivant at Llandaff, while James Campbell was appointed to
Bangor in the next decade. These men devoted their long lives
to the service of their sees, and stayed in them for an average of
thirty years. The days of rapid transfer to more lucrative benefices were gone. They reorganised their dioceses, rearranged
parishes and built churches where they were wanted to meet
the needs of a growing population. Yet reform alone did not
solve the problem in Wales, as was evident in the case of Thirlwall. He was one of the greatest churchmen of his age, a man of
towering intellectual ability; he even learnt Welsh and acquired
sufficient confidence to preach in it. But his relations with his
own clergy were singularly unfortunate. He expressed his contempt for them, their persons and their habits, in brutally frank
terms, and within a decade his coldness and reserve had completely alienated them, so that they responded with a dislike
which was little short of hatred. This could be remedied only
by bishops chosen from among the Welsh people themselves,
who appreciated their peculiar needs and difficulties. A group of
Welsh clergy in the West Riding of Yorkshire had drawn this
to the attention of Sir Robert Peel, then prime minister, as
early as 1835, but it was only after a similar memorial had been
presented to Gladstone by Dean Edwards of Bangor in 1870
that Joshua Hughes was appointed to St. Asaph in that year,
the first Welsh-speaking Welshman nominated to a Welsh
diocese since the reign of Queen Anne.

Of more immediate importance was the spread of the
Oxford movement in Wales. The most outstanding Welshman
in the movement was Isaac Williams, an early associate of
Pusey and Newman, and author of one of the 'Tracts.' On his
brother's lands in the vale of Clarach, near Aberystwyth, he
was instrumental in having built the church of Llangorwen, in
order to counteract the spread of nonconformity in Cardiganshire. Its chancel was modelled on Newman's church at Little-
more, and the lectern was a gift from Keble. But the tractarians
were most numerous in the diocese of Bangor, where they were
encouraged by Campbell's predecessor, Bishop Bethell. They
were not exceptional men, the most notable being Morris
Williams (Nicander), the incumbent of an Anglesey parish
for thirty years, but they formed a remarkable group. Their

chief importance lay in the reaction which they aroused in Wales, for they were regarded as progressing towards the Roman catholic church. The *Amserau*, in its original prospectus, declared one of its primary purposes to be 'to oppose the super-stitious, unchristian and papal doctrines and practices of both Oxford and Rome.' Even the methodists, who had been so reluctant to leave the established church, shared with the older dissenters a violent detestation of Roman catholicism. Besides, tractarianism was associated with extreme toryism in Wales, and, coinciding as it did with the emotional ferment caused by the education reports, it converted the methodists to the point of view of the older dissent, thus serving to unite the ranks of nonconformity into a strong radical political force. The radicalising of the methodists proved to be the most important development in the social history of rural Wales in the nineteenth century.

This was soon apparent in the agrarian problem. Conditions in rural Wales became greatly eased in the fifties; in fact it is doubtful whether there was any agrarian problem peculiar to Wales after this decade. But it was now that opposition to the landowners became most vocal, and this reflected both the growing political consciousness of the Welsh peasantry, and a realisation of strength on the part of the nonconformists now that they represented a majority of the Welsh nation. Hiraethog, in Llythyrau 'Rhen Ffarmwr, exposed the main grievance of both Welsh and English peasants—the advantage taken by their land-owners to raise their rents on account of improvements carried out by the tenants themselves. This was also the theme of two widely read pamphlets by S.R., *Farmer Careful of Cilhaul Uchaf* (1850), and particularly *A History of Diosg Farm* (1854), in which he related the experience of his own family.

For a time S.R. sought a solution of all the problems of the Welsh peasant in emigration. Throughout the century a constant stream of emigrants had left Wales, settling, almost without exception, in the United States of America. There, the land-hunger of generations of Welsh peasants was at last satisfied. S.R. adopted the idea of Morgan John Rhys, half a century earlier, and sought to settle the Welsh together in a community. So, in 1856, he purchased 100,000 acres of land in eastern Tennessee, and a party of emigrants set out under the leadership of his brother. S.R. himself followed with another party in the spring of 1857. But the experiment was a failure. Much of the land was poor; S.R. was soon involved in legal disputes about rights of ownership, and the outbreak of the Civil War brought complete disaster. The Welsh nonconformists strongly supported the northern states in this war, and S.R. incurred much obloquy in Wales because he was suspected of supporting the south. He defended himself on the grounds that war was as great an evil as slavery, and that one evil should not be used to wipe out another. His community was dispersed, and, in 1867, S.R. himself returned to Wales.

In the meantime a crisis had been reached in Wales. The land was swept in 1859 by one of the periodical religious revivals which are such a marked feature of its religious life. This coincided with a general election. The member for Merioneth in the previous two parliaments was W. W. E. Wynne of Peniarth, a very celebrated antiquary. But he was an ardent tractarian, and had been instrumental in introducing ritualistic changes in the neighbouring parish church of Llanegryn. The nonconformists, on this account, induced David Williams of Castell Deudraeth to contest the seat. This threat to their privileged position immediately roused the landowners to action. They instructed their tenants to vote for Wynne, and when nineteen tenants of the Rhiwlas estate, near Bala, asked permission to abstain altogether from voting, on conscientious grounds, they were each personally interviewed by the landowner. Wynne was returned by a small majority, but three of the Rhiwlas tenants who had abstained from voting and two who had voted for Williams were forthwith evicted from their farms. Moreover on the Wynnstay estate, eleven who had remained neutral had their rents raised and five who had voted for Williams were evicted, though Sir Watkin Williams Wynn was careful to explain that this had no connection with the election. A sinister attempt to exercise economic pressure in elections had thus become evident in Wales, and a further step was taken in the following year when a Cardiganshire landowner informed her tenants that they must either become members of the church of England or leave her estate.

Political pressure had hitherto been almost unknown in rural Wales, for the landowners had been sufficiently sure of their position. It was the loss of this security which now made them adopt repressive measures. It became evident that a trial of strength was impending, and this was brought nearer by the Reform Act of 1867, which greatly extended the franchise and gave Merthyr a second member. On this account the election of 1868 was a memorable one. The dissenters had made a careful choice of candidates, the most notable being Henry Richard, the candidate for Merthyr. He was already fifty-six years of age and had taken an active part in public life. The son of a Calvinistic methodist minister, he had himself become the pastor of an independent church in London. There he had championed Welsh causes, as for example, in the blue book controversy. At first a voluntaryist he had come to accept state aid for education. But in 1848 he relinquished his pastorate to become the secretary of the Peace Society, which had been founded in 1816 by Joseph Tregelles Price, the quaker iron-master of Neath, and others. He was returned to parliament in the 1868 election at the head of the poll for Merthyr, and he retained his seat till his death. He was the first real exponent in the house of commons of the point of view of Welsh nonconformity. He was also the first British member of parliament to keep the organisation of peace before the government of the country, in face of the wave of triumphant nationalism which swept over Europe, engulfing it in bloodshed.

The most stirring election in 1868 was, however, in Denbighshire. There the liberal candidate was George Osborne Morgan, the son of a vicar of Conway, who had had an unusually brilliant academic career at Oxford, and who had reacted so strongly against the tractarian movement in the university that, while remaining a member of the church of England, he was to become a champion of disestablishment in Wales. But more interesting than the candidate was his chief supporter, the Denbigh publisher, Thomas Gee. It was he who had assumed full financial responsibility for *Y Traethodydd* in 1845; in the following years he had published a Welsh encyclopaedia, *Y Gwyddoniadur*, involving an outlay of £20,000, and, in 1857, he founded a Welsh weekly, *Y Faner*, which, two years later, incorporated *Yr Amserau*, and, with the title of *Baner ac Amserau Cymru*, has continued until the present day. Thomas Gee became the acknowledged leader of political nonconformity in north Wales. He was, himself, a recognised methodist preacher, and he aptly illustrates the change which had come over Welsh methodism since the days of John Elias. In his hands the election of 1868 became a bitter assault on the landowners both on the platform and in the press. Sir Watkin Williams Wynn still succeeded in heading the poll, but George Osborne Morgan won the second of the two seats for the shire.

As a result of the 1868 election, Wales was represented in parliament by twenty-one Liberals and twelve Conservatives. There followed immediately widespread political evictions, no less than seventy in Carmarthenshire and Cardiganshire. This was denounced in parliament by Henry Richard and George Osborne Morgan, and their evidence helped considerably in securing the passing of the Ballot Act in 1872. Both members incessantly brought nonconformist grievances before the house. In no less than ten sessions they introduced burial bills, until, in 1880, the Burial Act authorised the use of any Christian form of service in parish churchyards. The Reform Act of 1884 again extended the franchise and increased the number of constituencies in Wales. Denbighshire was now divided into two single member constituencies, and George Osborne Morgan chose to stand for east Denbighshire, which was the centre of the Wynn influence. By his defeat of Sir Watkin in the election of 1885 he brought to an end a period of 182 years of unbroken representation by the Wynns. With the Local Government Act of 1888 most of the administrative work which had hitherto been done by the justices of the peace passed into the hands of popularly elected bodies. This deprived the gentry of much of their influence in their own localities, and the decline of squire-archy was nowhere better illustrated than by the election of the methodist, Thomas Gee, as the first chairman of the Denbighshire County Council.

These developments, however, coincided with an agricultural depression, which, once more, brought grievances to the surface. The rural population of Wales, which had shown an increase in every census until 1841, showed thenceforward a marked and continuous decline. It was evident that the social character of rural life was unsatisfactory, and that the superior economic and social opportunities of the towns and industrial areas were proving an irresistible attraction for the youth of the countryside. Rural crafts declined, and the trend was the more serious since the population left behind in the rural areas had a greater proportion of middle-aged and old people, and therefore had less efficiency. This migration was extremely marked in the eighties, because it coincided with an economic depression. The Franco-German war of 1870 had produced a sharp financial crisis, which had widespread consequences. But even more important was the opening up of new countries. Wheat from the vast cornfields of America and cattle from the endless grasslands now competed with home-grown products with disastrous effects. The depression was very acute in Wales in 1879, and continued throughout the next decade.

The growth of nonconformity made it certain that the financial stringency in rural Wales would lead to an increased reluctance to pay tithes, which the farmers had always regarded as an injustice. Meetings of protest against tithes were held from 1883 onwards, and some clergymen voluntarily agreed to rebates. Others refused, and in 1886, troubles began in the Vale of Clwyd. Attempts were made to distrain upon the goods of those who refused to pay, but they were frustrated by the local populace. In August, therefore, the device of importing an English auctioneer, protected by a squad of fifty policemen, was adopted at an auction at Llanarmon. The farmers retaliated by forming an anti-tithe society to reimburse those whose cattle were seized, and by arranging that, at the first indication of a sale, large crowds should be summoned from the surrounding farms by the blowing of horns. By November there were tithe troubles in nearly every shire in Wales. The Vale of Clwyd still remained the chief centre, and there, at Llangwm, an attempt, in May 1887, to hold a sale very early in the morning, and to take away two cows from a defaulting farmer, led to a scuffle between the crowd and the police in which many were injured. As a result troops were drafted into the area, and this greatly exasperated the people. So, when soldiers were brought to a sale at Mochdre in June, a skirmish took place and the Riot Act was read. This forced the government to appoint a commission to enquire into the disturbances. Nevertheless rioting broke out afresh in May 1888 in Llannefydd, and troops were again called in. Eventually, the Tithe Act of 1891, initiated by the newly-appointed bishop of St.

Asaph, A. G. Edwards, who was deeply concerned at the suffering of his own clergy through the loss of their revenues, made tithe payable by the landlord and not by the tenant. The landlord naturally reimbursed himself by increasing his rents accordingly, but it was now impossible for the tenant to refuse the payment of tithes without at the same time refusing to pay rent and thus losing his farm.

The 'tithe war' was the Rebecca Riots of north Wales, and like them, it drew attention to problems other than the immediate cause of the dispute. For it was the tithe riots which made both the land question and disestablishment matters of practical politics. The relations between landlord and tenant had become aggravated by long years of social and sectarian bitterness as well as by the economic depression. Rack-renting continued, for the land hunger of the Welsh peasantry kept up the demand for farms, and landowners took advantage of this competition to keep their rents high. The game laws were oppressive and a constant source of irritation, since in no other branch of their work did the landed gentry on the bench administer justice with such inexorable severity. An Agricultural Holdings Act of 1875 had sought to provide adequate compensation to tenants for improvements carried out by them on their farms, but its action was permissive only, and its provisions were adopted in Wales only on very few estates. A new act of 1883 made these provisions compulsory, yet many landowners still inserted into their agreements with their tenants patently illegal clauses contracting out of their obligations. Meanwhile an act of 1881 relating to Ireland had provided for the free sale by the tenant of his interests in his holding, for fixity of tenure and for the assessment of a fair rent by an independent tribunal. The enviable position of the Irish tenant had much to do with the demand for similar concessions in Wales.

No one had the example of Ireland more clearly in his mind than Thomas Edward Ellis, who, at the age of twenty-seven, became member of parliament for Merioneth in 1886. He was the son of a tenant on the Rhiwlas estate, and, in the year of his birth, four of his relatives had been among those evicted for their political opinions. His father had himself suffered through the petty tyranny of land agents and gamekeepers. Before his sixteenth birthday, Thomas Edward Ellis

became a student at Aberystwyth. He remained there for four
and a half years, and, after another five years at New College,
Oxford, he graduated in 1884. His academic career was undistinguished, but he prepared himself for political life both by his
wide reading and by his association with future political
leaders at Oxford. He was possessed of a rare charm of manner,
a wide culture, considerable sensibility in art and literature,
deep moral fervour and an intense passion for social justice.
His defeat of a Merioneth landowner in the election of
1886 was regarded not merely as a personal victory but as a
triumph for the peasantry of Wales.

Ellis immediately voiced the grievances of his people both in
regard to tithes and to land tenure, but with little effect until
Gladstone's fourth administration was formed after the election
of 1892. This election proved to be of the greatest importance to
Wales, for the government majority amounted to only forty,
and Wales had returned thirty-one Liberal members with only
three Conservatives. The election had been fought in Wales
over the two questions of land reform and disestablishment.
Ellis therefore persuaded Gladstone in 1893 to set up a royal
commission 'to enquire into the conditions and circumstances
under which land in Wales and Monmouthshire is held, occupied and cultivated.' This commission was composed of nine
men, and Daniel Lleufer Thomas was appointed its secretary.
It held eighty-six meetings throughout the length and breadth
of Wales and in London, and took evidence from over a
thousand witnesses. In 1896 it published a voluminous report,
together with five volumes of evidence and an invaluable
volume of appendices dealing with various aspects of Welsh
rural life.

The commissioners failed to agree in their conclusion, for
six advocated the establishment of a land court, as in Ireland,
while three were against it. Moreover the Liberal ministry had
fallen in 1895, and no legislation to introduce land reform could
be expected from a Conservative government. The enormous
labours of the commission had, therefore, no practical effect.
Nevertheless it had proved of great value, for it had given an
opportunity for a public discussion of grievances and had
effectively cleared the air. Cases of oppression which it revealed
related in most instances to earlier decades, but the commission

had brought the powerful force of public opinion to bear on the relations of landowner and tenant with beneficial effects. The Conservative administration lasted for ten years; when the Liberals returned in 1905 the state of agriculture had again improved, and the question of land reform was not raised.

The new Liberal government's concern in Wales was almost entirely with disestablishment, another proof that the problem of rural Wales was, in essence, not agrarian but religious. A movement for disestablishment had been growing in Wales throughout the century, but the real struggle came only after the success of the Irish Disestablishment Act in 1869. Once more it was the example of Ireland which inspired Wales. But Gladstone, although he had sponsored the Irish measure, was a devout anglican, and was lukewarm in his support, though he still retained his personal ascendancy over the Welsh members. Various bills were introduced to disestablish the church in Wales, but were all thrown out. The motion of Lewis Llewelyn Dillwyn, the member for Swansea, in 1886, that 'the established church in the Principality was an anomaly and an injustice which ought no longer to exist' was lost, although twenty-eight of the thirty-four Welsh members voted for it. The established church was meanwhile organising its defence, and in 1889 it secured an eminent leader in A. G. Edwards, the newly appointed bishop of St. Asaph. He was to prove a remarkable prelate, a brilliant and effective controversialist, and a man of great intellectual vigour. He was ably seconded by John Owen, later bishop of St. David's, a fervent orator who lacked the asperity of his leader and retained the affection even of his political opponents. Gladstone's majority in 1892 depended, as we have seen, on Welsh support, but he was still reluctant to commit himself on Welsh disestablishment. In 1895, as an ordinary member, he withdrew his support of the bill brought in by the Home Secretary, H. H. Asquith. With the fall of the Liberal government in the same year (to which Welsh disestablishment contributed) the question remained in abeyance for ten years.

The return of the Liberals with an enormous majority in 1905 made it certain that new measures would be introduced into parliament. But first of all, a royal commission was appointed in 1906 to obtain accurate information. Its figures showed that some 74 per cent of the full members of protestant churches in Wales were now nonconformist, as against 26 per cent who were anglicans. A bill, based on its report, was twice passed by the house of commons, only to be rejected by the lords, and it became law in 1914 through the operation of the Parliament Act. It both disestablished and partially disendowed the church in Wales, but it was decided that the date of disestablishment should be postponed until the end of the war which had broken out. For the purpose of disendowment the year 1662 was adopted as marking the final division of the Welsh people into two religious persuasions. All churches, parsonages and endowments given since that year were retained by the church. The ancient endowments, valued at some £4,000,000, were secularised. Two-thirds of these endowments were to be applied by the county councils to charitable purposes; the remainder passed to the University of Wales and the National Library.

No time was lost in providing the new church with a constitution in preparation for its disestablishment, and this prodigious task was undertaken by Mr. Justice Sankey, with the aid of other eminent jurists and scholars. The constitution provided for a Representative Body to have charge of church property and finance, and a Governing Body to deal with other matters. When the war came to an end the affairs of the nation were in the hands of a Welsh prime minister, David Lloyd George, who had ardently championed disestablishment. The bitterness of the struggle had, however, already been partly forgotten in the calamity of war, and the prime minister was anxious that it should not be revived. He therefore sponsored, in 1919, a Welsh Church Temporalities Act, which authorised the payment of a sum of £1,000,000 to the church, and in other ways mitigated the financial injury of disendowment. This caused deep chagrin to the more intransigent nonconformists but it was welcomed by the nation as a whole. The church in Wales came into existence on March 31, 1920. It was now entirely separated from the province of Canterbury, and Bishop Edwards became its first archbishop. A new diocese of Monmouth was formed in 1921, and another of Swansea and Brecon in 1923.

Thus came to an end a long chapter in the history of Wales, and the consequences of the change have proved to be profound.

Here it can only be noted that the clergy are no longer committed to one political party, as they had been for over a century through the exigencies of church defence, while the pastors, with the ending of the long and bitter struggle against the anglican church, have irretrievably lost their leadership in political affairs. Since then the correlation of nonconformity and politics in Wales has ceased to have any meaning.

CHAPTER XVII

THE GROWTH OF NATIONAL CONSCIOUSNESS

VARIOUS factors which have influenced the growth and development of the Welsh nation have been indicated in earlier chapters. Of these the most important is the anglicisation of the gentry, a process which was almost complete by the nineteenth century. It proved a marked loss to Welsh life, since it deprived native art and literature not only of the encouragement of the gentry but of their active participation. On this account the literary revival in Wales in the nineteenth century bore unmistakable indications of a peasant origin. Differences in class and language, as we have seen, were accentuated by religious divisions. Furthermore, both the anglican church and the nonconformist bodies were integrally associated with their counterparts in England, and thus hindered the growth of a separate Welsh nationality. In the course of the nineteenth century the industrialisation of Wales added a further division in so far as it brought in a large non-Welsh population which has never been assimilated. Besides, industrialism linked Wales with England as never before in its history. While Wales was isolated geographically, and was almost self-sufficing economically, the influence of England was not strong. But the building of roads and railways, and the enormous growth of Welsh industry as part of the economic development of Britain, profoundly affected Welsh life; so much so that there is still a marked tendency to regard Welsh culture as being in essence the culture of rural Wales and not of the industrial areas.

In addition to these factors there has been the absence of a unifying political organisation. England was welded into a conscious unit by its powerful rulers and its central administrative bodies. These Wales has lacked, and, early in the nineteenth century, it lost its one remaining instrument of government in the disappearance of the Courts of Great Sessions. They had always incurred the jealousy of the courts of Westminster, and their abolition was included among schemes for financial reform introduced at the end of the eighteenth century. A committee appointed to enquire into the working of the courts in 1817 brought to light several abuses. The Welsh judges could continue to sit in parliament, and appointments were frequently made as rewards for political support. Also, the judges could still practise at the English bar, and it was at least possible for a judge to be consulted in his capacity as counsel on a case which would later be tried before him. Since the judges went constantly on the same restricted circuit they became intimately acquainted with the gentry of the neighbourhood, and might find it difficult to be impartial in cases concerning them. No instances of corruption or of malpractice were produced, however, and it was pointed out that the courts were cheap, efficient and popular. The Welsh members of parliament were divided. The most prominent of those who defended the courts was John Jones, the member for the Carmarthen boroughs. But it is evident that he was not influenced by nationalist motives because he deeply deplored the application of Madam Bevan's legacies, now released from chancery, to establish Welsh schools, since these perpetuated the use of the Welsh language which he believed to be greatly on the decline. Despite some protests in Wales, the Courts of Great Sessions were swept away in 1830, and two circuits, subject to the courts at Westminster, were substituted for them. The union of England and Wales was thereby completed.

The foundation of national unity in Wales and of a consciousness of difference from England, despite these adverse factors, can be found, above all, in the persistence of the Welsh language. No figures are available, but it is probable that a very great majority of the people of Wales spoke Welsh at the beginning of the nineteenth century. This was true even of the industrial areas, for much of the migration into the coalfield up till that time was from rural Wales, as is shown by the number of Welsh chapels which were founded in these years in the towns and seaports. Yet there is very little evidence of a conscious desire to preserve the language, let alone to establish institutions with that end in view. There had, for a century, been a growing interest in Welsh antiquities, not least among the anglicised gentry, and, in 1707, Edward Lhuyd, in his *Archæologia Britannica*, laid the basis for all subsequent study of the Celtic languages. In his *Drych y Prif Oesoedd*, published in 1716, Theophilus Evans produced an uncritical history of Wales which gained much popularity because of its literary merit. Also, attempts were made towards the middle of the century to collect and copy old Welsh manuscripts. Much of this work owed its inspiration to the Society of Cymmrodorion, founded in London in 1751, which had Richard Morris as its first president. He was one of the three Anglesey brothers, who have already been mentioned, and who were, in their day, eminent in the literary life of Wales. In 1764 Evan Evans (Ieuan Brydydd Hir) published *Some Specimens from the Poetry of the Ancient Welsh Bards* which brought Welsh literature to the attention of English writers, while Goronwy Owen, a protégé of the Cymmrodorion, gave new life to the old metrical forms of Welsh poetry. These interests show the faint beginnings of romanticism even in the Augustan age, when classical standards of taste and criticism still prevailed.

For it was the romantic movement in thought and literature which gave an impetus to national sentiment in Wales, as in the other countries of Europe. An interest in all that was strange and remote led to pride in the legendary and historical past of the nation. This was particularly strong in a group of London Welshmen, for in them it combined with the attachment of exiles for the land of their birth. The Society of the Gwyneddigion, founded in 1771, was foremost in fostering a study of Welsh literature, and its two chief members, Owen Jones and William Owen (who later took the name of Pughe) published in 1789 an edition of the work of the mediaeval bard, Dafydd ap Gwilym. The society became radical under the influence of the French Revolution, itself the source of so many of the nationalist movements of Europe, but its primary interests were literary. It therefore undertook to collect all the Welsh prose and poetry of the middle ages, and published the result of its efforts in three volumes, entitled *The Myvyrian Archaiology*. For this task Owen Jones and William Owen (Pughe) had secured the assistance of 'the bard of liberty,' Iolo Morganwg, and he interspersed his own fabrications among the genuine old texts. Despite this unfortunate aspect of their work, the romantic movement thereby reintroduced into Welsh life the power of a great literary tradition as a national force, and henceforth the language, and the spiritual inheritance which found expression in it, became the symbol of Welsh nationality and the guarantee of its continuity. National consciousness has, indeed, existed apart from the language, but it has been weaker where this element was absent.

The chief product of the romantic revival in Wales was the eisteddfod. Meetings of the bards had been held in Wales, as elsewhere, in mediaeval times, and, in 1568, an eisteddfod was held at Caerwys in Flintshire, when a commission was granted by Elizabeth's government to certain north Wales gentlemen to grant licences to the bards, in order to distinguish them from the sturdy vagabonds who infested the countryside. There continued to be meetings of bards in the inns and taverns of Wales throughout the next centuries, but the modern eisteddfod dates only from 1789. The prime mover in its revival was Thomas Jones of Corwen, who, with the active support of the Gwyneddigion, arranged a meeting in his native town in May of that year. Later in the same year another eisteddfod was held at Bala, officially sponsored by the Gwyneddigion. At the same time there was a renewed interest in the religion of nature and in the cults of the druids. Iolo Morganwg sought to prove that literary traditions had continued unbroken since druidical times in his native shire of Glamorgan. He elaborated a ritual which purported to be that of the druids, and on June 21, 1792, he held the first 'gorsedd,' or esoteric coterie of bards, on Primrose Hill, in London. These inventions he succeeded in palming off on his contemporaries, and, at Carmarthen in 1819, the gorsedd became an integral part of the eisteddfod.

From this time on, regional eisteddfodau were held in various parts of Wales under the patronage of the local gentry, notably, Lady Llanover. Towards the middle of the century the institution came to reflect the growing national sentiment of Wales. The subjects set for the Llangollen eisteddfod of 1858 are instructive in this respect. For the chair the subject was the Battle of Bosworth (supposedly a Welsh victory), and for the crown the capture of Rome by Brennus, the Celtic chieftain. There were prizes for a lyric on Owen Glyn Dŵr, an epitaph on Llywelyn the Last, and an ode on the landing of Brutus in Britain, while the subject of the prize essay was the discovery of America by Madoc ab Owen Gwynedd. It was evident that the sponsors of the eisteddfod gloried in both the mythical and the historical past of Wales, and the institution, itself, did much to foster national sentiment. The Llangollen eisteddfod is notable also for the establishment of a committee to arrange a National Eisteddfod annually. This committee met with financial difficulties, but with the formation of the National Eisteddfod Association in 1880 (again through the efforts of the indefatigable Hugh Owen) a new period in its history was opened. The eisteddfod has acted as a great formative influence on Welsh life. It has centred the recreation of the Welsh people on literary and musical competition, and it has stimulated literary production. Above all it has contributed to the growth of national consciousness.

This national consciousness found expression in the mid-nineteenth century in a number of ways. The Cambrian Archaeological Association was founded in 1846 to study the antiquities of Wales. It received the patronage of the clergy and the gentry. In 1848 an attempt was made to counteract the anglicisation of this class by the foundation of the Welsh Collegiate Institution at Llandovery, where boys of the middle and upper class could be taught in a Welsh atmosphere and through the medium of Welsh. This was made possible through the munificence of Thomas Phillips, a surgeon in the service of the East India Company who was encouraged by Lady Llanover and others. 'The primary intent and object of the founder,' stated the trust deed, 'is instruction and education in the Welsh language,' and this was carried out in the early years, but with the appointment of A. G. Edwards (the future archbishop of Wales) as headmaster in 1875, the founder's intention was abandoned both in spirit and in letter. The adoption in 1856 of a national anthem, 'Hen Wlad fy Nhadau,' the words of which were written by Evan James, a weaver of Pontypridd, and the music composed by his son, James James, was another indication of growing national sentiment, and, in 1873, the Society of Cymmrodorion was revived to further the cultural needs of Wales.

Meanwhile national consciousness had been intensified by two factors. One of these was the influence of the blue book controversy after 1847. However justified the commissioners may have been in their strictures on the schools of Wales, they had produced also an indictment of the whole Welsh nation, an indictment which concerned matters where the emotions were most easily roused, that is, the language, religion and personal morality of the people. The comments of London newspapers served to embitter the Welsh, for, on the basis of the reports, the *Morning Chronicle* declared that they were 'fast settling down into the most savage barbarism,' while the *Examiner* thought that 'their habits were those of animals and would not bear description.' To the reports may be traced the antipathy felt in England towards Wales, an antipathy reflected, for example, in the attack of the *Times* on the eisteddfod in 1866, when the Welsh language was described as an anachronism, and Welsh literature as barbaric. To the reports, also, is due the intense anglophobia which provided the emotional impetus behind later autonomous movements in Wales.

The second factor was the influence of nationalism in Ireland and on the continent. The idealism of Joseph Mazzini, for whom the nation was but an instrument to serve the cause of democracy and of humanity, found a responsive echo in Wales, and the struggle of the Young Italy party against Austrian aggression roused great enthusiasm. Even more influential were the ideas which Thomas Davis, the Irish poet and politician, incorporated in a newspaper, *The Nation*, which he edited from 1842 until his death in 1845. These ideas became familiar in Wales through the writings of Gwilym Hiraethog, who was in correspondence with Mazzini. Hiraethog also championed the Hungarian revolt against Austria, and for a time the leading articles in *Yr Amserau* were devoted mainly to this topic. So strongly did he support the cause of the Hungarian exiles that he received their thanks in person through Kossuth's private secretary. Hiraethog was an immensely popular lecturer as well as a writer, and by innumerable lectures throughout the length and breadth of Wales, he made Kossuth and Garibaldi into heroes for the Welsh people. Analogies with the struggle of Italians and Hungarians against Austrian oppression, and with that of Irishmen against English rule, were not lost on his audiences.

Nationalist sentiment found practical expression in the work of an independent minister, Michael D. Jones. He was a leader of nonconformity, and his mother had been evicted by Sir Watkin

Williams Wynn, no doubt on account of her son's activities. Like S.R. he sought a solution to Welsh problems in emigration, but, in the United States, he came to realise that Welsh people there, in the second generation, lost their language and national characteristics. He therefore decided to locate his community in South America, for in that sparsely populated land he thought that it would take firm root. Favourable descriptions of Patagonia had appeared in English books of travel, and two emissaries, sent out by Michael D. Jones to investigate the land, also thought it suitable for settlement. Michael D. Jones thereupon made overtures to the Argentinian government with regard to the reservation of territory in the Chubut valley for the exclusive use of Welsh emigrants, and a party of 153 emigrants (which did not, however, include Michael D. Jones himself) left for South America on the *Mimosa*, arriving in the Chubut river on July 28, 1865. But the enterprise was ill-conceived and ill-planned. Although the community would have to live by farming there was only one farmer among the emigrants. They encountered great difficulties through drought and intermittent floods. On more than one occasion they determined to leave, but, after much recrimination, decided to stay. The colony survived largely through the bounty of the Argentinian government, and, ironically enough, through the help of the imperial government of Britain. In time a marked antipathy grew up between the Welsh and the Spaniards, but the community has maintained an uncertain existence until the present day.

The chief indication of the growth of national consciousness in Wales in the second half of the nineteenth century is the establishment of national institutions of higher learning. The provision of schools, and of normal colleges to train teachers, had arisen naturally out of the struggle between nonconformity and anglicanism. A demand for a separate university came only when the nation became conscious of a desire to preserve its own traditions. Characteristically, also, the first move came from a group of exiles, whose patriotic sentiment was heightened by absence from their native land. These were the Welsh clergy in the West Riding of Yorkshire, whose predecessors had already, in 1835, petitioned the government to appoint Welsh bishops in Wales. They submitted, in 1852, a further petition to parliament for the establishment of a Welsh university.

In the succeeding years various schemes were put forward, but there was little progress until 1863, when a number of London Welshmen, meeting in the Freemasons' Tavern in London, set up a committee to collect funds. The chairman of this committee was William Williams, now member for Lambeth, whose questions in parliament had led to the appointment of the education commission of 1846. He made a donation of £1,000. Four years later an opportunity came to secure a building. A firm of railway contractors were at this time erecting a huge hotel at Aberystwyth, and had already spent the sum of £80,000 on it when they became bankrupt. The promoters of a Welsh university were able to buy this edifice for £10,000 (£6,000 of which they borrowed), and it was this accident which led to the location of the first Welsh university college at Aberystwyth. Renewed appeals for government assistance proved unavailing, yet, in October 1872, the college opened with twenty-five students, and with Thomas Charles Edwards (the son of Lewis Edwards of Bala) as its first principal. For ten years more the college had to rely on voluntary help. David Davies of Llandinam made substantial endowments, but the college depended mainly upon small subscriptions (in one year there were no less than 73,000 of these), and, in a very real sense, it was supported by the 'pennies of the poor.' From 1872 onwards Hugh Owen, now in his seventies, devoted his whole time to the work of organising subscriptions. His figure was a familiar sight in the railway stations of Wales, as he travelled the length and breadth of the land, at his own expense, to rouse interest in the college. When he died in 1881 its fate was still uncertain.

The return of Gladstone to power in 1880 had given the Welsh educationalists renewed hope, and a departmental committee was appointed, with Lord Aberdare as its chairman, to enquire into intermediate and higher education in Wales. Its report, published in 1881, recommended the establishment of two colleges, one in north Wales and one in south Wales, and a grant of £4,000 to each. This financial provision made certain the continuance of higher education, but the recommendation of two colleges, although it found favour with most Welsh people, and was, in fact, in accord with the intention of Owen Glyn Dŵr almost half a millennium earlier, was undoubtedly ill-advised. The committee thought that Aberystwyth might serve as the north Wales college, or that the college already in existence there might be transferred elsewhere. After arbitration between various south Wales towns, the college for south Wales was located at Cardiff, and opened its doors in 1883. A conference called at Chester to arrange for the establishment of the college for north Wales ignored the possibility of locating it in Aberystwyth, and eventually Bangor was chosen as its site, the college being opened in 1884. The grant which had temporarily been given to Aberystwyth was thereupon transferred to Bangor. But the departmental committee had underestimated the strength of the attachment to Aberystwyth of a brilliant group of old students, who were determined that it should continue to exist, and the government compromised with a provisional annual grant to it of £2,500 in 1884. This was increased to £4,000 in 1885, and four years later the college received its charter, thus being placed in all respects on an equal footing with Cardiff and Bangor. Separatism, however, was not yet at an end, for, in 1920, a fourth college was founded at Swansea. Much university work is thus quadrupled in Wales, and the system has proved wasteful and inefficient. Had the departmental committee of 1880 decided upon one college for Wales numerous problems of administration and finance would not have arisen.

Unity, was, to some extent, preserved by associating the three original colleges in the University of Wales. This was primarily the work of John Viriamu Jones, who, at the early age of twenty-seven, had become Cardiff's first principal. He was a man of unusually brilliant intellect, and was possessed, also, of a rare gift of statesmanship. It is probably true to say that he is the one educationalist of undoubted genius that the Welsh national movement has produced. Considerable difficulty was encountered in obtaining a charter for the University, but the dependence of Gladstone's fourth ministry in 1892 on the support of Welsh members made it certain that the project would receive government support. The charter was therefore accepted by the house of commons without a division, but in the house of lords a resolution was passed, through the influence of the Welsh bishops, to defer its acceptance till provision had been made for the inclusion of Lampeter as a college in the University. The government decided to ignore this, and the University came into being by royal charter on November 30, 1893. Lord Aberdare became its first chancellor, and its first vice-chancellor was John Viriamu Jones, whose work was cut short by death eight years later at the age of forty-five.

The colleges, and the University which united them into a national body, were a spontaneous growth arising out of the desire of the Welsh people for higher education. They were both the product and the cause of an awakening unparalleled in the modern history of Wales. Poor in everything except in spirit, their very struggles for existence generated enthusiasm. Their influence was strengthened by that of an Oxford society, the society of Dafydd ap Gwilym, founded in 1886, which united the emotional susceptibilities of exiles to high standards of scholarship. Among its founders was the historian, Owen M. Edwards, the son of a Merioneth crofter, who had a poet's insight into the significance of the nation's past, and who, while remaining a teacher of history at Oxford, poured out in vigorous Welsh prose a remarkable quantity of writings, which did much to interpret to the Welsh people their literature and traditions. The University made possible, at last, an adequate study of the language and literature, and of the history of Wales. Prominent among its teachers were the grammarian, Sir John Morris Jones, and the historian, Sir John Edward Lloyd. Its astringent scholarship has destroyed many popular illusions, but it has helped to build up a sound national life grounded in the authentic tradition of Wales.

From the beginning it was realised that the University could not do its work effectively unless there were an adequate supply of schools to prepare its students before admission. The Aberdare committee turned its attention to this matter. It found that there were a number of grammar schools in existence though the endowments of some of them were used for elementary education. But, in view of the enormous growth of the population in the nineteenth century, and, especially, the growth of a middle class in Wales, they were far too few and far too small. The Aberdare report, therefore, recommended both the extension of the existing schools and the establishment of new ones by direct grant from the government. This was, in fact, a revolutionary proposal, for the state had not hitherto concerned itself with secondary education. The recommendations of the committee were incorporated in the Intermediate Education Act of 1889. Credit for its passing is due mainly to Stuart Rendel, who had become member of parliament for Montgomeryshire in 1880, ousting the Wynns, who had held the seat for eighty years without a break. He was a churchman, and was English by birth and association. Yet he so closely identified himself with Welsh life as to become 'the member for Wales.' The leader of the Welsh members at this time was Henry Richard, but he was far more nonconformist than he was Welsh, and was lukewarm in his support of any measures which related exclusively to Wales. Stuart Rendel, on the other hand, was an enthusiast for the cause of small nations. It was he who had rescued the college at Aberystwyth from extinction, both through his intervention with Gladstone, who was his personal friend, and through his own generosity. Despite the fact that a Conservative government was in power he skilfully piloted the Intermediate Act through parliament, and, for the purposes of secondary education, secured the inclusion of Monmouthshire as an integral part of Wales. The act made provision for the use of existing endowments. It empowered the county councils to raise a halfpenny rate for secondary education, and arranged that a Treasury grant should be made to each county equivalent to the amount raised. By 1902, when the system adopted in Wales in 1889 was applied to England, ninety-five intermediate schools, catering for 8,000 pupils, had been established.

Obviously it was necessary to co-ordinate the work of the schools by means of examination and inspection. There was no central authority to undertake this, for there were no state supported grammar schools in England. Viriamu Jones therefore strove hard to knit the whole educational system of Wales into one unit by seizing this opportunity to make the supervision of the schools a function of the University. In this he was not successful, so a separate body, the Central Welsh Board, was created in 1896. It was composed mainly of representatives of the governing bodies of the schools in each county, and it was financed by contributions from the rates and by a Treasury grant. Owen Owen became its first chief inspector in 1897. For fifty years, the Central Welsh Board controlled secondary education in Wales. Its founders had intended that technical education should be adequately provided in the schools, but, in accordance with the wishes of the people, Welsh secondary education became almost exclusively academic. At an early stage the Board recognised the need for instruction in the language, literature and history of Wales.

Welsh national aspirations were, therefore, mainly cultural. For a brief period at the end of the century, however, they became more political in character. Here again the influence of Ireland, in the heyday of the Irish home rule movement, was evident. A hatred of Roman catholicism had hitherto kept Wales aloof from support of Irish causes, but its attitude had become softened with the course of time, and the growth of nationalism in Wales itself had made possible a deeper understanding of the Irish problem. This was reinforced by the influence of Irish protestant leaders, in particular that of Thomas Davis. The nationalism of Michael D. Jones was stronger than his protestantism, and he was instrumental in obtaining a hearing in Wales even for the Irish revolutionary, Michael Davitt. A younger writer, Robert Ambrose Jones (Emrys ap Iwan), a Calvinistic methodist preacher, also helped to eradicate the antipathy of the Welsh people towards Roman catholicism. He was partly French in blood, and had spent some years of his youth on the continent. By his writings continental currents of thought became familiar to the youth of Wales other than through the medium of English books, and in a series of incisive letters in *Y Faner* he combated what he considered to be the 'anglo-mania' of Welsh leaders in religion and politics. He admired Charles Stuart Parnell and his obstructionist tactics in parliament, for he held that neither party, Liberal or Conservative, was more favourable than the other to the interests of Ireland and Wales. It was he who coined the Welsh word for self-government (ymreolaeth), and he argued that both disestablishment and the movement for land reform distracted attention from this, which was the real problem of Wales.

These various trends of thought culminated in 1886 in the formation of a Young Wales movement, Cymru Fydd, in imitation of Young Italy and Young Ireland. The time was opportune, for in the eighties the older leaders of Wales passed away. Sir Hugh Owen died in 1881, Hiraethog in 1883, S.R. in 1885, Lewis Edwards in 1887 and Henry Richard in 1888.

Younger men were taking their place in all aspects of public life, notably Thomas Edward Ellis, Owen M. Edwards, John Viriamu Jones, David Alfred Thomas and David Lloyd George. Cymru Fydd, in fact, was itself not essentially political in origin, although it owed allegiance to the Liberal Party. Its main insistence was that the Liberal Party should pay greater attention to Wales, and it brought to the surface a conflict between Welsh and English Liberalism.

Its foundation coincided with the election of Thomas Edward Ellis as member for Merioneth. Two years later he was joined in parliament by D. A. Thomas, member for Merthyr Tydfil, and in 1890 the youthful Lloyd George became member for the Caernarvon boroughs. These were only the more outstanding men in the most remarkable group of representatives that Wales has sent to parliament in the whole of its history. The leader of the group was Thomas Edward Ellis. 'For many years,' he wrote, 'my two teachers in politics have been Joseph Mazzini and Thomas Davis'; he was, therefore, a strong advocate of home rule for Wales. The example of Ireland was the formative influence in his life, and he had become a great admirer of Parnell even before he entered parliament. In 1888, during a Conservative administration, the Welsh members decided to have whips of their own, in imitation of the Irish, so that the Welsh party in parliament would have to be reckoned with by both sides. But it was soon evident that Thomas Ellis had very little of Charles Stuart Parnell in him, and that he was not likely to beome 'the Parnell of Wales.'

The election of 1892 was to prove a crucial one. It was fought, in the country as a whole, over the question of Irish Home Rule, but, in Wales, over disestablishment and land reform. As we have seen, Gladstone's majority proved to be only forty, and of the Liberal members Wales returned thirty-one. The danger to the government of the formation of a Welsh party on Irish lines was therefore obvious, and Gladstone skillfully obviated this by acting on the advice of Thomas Ellis's Oxford associates and offering him the post of junior whip. Thereby the prime minister would secure the loyalty of the Welsh members, and make impossible the formation of a sectional Welsh party. Flattered by the offer, for he was but thirty-three years of age, and torn in his own mind as to whether he could best serve Welsh interests from within the government or as leader of a separate group, a matter which is still debatable, Ellis accepted. Henceforth his loyalty to the Liberal Party was never in question. Gladstone proved amenable to Welsh requests for a land commission and a university charter, but he was reluctant to bring in any measure for disestablishment. Therefore, in September 1893, a proposal to form an independent Welsh party received the support of seven members, including D. A. Thomas and Lloyd George, but was defeated through the loyalty of the older men to Gladstone. In the following year D. A. Thomas, Lloyd George and two others did break away from the Liberal party, and started a campaign in Wales on their own account. But their revolt was short-lived. Rosebery, who had succeeded Gladstone as prime minister, agreed to bring in a disestablishment bill, and made Thomas Ellis chief whip. The son of a Merioneth tenant farmer thus found himself placed in a position of authority over descendants of the great English Whig landowners. Even more important in explaining the collapse of the Welsh movement was the defeat of the Liberal Party in 1895, and its long period of ten years in the wilderness. On this account minor differences between Welsh and English Liberals were merged in opposition to the party in power. Cymru Fydd, as a popular movement, also came to a sudden end. It had flourished so greatly in 1894 and 1895 that a salaried organiser was engaged, and numerous branches were formed in both north and south Wales. But it had no solid foundation in political belief and it disintegrated. The Welsh political movement suffered from the fact that in a group remarkable for its character and ability there was an inevitable clash of personalities, especially between the powerful industrial magnate, D. A. Thomas, and the ambitious country attorney, David Lloyd George. No one emerged who, by experience, success or age, was an obvious leader, and who could weld the group into a solid unit. Thomas Ellis's very youth was against him. Besides, he died in 1899, soon after reaching his fortieth birthday, at too young an age for any real estimate to be made of his qualities of statesmanship. His early death, however, served only to enhance his value as a symbol of the Welsh renascence in the affectionate regard of his fellow-countrymen.

Political nationalism, even in this mild form, was therefore short-lived in Wales, and attention was once more concentrated on culture and education. In the primary schools, payment by results had led to the teaching of reading, writing and arithmetic to the exclusion of everything else. Not only did Welsh find no place in the curriculum, but children were severely punished for speaking Welsh in the classroom or the playing yard. This continued even after education became free and compulsory. Children were taught in a language which they understood only imperfectly, with serious consequences to their progress. To remedy this was one of the chief purposes of the Welsh Language Society formed in 1885, and within three years it had secured the inclusion of Welsh as a class subject in the schools. The Education Act of 1902 established in each shire Local Education Authorities, which varied greatly in their attitude towards the Welsh language. In the general election of 1906, Wales did not return a single Conservative member. The new Liberal Government thereupon acknowledged the cultural autonomy of Wales by the formation in 1907, within the Board of Education, of a separate Welsh department, whose secretary had direct access to the minister. This department secured the services of Owen M. Edwards as its first chief inspector, and he, by his charm of manner and personal qualities of inspiration, almost revolutionised the attitude of both teachers and education authorites towards the place of Welsh in the schools.

The year 1907 also saw the granting of charters to the National Library of Wales and the National Museum of Wales. Both institutions owed their inception to the same group of men who had striven for a University of Wales. At an early date these men had realised the desirability of forming a national collection of books and manuscripts, and the nucleus of such a collection was housed in the newly established college at Aberystwyth. Thus it was that the circumstances which decided the location of the college also predetermined the site of the Library. The claims of Aberystwyth were, indeed, contested by Cardiff on the grounds of the corporation's own magnificent collection of books and manuscripts and of the greater accessibility of Cardiff to the majority of the people of Wales. However, certain benefactors, notably Sir John Williams, the owner of a great private library, would give their collections to the nation only if the Library were located at Aberystwyth. Members of parliament had meanwhile urged the claims of Wales to a share in the grants voted annually for the maintenance of libraries and museums, and a committee of the privy council was appointed to consider the matter. It recommended that a Library be established and that it should be located at Aberystwyth. A site for it was presented by Lord (Stuart) Rendel. The miners of Glamorgan and Monmouthshire generously agreed to a levy of a shilling a head on their wages towards a building fund, even though the privy council's decision in favour of Aberystwyth had gone against them, while thousands of other small subscriptions were made. Largely through the efforts of Sir Herbert Lewis, the Library was placed in 1911 on an equal footing with the other great public libraries, by being given the right to claim a free copy of almost every book published in the United Kingdom. The National Library has thus become unrivalled as a repository for books, manuscripts and records relating to Wales, and as a centre for the study of its language, literature and history.

The privy council committee at the same time recommended that the Museum should be located in Cardiff, and the city thereupon presented to it a site in Cathays Park, together with its own collection of natural history, arts and antiquities, as well as sums of money amounting to some £13,500, and the annual proceeds of a halfpenny rate. The work of the Museum supplements that of the Library in furthering a scientific study of the natural history, archaeology, art and folk culture of Wales. It also fosters a popular interest in these subjects for it is visited annually by some 300,000 people. In 1946, a new development took place, through the generosity of Lord Plymouth, who gave St. Fagans Castle to the nation, to enable the establishment, amid beautiful surroundings in the Vale of Glamorgan, of an open-air museum to illustrate the life of the people of Wales throughout the ages, the first of its kind in the British Isles.

The quarter of a century which preceded the outbreak of the Great War was, thus, a period of great achievement in Welsh life, and is in strange contrast to the ineffectiveness of the quarter of a century which followed. Three great national institutions had been founded, the University, the Library and the Museum, to foster the indigenous culture of Wales, and the schools, which provide the basis of national life, had been granted a large measure of autonomy through the formation of a separate Welsh Department. Even disestablishment, which erected Wales into a separate ecclesiastical province, helped to unify it by severing links with England. In this new province, Monmouthshire was included as an integral part without question or even discussion. In a different way the new county councils fully realised such desires as many people had for self-government in the ordinary affairs of every-day life. Political nationalism therefore receded in importance, and when, in March 1914, the Middlesbrough ironmaster, E. T. John, member of parliament for east Denbighshire, introduced a measure for Welsh home rule, he obtained singularly little attention from his fellow-members or from the Welsh people. The outbreak of war soon afterwards brought with it new problems to Wales, and other solutions for them had to be found.

CHAPTER XVIII

EPILOGUE

LIFE in Wales in the quarter of a century after 1914 was entirely dominated by the First World War and by its consequences. The basic industries of coal mining and steelmaking were of vital importance in warfare, and they therefore expanded rapidly in the war years, as did the engineering and shipbuilding industries which were dependent upon them. With government encouragement they increased their equipment and incurred liabilities far in excess of what was justified by the peacetime demand for their products. Wages, also, were high, and here again the government encouraged the rapid entry of labour into these industries to meet the needs of war. Nor did this artificially stimulated industrial activity cease immediately when the war came to an end. The destruction of the mines of Belgium and France had created a coal famine in Europe, so that there was a continued demand for Welsh coal, and quantities of steel were required to rebuild the devastated areas.

There was the same artificial prosperity in rural Wales. High prices were obtained for agricultural products, and much land was once more brought under the plough. These prices continued to rise in the years 1918, 1919 and 1920, for they were pushed up by the general inflation which prevailed. The period was, in fact, of the highest significance in the social history of rural Wales, for it saw the culmination of social trends which have been described in the earlier chapters of this book. Taking advantage of these high prices a great number of gentry sold their lands, and it may be said that large estates now virtually ceased to exist in Wales. Four centuries had therefore seen the rise of a class of gentry, its acquisition of political power, the decline of that power and the final disappearance of the class. The change was not, however, entirely in the interests of the farmers. They were relieved of any petty tyranny they may have suffered at the hands of land agents and gamekeepers, but they bought their land at highly inflated prices, at the cost of heavy mortgages, and from this time onwards the real landlords of Wales were the banks.

The boom collapsed in 1923, and there began for Wales a period of almost unrelieved depression which lasted until the outbreak of the Second World War. The causes of this collapse were general, but it was the misfortune of Wales that there they were all intensified. Primarily this was due to the entire dependence of south Wales on the basic industries of coal, iron, steel and tin-plate. This dependence was characteristic of other industrial regions in Britain, but it is south Wales which provides the extreme example of it. Areas in which there was a greater variety of industries offered far more resilience to the depression, and provided alternative occupations for workers who found themselves unemployed. Even in Wales itself the depression was less felt in the hinterland of Swansea where there was greater variety. Moreover Welsh industry was concerned largely with the extraction of raw material, such as coal, and the production of the basic material for other industries, such as steel bars, rather than with the production of finished goods. Many of the products of south Wales were sent abroad, for it was a natural exporting area. But the return to the gold standard in 1925 seriously over-valued British currency in comparison with that of other countries, and export therefore became difficult because of the high price of British goods. This coincided with the undervaluation of the franc, so that the French market was lost. Other markets, such as those in the South American republics, which had always had the closest links with south Wales, were lost during the war to the United States and were never again regained. Finally, the wave of political nationalism, which had culminated in the First World War, brought with it intense economic nationalism, and the establishment of high tariff barriers which strangled world trade.

The basis of Welsh prosperity was coal, and it was in the coal trade that the slump was most marked. The United States had captured the Canadian market, as well as those of Central and South America. Next to these the chief markets for south Wales coal had been France and Italy, but the peace settlement arranged for the delivery of vast quantities of German coal to both countries as reparations payments, so that the demand for Welsh coal was seriously curtailed. Even when conditions became more stable, Wales again suffered through the competition of the German and Polish mines. The government decontrolled the mining industry in March 1921, and this was immediately followed by a dispute between the coal-owners and the miners, leading to a stoppage for three months. Together with the General Strike of 1926 this considerably aggravated the position of the south Wales coal industry as a competitor for world trade. In this period, also, the British navy, which had been one of the largest consumers of south Wales steam coal, turned to the use of oil, and was followed in this by most other navies, while within a few years half the merchant shipping of the world had done the same. The bunkering trade of south Wales therefore seriously declined. The development of motor transport and of hydro-electric power lessened the consumption of steam coal at home. Both the output and the export of anthracite coal remained throughout these years above the 1913 level, but the position in the steam coal industry in south Wales is clearly shown by the fact that while, on the eve of the First World War, 56·8 million tons were produced annually and 234,000 miners were employed, on the eve of the Second World War, a quarter of a century later, output had fallen to 35·3 million tons and the number of miners employed to 136,000.

The prosperity of the ports depended upon that of the coalfield, and the peak of the trade of Cardiff was reached in 1920. But the imports of Cardiff never amounted to more than fifteen per cent of its maritime trade, and, even so, half its imports covered materials necessary for industries which were dependent upon export. Therefore, when exports declined, Cardiff shipping came almost to a standstill.

World factors also accounted for the decline of the steel and tin-plate trades. India, China and Australia developed their own industries, and other markets were captured by the United States. Nearer home, Belgium proved to be a formidable competitor. Its industries had been destroyed in the war, and were now magnificently re-equipped at low cost by means of reparations payments. The somewhat antiquated plant of south Wales found it difficult to compete with them, especially as the Belgian wage level was the lowest in Europe. Therefore, one great steel works after another was closed. Cyfarthfa, which had been restarted during the war by Guest, Keen and Nettlefolds, was again closed in 1921, and in 1930 the Dowlais steel works was closed, causing the unemployment of between three and

four thousand men. In the same year took place the merging of
the two firms of Guest, Keen and Baldwins, with considerable
reorganisation. Production was restricted in the tin-plate
industry by a pooling scheme, and several small works which
had hitherto flourished were bought up by the larger firms, such
as Richard Thomas, in order that they might be closed.

The unfavourable conditions which prevailed in south
Wales were intensified by the world depression which lasted
from 1929 to 1934. In order to foster the internal recovery of
the country in face of this depression the government introduced tariffs on imported goods, but these only aggravated the
difficulties of a region which was dependent upon export.
Therefore, although there was considerable improvement in
British industry after 1934, the recovery of south Wales was
much less clearly marked.

Rural Wales was seriously affected by the repeal, in 1921, of
the Corn Production Act, which had guaranteed high prices for
cereals. Much of the land which had been ploughed during the
war thereupon went out of cultivation. The prices of other
agricultural products fell at the same time. A great proportion
of rural Wales therefore turned to milk production, and the
change was accelerated by the growth of motor transport,
which made possible the collection of milk from the farms.
Milk production required fewer workmen than tillage or stock
breeding, and the constantly increasing mechanisation of agriculture in these years still further reduced the number of men
required. The wages of farm labourers remained at an average
of thirty-four shillings a week, so that there was a constant
drift away from the land.

The primary factor in the social life of both rural and
industrial Wales in the years between the wars was, therefore,
the existence of acute unemployment. Throughout this period
the unemployment rate for Wales was consistently far higher
than for any other region in the United Kingdom. It reached its
peak in August 1932, when there were 245,000 unemployed in
Wales and Monmouthshire, out of a total population of two
and a half million. The moral and economic difficulties caused
by the enforced idleness of large numbers of people over a long
period of years were thus intensely felt in Wales. The most
spectacular of the consequences of unemployment was a migra-

tion of workers to the Midlands and to south-east England, drawn especially by the growth of light industries in and around London, thus reversing the trend of the previous century. In the ten years between the census of 1921 and 1931, no less than 259,000 persons migrated from Wales, 242,000 of whom were from the industrial south. The fertility rate in south Wales was high, and this loss was counteracted by the natural increase of the population, yet the census of 1931 showed a net decline of 65,000 persons in Wales. This was the first time that a decrease had been shown in the population of Wales since the first census was taken in 1801. The loss was not evenly spread. Flintshire, for example, showed a marked increase, due to the establishment of new industries, whereas Glamorgan showed a net loss of 46,000 and Monmouthshire of 22,000. Figures for subsequent years made it abundantly clear that migration still continued at a rapid rate, and it was calculated that by the end of 1938, 430,000 people had left Wales, involving a net loss of population of 191,000.

Migration partly solved the problem of unemployment, but it brought other problems in its train. For migration affected the younger men and women. The decrease was confined to persons up to the age of forty; above that age the population actually increased. It was therefore the vigorous and resourceful section of the community which left, leaving an ageing population behind. Besides, migration involved a great loss of social capital in the form of houses, schools and public utilities. This was particularly serious as Welsh workmen had taken pride in owning their own homes. Religious and charitable institutions suffered, and became dependent upon aid from outside. The loss of contributions to their funds made them unable to render service when this was most needed. The diminishing purchasing power of the workers also affected the shopkeepers and professional classes.

Nor was migration without its effect on the fortunes of the Welsh language. While each succeeding census had shown that the proportion of Welsh-speaking to English-speaking persons in Wales had decreased, the actual number of those who spoke Welsh had constantly increased until 1921, because this natural increase of the population could, up to that date, be retained within the country. The census of 1931 gave the population of

Wales and Monmouthshire as 2,593,000, of whom 2,472,000 were aged three and upwards. Of these 811,000 were returned as bilingual, while 98,000 spoke only Welsh. This showed a net loss of 13,000 persons able to speak Welsh as compared with the census figures for 1921. Anglesey, Caernarvonshire, Merioneth, Cardiganshire, Carmarthenshire and north Pembrokeshire remained preponderantly Welsh in speech, while Radnorshire and Monmouthshire had become essentially English. The net loss was undoubtedly due, in large degree, to migration, but the significant fact remained that nearly a million people in Wales spoke Welsh, while, if the Welsh speaking communities in England and abroad were included, the figure would be over a million.

All social and political developments in Wales between the wars were conditioned by the overwhelming fact of unemployment and its consequences. One result was the rapid growth of the Labour Party. The political trend of Wales in the years before the First World War had been shown by the election of 1906, when no Conservative candidate was returned, while there were twenty-nine Liberal members and six Labour members. For a time the industrial areas were content with an accelerated radicalism, but this ceased to be the case in the face of intense social distress. Liberalism continued to be the political creed of the rural constituencies of Wales, but the outcome of the election of 1929 was as unequivocal as that of 1906, for while one Conservative member was returned and nine constituencies remained Liberal, there were no less than twenty-five Labour members. Moreover, when the Labour Party was heavily defeated two years later in the country as a whole, on the formation of the National Government, it still retained twenty seats in Wales. The party did not adopt any essentially Welsh attitude towards politics. The representatives of industrial constituencies sought a remedy for unemployment in measures which related to the whole kingdom, and were generally impatient towards particular Welsh claims. Nevertheless an extension of the Liberal programme of pre-war days was visible in the demand, supported by some Labour members, for a secretary of state, with ministerial rank, who would co-ordinate the activities of the various government departments in relation to Wales. Moreover there was a demand for the repeal of the language clause in the Act of Union of 1536, by which all proceedings in the law courts had to be conducted in English. This was done by the Welsh Courts Act of 1942, though the records of the courts were still to be kept in English.

Of more significance than these measures was the growth in Wales of an independent Nationalist Party. It was founded in 1925 with the purpose of making Wales a self-governing dominion within the British Commonwealth. The demand for autonomy was strengthened by the depression, in so far as the economic advantages of association with England now became less obvious. On the other hand the disadvantage of being embroiled in the wars of a great power was obvious enough, and the party had, from the start, a strong pacifist element, attracting to itself many nonconformist ministers who no longer had much affinity with Liberalism. The development in the smaller countries of Europe, where a desire to preserve the national language and cultural institutions had been succeeded by political nationalism, was paralleled in Wales. It was claimed that the cultural nationalism of the pre-war period was unsatisfactory, for culture was but one aspect of the social life of a people, of which political activity was another, and a healthy national life required both. Without political machinery, even culture must become provincial and unimportant, dominated by that of the more powerful partner within the state. Only through complete national unity, it was argued, could a sense of social responsibility be developed which would be strong enough to counteract the disintegration caused by a long period of depression and unemployment. When the danger from Nazi Germany led the government to embark upon rearmament, its policy met with bitter protest from the Nationalist Party, and on September 8, 1936, three of its responsible leaders resorted to violence and set on fire a bombing school at Penyberth in Lleyn, appealing to conscience and the moral law in justification of their breach of the law of the land. The attempts of the party to contest various consituencies in parliamentary elections were not successful until 1967.

The intensity of the depression called for special measures from the government, and an entirely new procedure was created by the introduction of legislation intended to protect certain communities which had suffered through eonomic changes, just as the Factory Acts had protected individuals. So, in December 1934, part of the south Wales coalfield was declared a 'special area,' and great efforts were made to introduce a variety of industries. But these were almost entirely confined to towns in the coastal belt, since proximity to the main railways and docks is essential to the prosperity of modern light industries. A trading estate was established at Treforest, some ten miles from Cardiff docks in the direction of the mining valleys, and several firms started factories there. They drew their labour supply from the lower ends of the mining valleys, but the total number of men and women employed was small. Attempts were also made to settle miners and their families on the land in the Vale of Glamorgan.

The most striking instance of government intervention occurred in connection with the location of a strip mill at Ebbw Vale. Richard Thomas and Company announced in 1935 their intention of opening a strip mill on the American pattern for the manufacture of tin-plate at Redbourn in Lincolnshire, where there was a considerable supply of iron ore. This would concentrate all the processes in the production of steel and tin-plate on one site, and by making these processes continuous, would make possible the avoidance of waste and the production of a colossal output with the minimum amount of labour. The proposal caused consternation in south Wales, for it was feared that the tin-plate industry again would be lost, with still more unemployment and migration of labour. A vigorous campaign was started by local authorities, members of parliament and various public bodies. It was argued that the revival in the iron and steel industries had been due to the tariff which had eliminated the competition of cheap steel from Belgium and elsewhere. The tariff had adversely affected small independent tin-plate manufacturers who could no longer get their raw material in the form of steel bars from abroad. The renewed prosperity of the steel industry had therefore been won not through normal competition but at the expense of higher costs to the community. The industry therefore was under an obligation to the community, and could no longer locate its plant where it pleased. After the personal intervention of the prime minister, Richard Thomas and Company abandoned their Redbourn project and decided to open their new works at Ebbw Vale, where they acquired the derelict steel works of the Ebbw Vale Company. In this way employment would be provided for workers at the upper end of one of the mining valleys, where the hard core of unemployment had been most difficult to reduce. The development was an interesting one, for it entirely reversed the trend of south Wales industry, which, for half a century, had moved from the northern rim of the coalfield to the coast, and this emphasises the fact that the decision was made for social and not for economic reasons.

Unemployment was considerably reduced by the rearmament programme, but, at the outbreak of the Second World War, the figure for Wales stood at well over a hundred thousand. Many persons had been without work for five years and more. Efforts to alleviate the social distress which prevailed continued to be made by voluntary bodies, and 'settlements' were opened in several industrial towns to provide facilities for study and recreation. A remarkable development in the inter-war years which helped to counteract social disintegration was the growth of the Urdd, or Welsh League of Youth. It was founded in 1922, and, in time, became over 50,000 strong, in addition to the adults who acted as leaders and advisers. Without any political affiliation, the League has sought to develop a healthy national life by instilling into the youth of Wales an interest in their own traditions together with a sense of their kinship with other countries, and engraining in them a devotion to the service both of Wales and of humanity. By its own national eisteddfod and its mabolgampau (olympic games), it has provided the youth of Wales with a stimulus to healthy mental and physical recreation, and has brought together north and south, rural and industrial Wales, English-speaking as well as Welsh-speaking, into close unity of purpose. An interesting experiment on a smaller scale to rehabilitate older workers from mines, factories and farms, and provide them with a brief opportunity to study and broaden their intellectual interests, has been provided by the workers' residential college at Harlech.

Not until the transition to a full war economy had been completed was the mass of redundant labour absorbed. By the middle of 1941 only about 35,000 people were out of employment. The virtual elimination of large-scale and sustained unemployment, that scourge of the inter-war years, was by far the most important consequence of the war. Only rarely, as in 1963 when it reached the figure of 59,000, did it rise very substantially above about 40,000, and during boom years, as in the mid-fifties, it was sometimes below 20,000. In 1955, for example, when it fell to just under 15,000, it was the lowest ever recorded in peace-time. But these figures concealed two factors in the economic revival which were of great social importance. First, unemployment varied enormously as between region and region and from industry to industry. Parts of north Wales, especially the slate-towns of the north-west, and certain towns and villages in south and south-west Wales affected by the drastic and very rapid reorganization of the coal and tinplate industries, experienced levels of unemployment which to those who lived in those communities seemed highly reminiscent of the bitter 1930s. It was also a persistent characteristic of the pattern of post-war unemployment that the rate was consistently at least twice the average rate for Britain as a whole. It was observed also that the Welsh economy, though coming increasingly to resemble that of England in the diversity of its major products, yet seemed more erratic than that of England and more subject to the slumps in the trade-cycle. In addition to this, the long and persistent decline in agriculture, which had been interrupted by the war, continued unabated and with increasing pace after 1945, and since unemployment in rural areas invariably involved the consequential evil of migration, rural depopulation remained throughout the period a major preoccupation.

Despite these continuing weaknesses, there had been a remarkable change for the better in the economic fortunes of the principality.

The explanation for it lay in the different pattern of industry which emerged during and after the war. During the war strategic considerations had necessitated the transplanting of armaments factories and other essential industries from their traditional locations to places in Wales where they would be less vulnerable to enemy attacks. After the war, many of these factories and plants were put to new purposes, and others were encouraged by successive governments to settle in Wales. The old legislation which had established the Special Areas of the inter-war period was greatly extended to enable this to be done, and by 1966 most of Wales had been designated a Development Area. By this and other legislation the old trading estates were expanded and new ones established, advance factories built and government incentives offered to encourage suitable firms to settle and expand where the need was greatest. Somewhat more tardily investment in transport facilities to serve these new industrial centres began in earnest in 1953, and by the end of the sixties the Severn Bridge had been opened and new roads built to motorway standards linking south Wales to the Midlands (but not south Wales to north Wales) had been completed.

Contemporaneously, the old pillars of the Welsh economy – coal and steel – were being reshaped. The relative and absolute decline of the coal industry was spectacular. Among the first of the basic industries to be nationalized in 1947 it was the first to have enforced upon it a contraction of almost cataclysmic proportions. This began in the late fifties when the insatiable demand of the immediate post-war years for energy had slackened off and technologically and economically more attractive forms of energy, such as oil, had become available. By 1970 total output, which had been 20 million tons in 1945, was down to 13 million tons, and the labour force reduced from 100,000 men to 41,000. A similar, if more drastic, fate befell the tinplate industry. Still almost exclusively a Welsh industry, production was scattered among a number of relatively small units – the so-called 'hand-mills', most of which were technically obsolescent – and in the recently modernized strip-mill at Ebbw Vale. After 1952 new and even more efficient strip-mills were constructed at Trostre, near Llanelli, and Velindre, near Swansea. Both were closely integrated with the new steel works at Margam – at the time of its building, the largest in Europe – and by 1958 when world demand for tinplate had begun to contract, nearly all the old hand-mills had been closed and the Welsh monopoly in tin manufacture concentrated in the two new strip mills. Hence, by the 1970s the economic character of Wales had been changed. Steel production along with its associated tinplate, had been concentrated in vast new plants near the Bristol Channel ports at Port Talbot and Llanwern (Mon). Only Shotton, in Flint, and Ebbw Vale in Monmouthshire lay marginally outside the pattern, and were correspondingly vulnerable when further measures of rationalization were proposed in the mid-1970s. Coal production, likewise, was now concentrated in far fewer pits, some of them entirely new and all of them highly mechanized. New factories, many of them employing women, had been established in the industrial north-east and south. These ranged from aluminium smelting in Holyhead, nylon spinning in Flintshire and Pontypool, oil and its products in Pembrokeshire and Glamorgan, washing machines at Merthyr, and car-parts on a very considerable scale at Llanelli, Swansea and Cardiff. No longer was Wales economically uniform and monolithic. The economy had been diversified to an extent undreamt of by previous generations and the concurrent relative prosperity seemed proportionately the more secure.

One of the most important consequences of these changes was an intensification of that movement of population which had always been a characteristic of the industrial process. The total population of the country was no longer declining, though it was clear that this was due not to the return of Welshmen who had left the country during the depression but rather to a fresh immigration of labour to the new and reviving industries and, in north and west Wales, to the existence of an increasing class of rentiers. Total population rose from 2,584,000 in 1951 to 2,734,000 in 1971, but now a higher proportion lived in the four industrial counties of Glamorgan, Monmouthshire, Denbighshire and Flintshire than ever before. No less than 1,255,400 people, or 46.1 per cent of the total population of Wales in 1971, lived in Glamorgan alone. Within the industrial counties themselves similar shifts reflecting the changing industrial pattern took place, old industrial towns and villages at the heads of valleys losing population to the new industrial complexes near the coastal areas where conurbations were beginning to form. At the same time the rural counties of mid-Wales were losing population, and this was particularly disturbing as the loss tended to be in the 15 to 34 age group. The 'heart-land' of Wales was not only losing people, but those who remained were the older people, their numbers steadily swelled by an influx of retired folk from England, thus producing virtually geriatric communities with the social problems that that involved. Also, vast areas of central Wales and the moorlands of south Wales were given over, often despite the bitter objections of the farming communities, to the Forestry Commission. In 1960, when the

Commission celebrated its fortieth birthday, it owned a quarter
of a million acres of land in Wales, or 5 per cent of the total land
surface. Many people, representing all shades of political
opinion, argued that the social effects of rural depopulation were
so portentous that special policies designed to reverse the process
or to compensate for its most deleterious effects ought to be
adopted. These ranged from the establishing, with central
government's aid, of small, rural craft industries, to the creation
of new towns or the encouragement of growth in the region of
existing towns, and the improvement of the transport systems.
But this remains an apparently insuperable problem and
perhaps an inevitable concomitant of the heavy industrialization and urbanization of the south and the north east. Only in
Pembrokeshire, where Milford Haven began to be developed in
the 1960s as a deep-sea oil-port and refining centre, was there
investment on a truly magnificent scale. But even this was
scarcely commensurate with the problem and the capital
intensive and highly sophisticated technologies used in this new
industry provided permanent employment for relatively few
people. The Victorian dream of a new Merseyside on the banks
of the Cleddau seemed as remote and as unattainable as ever.

Even as the depression of the inter-war years had threatened
the existence of the Welsh communities which industrialization
had created, so now the post-war prosperity seemed to many to
pose threats as powerful and destructive, albeit more
subtle, to the traditional society or what remained of it. Rapid
urbanization based upon highly sophisticated industries located
away from the old centres of population, the continued drift of
people out of the mining valleys, and the even more rapid
depopulation of the rural counties, were felt to be inherently
destructive of the Welsh culture. The most unmistakable in-
dicator of this was an intense awareness of the minority status
of the Welsh language and a growing concern regarding its
future. As early as 1931 it had seemed to have been in a state
of irrevocable decline. By 1971 it was spoken by only 21 per
cent of the total population compared with an estimated 50
per cent seventy years previously. More ominously, there were
by 1971 clear indications that it was shrinking geographically
even in those areas in the west of the country where it had
always hitherto been strongest. 'Welsh Wales' was no longer

west-Wales, but north-west Wales and south-west Wales divided by a corridor of Anglicization along the Severn-Dyfi routeway into mid-Wales. These were the regions where population was thinnest, the social infrastructure most expensive to maintain, where relative poverty and deprivation were most in evidence, and which were therefore least able to maintain their individuality and sustain their unique culture.

Concern for the fate of the language – and with it all that is most distinctive in the culture of Wales – was widespread, a constant preoccupation of official and unofficial, political and religious, bodies. The period saw a significant extension to the educational means which had been devised in the course of the century by the Ministry of Education to ensure that Welsh continued to be taught in the schools of Wales. One new departure was the foundation, at first by private initiative and later by L.E.A.s, of schools in which the medium of instruction should be Welsh. The Urdd had opened such a school at Aberystwyth in 1939, and ten years later similar primary schools, and, from the mid-fifties, secondary schools also, had been established in English-speaking parts of the country. Official approval and encouragement were given to this interesting development by the Gittins Committee (the equivalent for Wales of the Plowden Committee) which published its report early in 1968 and which was immediately accepted by the Minister of Education. The University in common with the Training Colleges also accepted its responsibilities in these respects and in 1955 began a policy of appointing lecturers to teach through the medium of Welsh. Other means of fostering the language adopted during these decades included financial assistance to publishers of books in the vernacular, and a very substantial extension of the work of the Welsh Arts Council. Above all the Welsh Region of the BBC, particularly after the setting up of the Broadcasting Council for Wales in 1952, devoted far more time than it had hitherto to Welsh affairs and to programmes through the medium of the Welsh Language. Other Welsh language institutions, such as the Eisteddfod and Welsh League of Youth, continued to thrive, but with the continued decline in the numerical strength of the Welsh language, and of those religious institutions with which it had been most organically connected in the past, these too became more and more dependent upon official forms of patronage and were particularly sensitive to the growing inflation of the period.

The decline in organized religion, which had begun in the inter-war period, likewise became very marked during these years. It affected all denominations and appeared to be qualitatively different from any of those periodic withdrawals from religion (followed by fresh revivals) which had been so characteristic of the Welsh religious experience in the past. In urban areas, particularly in the coal valleys and in the industrial towns, this decline was of cataclysmic proportions, and insofar as it was associated in these places with an equally severe decline in the use of the language, it represented a fundamental' change in the character of the communities affected. The decline was less marked in those urban areas which retained their Welshness, as in the anthracite coalfield, and in rural areas chapels and churches retained much of their popularity and continued to fulfill their traditional roles. But over the country as a whole the decline was so rapid and so widespread as to amount to a cultural change of major proportions which would inevitably have profound effects on moral and political, as on religious, attitudes and behaviour.

Such basic cultural concerns were reflected in the political life of the principality. This was especially the case when the resentments which they sometimes engendered in particular groups came to be combined with a growing sense of economic grievance, in particular, the belief, widely shared, that the country was being unfairly discriminated against in the allocation of financial and other resources and exploited in respect of the disposal of its own natural resources. Much of this debate was conducted on the basis of unsatisfactory evidence and a great deal of guesswork, for it was not until 1954 that an annual Digest of Welsh Statistics came to be published. Agitation for the appointment of a Secretary of State on the Scottish model by a resurrected Undeb Cymru Fydd, aided by a number of M.P.s, in the belief that this would lead to better administration was not sympathetically regarded by the first post-war Labour government, and the appointment of a Council of Wales, a nominated body meeting in private, and having advisory powers only, was scarcely regarded as a substitute for the devolutionary measures which were increasingly being favoured by a wide spectrum of opinion. There was an all-party conference on Home Rule in 1949, and another, more carefully organized, in 1954 in which prominent members of the Labour Party took part. In fact, it was a Conservative government which took the first serious step in that direction when Churchill created a Ministry of Welsh Affairs in his 1951 administration, its incumbent then and until 1964 invariably holding another office as well. There was also a minister of State appointed to the Ministry from 1957. Though these changes made little impact at the time, and affected only marginally the popularity of the Conservative Party in Wales, they nonetheless represented considerable advances in the direction of a gradual and moderate devolution of administration. By 1964, in addition to health, trade and labour, which had been partially devolved before and during the war, the Welsh Office had assumed responsibility for housing, agriculture and fisheries, and transport. Cardiff, which had been proclaimed (not without considerable opposition from north Wales) the capital city in 1954, was thus becoming an important centre for government and the nationalized industries. Less confidently, it was also beginning to take on some of the cultural roles which it had so conspicuously neglected in the past.

Complementary to these developments was a constitutional innovation of quite considerable potential importance, namely, the establishing of a standing committee of the House of Commons, known as the Welsh Grand Committee. It was empowered to call for expert evidence and to question any minister on the implications for Wales of any departmental activities for which he was responsible. All these developments came to a head in 1964 when the newly-returned Labour government, in fulfilment of its pledges, appointed a Secretary of State for Wales with a seat in the cabinet.

Politically and culturally, therefore, these were years of innovation and of new developments when the country seemed to be achieving, without violence and within the accepted constitutional machinery, degrees of national recognition and self-consciousness to which it had long aspired but without success. The programme to which the Labour Party was pledged, and which James Griffiths, the first Secretary of State, was busy implementing, was certainly more radical than any hitherto formulated, and it is highly probable that it was its emphasis on economic reform with large-scale investment in mid-Wales and in the run-down areas of the country that ensured a massive Welsh Labour vote in 1966. Of the votes cast in the general election of that year 60.7 per cent were polled for Labour, 27.8 per cent for the Conservatives, 6.3 per cent for the Liberals, 4.3 per cent for Plaid Cymru, and 0.9 per cent for the Communists. 32 out of the 36 seats went to Labour – a result which confirmed a Labour ascendancy as great as that of the Liberals sixty years previously. On the cultural side the appointment of the David Hughes-Parry Committee to enquire into the legal status of the Welsh language seemed to take the steam out of the boilers of the young extremists of the newly-formed Welsh Language Society as effectively as the policies of the government seemed to undermine the progress of the Welsh Nationalist Party.

In fact, the remaining decade was to be enlivened and sometimes dominated by the unexpected growth of the Nationalists and the growing agitations of the Welsh Language Society. The return of Gwynfor Evans, president of Plaid Cymru since the end of the war, as member for Carmarthen at a by-election in 1967, marked a water-shed in the history of the party and the political history of Wales. It coincided with both a remarkable extension in the geographical and sociological appeal of the party from predominantely Welsh-speaking, educated, middle-class people to English-speaking working-class people, especially the young, in industrial south Wales. Its programme and the ideology underlying it changed also. It issued a series of highly sophisticated reports on various aspects of the economy, and published impressive investigations into current social problems which appeared to have an originality and freshness of approach lacking in those of the other parties. Concentrating its efforts mainly in anglicized, industrialized Wales it gave less emphasis than had ever been given before to language and culture generally. By the 1970s, in some constituencies, both in parliamentary and local elections, Plaid Cymru had come to constitute a major threat to the ruling Labour Party, and even to replace the Conservatives as the main party of opposition.

The Welsh Language Society, by contrast, had been founded in 1963 with the simple and uncomplicated aim of gaining equal status with English for the Welsh language. Its basic philosophy was articulated in a lecture on the fate of the Welsh language given shortly before by the poet and critic, Saunders Lewis, who was an original founder of Plaid Cymru and one of the men prosecuted for his part in setting fire to the bombing school near Pwllheli in 1936. Exclusively concerned with this one issue, the Society adopted militant methods of agitation and its young members by 1970 were attacking English road signs, demanding bilingual official forms and generally setting out to cause maximum embarrassment to official bodies. Whatever practical effect they may have had – and Plaid Cymru became increasingly embarrassed by the campaigns – the Society certainly succeeded in enlivening the political scene and in keeping in the foreground issues of considerable cultural importance. Repudiating the use of violence against people, though not against property, its militant attitudes and activities – above all the single-minded belief of its adherents that the fate of the language was sufficient justification for the abandonment of constitutional methods of persuasion – contributed somewhat to the atmosphere of violence which unhappily seemed to characterize the following decade.

Two measures, the one constituting a break with the past, the other foreshadowing changes of immense significance for the future, must finally be mentioned. The first was the creation, in common with the rest of the United Kingdom, of new local government areas and a new structure of local government. The change was opposed to the bitter end by the inhabitants of some ancient counties who resented the loss of their venerable institutions and distrusted the huge bureaucracy which would inevitably result from the creation of new ones. The other measure is still under debate at the time of writing, and concerns the extent to which the recommendations of the Kilbrandon Commission on the constitution will be instituted. The Commission was set up in 1968–9 to consider whether any changes in the present constitutional and economic relationships between the various parts of the United Kingdom were desirable. It reported in favour of a large measure of devolution for Wales, and the Labour Government in due course proposed an elected assembly sitting at Cardiff, with power over a vastly extended range of governmental functions, but lacking full powers of legislation and taxation. Less thorough-going than the proposals for Scotland these nevertheless represent a great step forward in the direction of self-government. Home Rule has still not been achieved, but it is now a commonplace of political discourse that Wales is a nation, that it has its own peculiar problems, and that it ought to possess institutions of its own to govern itself within the larger community of the realm. Precisely how it will come to do this remains very much in the future: no one would any longer doubt the ability of its people successfully to do so and to build a society at least as culturally rich and resilient as that which it has inherited from the past.

BIBLIOGRAPHICAL NOTE

It is unnecessary to append an extensive bibliography, for such a work is available in *A Bibliography of the History of Wales* (Cardiff, University of Wales Press, 2nd ed., 1962, and Supplements in the *Bulletin of the Board of Celtic Studies*, 1963, 1966, 1969, 1972, in progress.) This is indispensable to all students of Welsh History. Use should also be made of *The Dictionary of Welsh Biography*, 1959. The *Welsh History Review* (Vol. 1, 1960, in progress) appears twice a year.

GENERAL

For a general discussion of all aspects of the history of modern Wales, A. J. Roderick (ed.), *Wales through the Ages*, Vol. II, 1960. See also, E. G. Bowen (ed.), *Wales: A Physical, Historical and Regional Geography*, 1957.

CHAPTERS I, II AND III

Medieval Welsh Society. Selected Essays by T. Jones Pierce, ed. J. Beverley Smith, 1972. For administrative history, W. Ogwen Williams, *Tudor Gwynedd*, 1958, and Penry Williams, *The Council in the Marches of Wales under Elizabeth I*, 1958. For Tudor policy, Sir Frederick Rees, 'Tudor Policy in Wales', *Studies in Welsh History*, 1948, and William Rees, 'The Union of England and Wales', *Transactions of the Honourable Society of Cymmrodorion*, 1937.

CHAPTERS IV AND V

The indispensable work is Glanmor Williams, *The Welsh Church from Conquest to Reformation*, 1962. For Tudor Puritanism, David Williams (ed.), *John Penry: Three Treatises concerning Wales*, 1960.

CHAPTERS VI, VII AND VIII

G. Dyfnallt Owen, *Elizabethan Wales*, 1962, deals with social history. T. Jones Pierce in his introduction to *Clenennau Letters and Papers*, 1947, traces the emergence of a typical landed estate. For political history, A. H. Dodd, *Studies in Stuart Wales*, 1952. For the Civil War, Sir Frederick Rees's three essays in *Studies in Welsh History* (as above). See also Hugh Thomas, *A History of Wales 1485–1660*, 1972. The six volumes of Dr. Thomas Richards deal exhaustively with the history of Puritanism in Wales. (See the *Bibliography*, as above.)

Chapters IX and X

M. G. Jones, *The Charity School Movement*, 1938, has an admirable chapter on Wales. See also, Mary Clement, *The S.P.C.K. and Wales, 1699–1740*, 1954. G. T. Roberts, *Howell Harris*, 1951, is a brief introduction to the Welsh Methodist Movement.

Chapter XI

Glyn Roberts, 'Political affairs from 1536 to 1900', *A History of Carmarthenshire*, Vol. II, 1939, covers the whole period with respect to one shire and brings out the general principles involved.

Chapter XII

G. Nesta Evans, *Social Life in Mid-Eighteenth Century Anglesey*, 1936, deals with Wales in the period before the industrial changes. D. J. Davies, *The Economic History of South Wales prior to 1800*, 1935, is a general survey of economic development. A. H. Dodd, *The Industrial Revolution in North Wales*, 1933, is admirable on all aspects of industry and agriculture in the period from 1750 to 1850. His generalisations are applicable to a wider field than North Wales.

Chapters XIII, XIV and XV

For popular disturbances, David Williams, *John Frost: A Study in Chartism*, 1939, and, id., *The Rebecca Riots*, 1955; D. J. V. Jones, *Before Rebecca. Popular Protests in Wales 1793–1835*, 1973. See also, Glanmor Williams (ed.), *Merthyr Politics. The Making of a Working Class Tradition*, 1966. For industrial development, A. H. John, *The Industrial Development of South Wales*, 1950. The early chapters of A. W. Ashby and I. L. Evans, *The Agriculture of Wales and Monmouthshire*, 1944, are historical.

Chapters XVI, XVII and XVIII

T. I. Ellis, *The Development of Higher Education in Wales*, 1935, for the University movement. For the growth of national sentiment, Sir Reginald Coupland, *Welsh and Scottish Nationalism*, 1954. For political development, K. O. Morgan, *Wales in British Politics*, 2nd. edn., 1970. See also, Alan Butt Philip, *The Welsh Question. Nationalism in Welsh Politics 1945–1970*, 1975, and R. Brinley Jones (ed.), *The Anatomy of Wales*, 1972.

INDEX

INDEX